MAKING COMMON SENSE
COMMON PRACTICE

models for manufacturing excellence

MAKING COMMON SENSE COMMON PRACTICE
models for manufacturing excellence

R O N   M O O R E

Cashman Dudley
An imprint of Gulf Publishing Company
Houston, Texas

MAKING COMMON SENSE COMMON PRACTICE

models for manufacturing excellence

Gulf Publishing Company
Book Division
P.O. Box 2608 ☐ Houston, Texas 77252-2608

10 9 8 7 6 5 4 3 2 1

Library of Congress Cataloging-in-Publication Data

Moore, Ron.
    Making common sense common practice : models for manufacturing excellence / Ron Moore.
        p.   cm.
    Includes bibliographical references and index.
    ISBN 0-88415-899-3
        1. Manufacturing industries—Management.
    2. Manufacturing processes. 3. Production management.
    4. Manufactures—Quality control. I. Title.
    HD9720.5.M66 1999
    658.5—dc21   98–54948
                                                        CIP

Printed in the United States of America.

Printed on acid-free paper (∞).

Contents

7

8

9

10

16

17

18

APPENDIX A

APPENDIX B

Acknowledgments

Thanks to those in manufacturing plants who, given the proper tools, encouragement, and leadership, can and are providing manufacturing excellence; folks like Larry Funke and Mike Barkle; Mickey Davis; John Kang; Lester Wheeler, Joe Robinson, and Jerry Borchers; Glen Herren; Bob Seibert; Chuck Armbruster, Pat Campbell, and Al Yeagley; Ian Tunnycliff, James Perryer, and Andy Waring; Chris Lakin and Paul Hubbard; Wayne Barnacal, Rozano Saad, David Callow, Ben Coetzee, Xavier Audoreen, Bill Beattie, Jim Holden and Otto Moeckel; John Guest, Ron Morgan, Bill Elks, and Dan Merchant; Ron Rath, Ken Rodenhouse, Bill Karcher, Chris Sigmon, and Mike Mercier; Dan Duda; Reggie Tolbert and Don Niedervelt; John Lightcap, Gary Pellini, and Bill Blanford; Chris McKee; Ken Lemmon; Phil Bates; Jim Lewis; Rob Grey; Jim Schmidt; George Schenck; Martin Markovich; Jerry Putt; Eric Sipe, Stefan Stoffel and Bernold Studer; Bryan Mears and Leonard Smith; Bob Hansen and Ian Gordon; Larry Payne; and literally hundreds of others.

Thanks to those in the "corporate office" who, in spite of a sometimes thankless task, work diligently with those in the plants to facilitate the improvement process, folks like Rick Thompson; Harry Cotterill; Steve Schebler; Bob Pioani; Jerry Haggerty; Joe McMullen; Stu McFadden and Butch DiMezzo; Carl Talbot; Dick Pettigrew; Kevin Bauman, Joe Wonsettler, Rick Tucker, and Erich Scheller.

Thanks to executives who have the courage to think a little differently about manufacturing excellence and reliability—Rick Higby; Sandy Anderson; Warren Wells and Ron Plaisier; Adrian Bromley and Doug Coombs; Suhardi; Thomas Bouckaert; Diane Newhouse; Larry Jutte; Ken Plotts; Eion Turnbull; Bob Williams; R. Paul Ruebush; K.B. Kleckner; and John Manning.

Thanks to those who created the original reliability-based maintenance strategy and paper—Forrest Pardue and Ken Piety—and to those who helped further develop the concepts—Jeff Wilson and particularly Alan Pride for adding depth of knowledge to reliability requirements.

Thanks to all the folks who have been especially influential in helping create a vision for the way manufacturing plants ought to be run and continue to sustain and take reliability methods forward, regardless of any position in corporate hierarchy—David Burns and Bill Holmes; Andrew Fraser, John Billington, and David Ormandy; Red Slater; Bob Hansen; Tim Murnane; Tommy Fagan; Stu Teffeteller; Joe Petersen and Kay Goulding; and Vince Flynn, Roy Schuyler, and Ed Jones.

Thanks to Carol Shaw and Laura Hooper at the University of Dayton for helping create the manufacturing reliability series and making manufacturing excellence as an integral part of the University's vision.

Thanks to Alan Pride for contributing portions of certain chapters; to Winston Ledet, Jr., David Ormandy, Ron Rath, and Andy Remson for providing feedback on the manuscript, and making it a better product.

Thanks to Mike Taylor and Chris Crocker for providing the statistical analysis of Appendix A.

Thanks to Kris Jamsa, Tim Calk, Leigh Owen, Cheryl Smith, Phil Carmical, and all the staff at Gulf Publishing for their hard work in getting this book completed; and advising along the way.

Thanks to Mom and Dad for teaching me that you're only limited by your willingness to try.

Thanks to my children (grown now) who taught me more about management and leadership, and the difference, than all the business management books written.

Thanks to those who I may have forgotten. Please accept my apology and my thanks to you, too.

And finally, my biggest thanks to Kathy, my wife and best friend, for all her love, patience, encouragement, guidance, and belief in me.

Preface

This book is about maximizing manufacturing business performance through superior (and yet very basic) practices that allow a given company, industry, and economy to prosper in an increasingly competitive world. Key to this wealth creation are concepts related to uptime and asset utilization rates as compared to ideal, accounting for losses from ideal, *unit cost* of production (vs. costs alone), applying best practices to minimize losses from ideal, integrating the various manufacturing functions using a reliability-driven process, and finally, but certainly not least, integrating the marketing and manufacturing strategies. It is based on the best practices of some of the best plants in the world, and serves as a model for those seeking to achieve world-class performance in a manufacturing business.

It is fundamentally simple in concept, but far more difficult in execution. Indeed, the striking difference between the best manufacturers and the mediocre ones is that the best companies do all the little things exceptionally well and in an integrated way. Others may only feign their understanding of excellence. The practices described require leadership (more so than management), tenacity, teamwork, respect for the dignity and contribution of each individual, and fundamentally a shift from the historical mode of managing through straight cost cutting to a more successful method of managing through improving processes for manufacturing reliability, and *expecting* the costs to come down as a consequence. I have worked with many manufacturers, and most of them have been about average. A few have been very poor, and even fewer still have been excellent. The models presented represent a mosaic of the best practices of the best plants encountered. The case histories provide examples of some of the less-than-best practices encountered. I know of no single plant that does all the best practices outlined. I challenge all who read this book to become the first—you will be well rewarded.

There are, as you know, many books on manufacturing and operations management, and I thank you for choosing this one. What makes this one different? I believe that it fills a void in current literature on manufacturing practices, particularly in how we design, buy, store, install, operate, and maintain our manufacturing plants; and more importantly in how we integrate these activities, including the integration of the manufacturing function with marketing and research and development. There are many books on operations management, TPM, Kaizen, etc. However, in my view most of these focus on production flows, organizational structures, material management, etc., and therefore ignore other major issues that this book addresses, particularly the integration of these practices. Indeed, if those books, and the understanding of manufacturing practices they bring were so good, why does the typical manufacturer have an asset utilization rate, or alternatively overall equipment effectiveness rate, of some 60% of ideal for batch and discrete manufacturers, and 80% for continuous and process manufacturers; whereas, world-class manufacturers, few that they are, typically run in the range of 85%–95%? Clearly, this gap is too large to have been accommodated by current knowledge and practices. I hope to close that gap with this book, because it is about the practices of those who have achieved 85–95%, as well as those who are moving in that direction.

This difference could indeed represent a competitive edge for a company, an industry, or even a country. *Business Week* has often reported that manufacturers are operating at 83%+ of capacity, suggesting that this is the point at which inflationary pressures increase. While this may be true of their historical capacity, it is not true of their real capacity. Most manufacturers have a "hidden plant" within their operation that could lead to a better competitive position for them, their industry, and ultimately for greater economic strength of this country, or for the companies, and countries, who achieve superior performance. Imagine the economic advantage of this country if we combined our innovation, marketing, and distribution skills with superior manufacturing capability. Imagine if we don't and others do.

This book could well have been called "The Manufacturing Prism" based on my observations of the behavior of manufacturing managers, particularly the more senior managers. Merriam Webster's *Collegiate Dictionary (1996)*, defines a prism as (among other things) "a medium that distorts, slants, or colors whatever is viewed through it." This definition fits my observations very well in that every manager (and individual) "distorts, slants, or colors" whatever is viewed by them according to their own position in the business spectrum. Each one filters light (or information) based on a unique position, experience, value system, etc., in the organization. Because we all do this to one extent or another, I find no particular fault with this behavior, except, that many fail to recognize the other functions, or "colors," associated with running a world-class organization, and the implications of their decisions on the organization as a whole. Even when these "colors" are recognized, most also tend to draw distinct boundaries "between colors," where in fact the reality is a continuum in which one color "melts" into another. Typically, each function, department, group, etc. operates in a "silo mentality" (the only color), optimizing the processes in their silo. Unfortunately, this generally fails to optimize the system as a whole, and most systems analysts advise that all systems must be optimized as a whole to assure truly optimal performance. I hope the models in this book help assure that optimizing your manufacturing organization is an integral part of a business system.

Alan Greenspan is reported to have said that there are three ways to create original wealth—mining, agriculture, and manufacturing. With the dramatic expansion of global telecommunications, the blossoming of the internet, etc., he may have since modified that opinion to add information systems. Nonetheless, it is clear that an economy's health and the creation of wealth is heavily dependent upon its manufacturing base. Indeed, according to Al Ehrbar, manufacturing productivity is the single most important factor in international competitiveness. I hope this book will help enhance your competitive position, as well as your industry's, and your country's.

In *The Borderless World*, Kenichi Ohmae seems to express the view that manufacturing is not necessarily the key basis for wealth creation, but rather that trading, distributing, servicing, and supporting may actually be greater ways of adding value in a given economy. While his points are well taken, I personally believe that all countries, and particularly the United States, must have an excellent manufacturing base as part of an overall infrastructure for original wealth creation. This is true in two ways. First, it is at the heart of the long-term health of a given economy, and improves the opportunity for greater overall economic success and power. Not to do so, and to simply rely on second-order effects related to distribution and support, places any economy at a greater risk long term. Second, it places that country in a better position to exploit opportunities in other markets, either by using existing manufacturing assets, or by creating new ones closer to those markets of interest, which are more competitive.

The world is indeed increasingly competitive. The advent of GATT, NAFTA, and other trade agreements are clear indicators of increased trade, and competition. But, having traveled literally all over the world, I believe that there is something more fundamental at play. Increasingly, the application of global telecommunications technology has made the access to knowledge—of markets, of technology, of almost anything—readily accessible. This means that you could be on the island of Borneo, and readily access the latest technology in Houston for improving manufacturing productivity. (I've seen and helped it to be done.) It also means you have access to capital not heretofore as readily available. Stock markets in Tokyo, New York, London, Moscow, etc. are routinely accessible through global media, forcing all companies world wide to compete for the same capital, and to perform at a superior level to be worthy of that capital investment.

In his book *Post Capitalist Society*, Peter Drucker states that the key to productivity is no longer land, labor, or capital, but knowledge. Knowledge leads to increased efficiency and increased access to capital. He further states that "The only long-term policy which promises success is for developed countries to convert manufacturing from being labor based into being knowledge based." I couldn't agree more. However, most cost-cutting strategies as currently practiced do not facilitate becoming knowledge based. Indeed, just the opposite may be true, because cost cutting typically results in even less time to improve knowledge, skills, processes, etc., and frequently results in the loss of knowledge of skilled workers to assure competitive position. The thrust of this book is to provide you with the basic knowledge required to assure superior manufacturing performance, so that you can compete in the global market place, can attract investment capital, can assure wealth creation, and can understand and sustain world-class performance. Perhaps Larry Bossidy, chairman & CEO of AlliedSignal said it best in 1995—"We compete in world-class markets in which capacity often exceeds demand. It is essential, therefore, that we become the low-cost producer." Granted there are other issues related to marketing, R&D, etc., that are also essential, but manufacturing excellence and low-cost production surely places those companies that achieve it in a superior position for business success.

This book began around 1990. For two years, I had been the president of a small, high technology company that supplied instruments and software to large industrial manufacturers to help them monitor the condition of their equipment and with that knowledge minimize losses due to unplanned downtime and catastrophic failures. We had recently developed additional products, not because of any grand strategic plan, but because we just "knew" our customers would need them. However, it soon became apparent that it would be very difficult to sell these products if we didn't have a systematic approach that demonstrated how these products related to one another in a manufacturing environment, and how they fit into the broader requirements of a manufacturing business. Contrary to our marketing and sales manager's opinion, we couldn't just walk into a manufacturing plant loaded like a pack mule with the latest technology, showing them the "neat stuff" we had to sell. We had to have a strategy. To his credit, that manager rose to the occasion.

About that same time, and through the creative thinking of the staff of that same marketing manager, we had also launched a program to identify, and give an award to, those companies that had made best use of our technology—higher production rates, lower costs, better safety, etc. Frankly, the thrust of this effort was to identify these best companies so that we could hold them up to prospective customers, and be able to say in effect "See what they've done, you can do this too!" It was part of our effort to further expand a growing market for our products, and to garner more sales for our company.

Fortunately, the need for a strategy combined with the creation of a program to identify some of the better manufacturing companies in the country led to an understanding of some of the best manufacturing practices, which are still surprisingly absent in typical manufacturing plants. What ultimately resulted from these initial efforts, including many lively discussions, was a paper titled "The Reliability-Based Maintenance Strategy: A Vision for Improving Industrial Productivity," a descriptor of some of the best practices in some of the best manufacturing plants in the country at that time. If that paper was the beginning, then this book is an intermediate step.

Some will say the content of this book is just common sense. I couldn't agree more, but in light of my experience in working closely with dozens of manufacturers, and having a passing knowledge of hundreds of manufacturers, *common sense just isn't common practice*—hence the title of this book for making common sense common practice. If manufacturers would just do the basics very well, their productivity would increase substantially, almost immediately. I have no doubt of this. This view is developed and reinforced by the experiences of this book, and coincides with the experiences of others. In *The Making of Britain's Best Factories* (Business Intelligence, Ltd., London, 1996), the overwhelming conclusion is that most factories don't do the basics well, and that conversely, the best do. Put another way, if people in manufacturing plants simply treated the plant (or were allowed to treat the plant) with the same care and diligence as they do their cars or homes, an immediate improvement would be recognized. Why then doesn't this happen? Perhaps the book will shed light on the issues, but creating a sense of ownership in corporate assets and performance is an essential element. Creating this sense of ownership requires respect for the dignity and contribution that each person makes to the organization, and trust between the shop floor and management, something which is lacking in many companies.

People who feel a sense of ownership and responsibility for the care of the place where they work achieve a higher level of performance. I've often told people, particularly at the shop floor level, "If you don't take care of the place where you make your living, then the place where you make your living won't be here to take care of you," an ownership philosophy strongly instilled by my parents. By the same token, most managers today are driven by cost cutting and labor force reductions in an effort to improve productivity and the proverbial bottom line. Do these actions create a sense of ownership and responsibility on the part of the individual on the shop floor? Do they feel "cared for" and therefore "caring for" the company where they work? Generally not. An individual who has gained a certain notoriety for improving corporate performance has the nickname "Chainsaw," presumably for his severe approach to cost cutting. Will the "chainsaw" approach to corporate management work? Can you cost cut your way to prosperity? He appears to have personally succeed in this, but will it work for a company, over the longer term? Perhaps, especially when a company is in dire straits, but not likely for most companies according to the following data.

The real issues are related to whether or not the right processes have been put in place to address the right markets for the company, long-term; whether the marketing and manufacturing strategies have been fully integrated into a business strategy; and whether employees have the understanding and motivation to implement the right processes to achieve world-class performance. If these issues are addressed, success will be achieved, costs will come down as a consequence of good practice and expectations, not as a fundamental strategy, and the company will have a sustainable business culture for the long haul.

Several recent studies suggest that cost cutting is not a very effective long-term tool for assuring business success. For example, in a study of several hundred companies who had gone through major cost-cutting efforts from 1989–94, and published by *The Wall Street Journal* on July 5, 1995, it was found that only half improved productivity; only a third improved profits; and only an eighth improved morale. In a study published in *The Australian* newspaper in September 1995, it was found that in those companies who engaged in substantial cost cutting, their share price lead market indices in the first 6 months following the cost cutting, but lagged market indices in the following 3 years.

In another study published by the US Conference Board, and reported on August 15, 1996 in *The Age,* also an Australian newspaper, it was found that in those companies who had undergone substantial layoffs in a restructuring, 30% experienced an increase in costs; 22% later realized they had eliminated the wrong people; 80% reported a collapse in employee morale; 67% reported no immediate increase in productivity; and more than 50% showed no short-term improvement in profits. Finally, the Queensland University of Technology, Australia, reported in June 1998 that only about 40% of firms that downsize manage to achieve significant productivity gains from downsizing; that only half the organizations that downsize cut costs; and that downsizing can result in a downward spiral into decline.

With data like these, why do executives continue to use cost cutting as a key "strategy" for improvement? Perhaps, as we who are blessed with healthy egos tend to do, each of us believes that we know better than the others who have tried and failed, and we can beat the odds. Perhaps, it is because we know of nothing else to do. A friend of mine once remarked that "insanity is repeating the same behavior, but expecting different outcomes." In any event, with these odds, simple cost cutting appears to be a poor bet. Rather, it is critical to put the right systems, processes, and practices in place so that costs are not incurred in the first place; and to set clear expectations for reduced costs as a result of these actions.

Perhaps, we are just beginning to re-think the cost cutting "strategy." *The Wall Street Journal* (November 26, 1996) headlined "Re-Engineering Gurus Take Steps to Remodel Their Stalling Vehicles" (and Push Growth Strategies)," acknowledging that re-engineering as it has been practiced hasn't met expectations in many companies, and to a great extent has ignored the human element in its approach. I would add that not achieving ownership and buy-in for the re-engineering process is a key fault in many companies that have tried it. In my experience, this sense of ownership for the change process is especially needed at the middle management level.

Further, capital productivity in a manufacturing plant can be more important than labor productivity. Both are important, no doubt. But, "How much money do I get out for the money I put in?" is more important than "How many units were produced per employee?," especially when many of the people working in the plant are contractors and don't count as employees. Putting the right processes in place to assure capital productivity *will* assure labor productivity. In my experience, cutting head count adds far less value to an organization than putting in place best practices, improving asset utilization, gaining market share, and then managing the need for fewer people using attrition, reallocation of resources to more productive jobs, improved skills, reduced contract labor, etc. Indeed, as the book illustrates, cutting head count can actual reduce production and business performance. Labor content in many manufacturing organizations is only a small fraction of the total cost of goods manufactured. Concurrently, as noted, asset utilization rates in a typical manufacturing plant run 60–80% of ideal, as compared to world-class levels of 85–95%. Given that you have markets for your products, this incremental production capacity and productivity is typically worth ten times or more than could be realized through cost cutting. And even if markets are soft in the short term, it still allows for lower production costs so that greater profits are realized, and strategically market share is enhanced.

Put the right processes in place, get your people engaged in a sense of ownership, create an environment for pride, enjoyment, and trust, and the costs will come down. Operating capital assets in an optimal way will provide for minimum costs, not cost cutting. Consider the US economy, which has a manufacturing base of well over $1 trillion. Imagine the impact on a given manufacturing plant, industry, or even economy, if it could even come close to world-class performance. For a typical manufacturing plant it means $millions; for the US economy, $100's of billions. As a bonus, we get lower inflation, lower interest rates, and greater competitive position, etc.

This book is an effort to provide ideas to those who are engaged in trying to become world-class performers as to how some of the best companies have accomplished this. Each chapter has been written such that it could stand alone, so you may see some overlap between chapters. I hope this will only serve to reinforce the principles espoused. However, the book is best when read in its entirety to provide a complete understanding of manufacturing, and how it fits into business excellence. The processes provided have been shown to work, as the case histories will illustrate, but should not be applied as a literal recipe. Each plant or company has its own culture, its own needs, markets, etc., and therefore, this book should be used as a guide, not as a literal mandate. As you read the different sections, you should ask yourself "Are we doing this?" and if not, "Should we be doing this?" and if so, "What is my *personal* responsibility to make sure this gets done?" Or, if you disagree with the models presented (because they may not always apply to all situations), use your disagreement to develop your own, and act on them. At its heart, manufacturing excellence requires leadership, but also that each individual assume a personal responsibility for excellence, working hard individually, and with others, to get as close to ideal performance as reasonably possible.

Finally, W. Edwards Deming once said that "Profound knowledge comes from the outside and by invitation. A system cannot understand itself." I hope this book, which is inherently by invitation, offers you profound knowledge that supports a journey to world-class performance. I thank you for the invitation to share this with you.

Ron Moore
Knoxville, Tennessee

Manufacturing and Business Excellence

> You don't do things right once in a while, you do them right all the time.
>
> *Vince Lombardi*

The Scene

Kaohsiung Industries, an international manufacturing company, has recently made substantial inroads into US and European markets, shaking the confidence of investors in competing US and European manufacturers. Around the globe, manufacturers like Kaohsiung are capitalizing on lower trade barriers, a growing global economy, and substantial growth in the Asia-Pacific economies, challenging other manufacturer's long-standing position in their traditional markets.

Beta International, a large manufacturing conglomerate, is under intense pressure from domestic competitors with newer technologies, from foreign competitors with cheaper products, and from within—there's so much politicking that much of the work that's done by many individuals is related to positioning for survival in a streamlined organization. They have just named a new CEO, Bob Neurath, who is determined to get the company back on track and reestablish itself as the leader in its markets, especially its chemicals sector.

On reviewing current marketing plans, the new CEO has found that the marketing division is really more like a set of sales departments, focused more on selling whatever products R&D develops for it than on understanding and targeting markets and then developing their marketing and sales strategy accordingly. The R&D department has lots of neat ideas, but too often these ideas are not fully linked to a thorough market analysis and understanding of customer wants and needs. Manufacturing is not integrated into either process. There seems to be a "silo" approach to the business. Everybody's in their silo doing their very best to survive first, and assure their silo's success second, but few take an integrated perspective of the business as a whole and how they support the company's success.

Several issues have been developing for some time in its manufacturing division, and much of this is coming to a head at its new Beaver Creek plant. It's not yet apparent to the new CEO that the Beaver Creek production plant, which manufactures one of its new premier products, is in deep trouble—the process isn't performing as expected, the plant is frequently down because of equipment failures, the shop floor is hostile toward management, and morale is at an all-time low. This plant was to be the standard by which its other plants were operated, but has fallen far short of its goals. A new plant manager has been recently assigned to correct these problems, and seems somewhat overwhelmed by the magnitude of the job. Moreover, it's his first assignment as a plant manager for a plant this size and complexity, having spent most of his career in purchasing, quality assurance, and then marketing. While there are spots of isolated excellence, most other plants in the corporation are not faring much better, as evidenced by the fall in the company's share price over the past several quarters. Further, recent pressures on interest rates have added even more angst to this capital intensive company.

Most analysts recognize the problems facing Beta, and see intense international competition as a continuing threat to Beta International's long-term success, and perhaps even its survival in its current form.

Inside the Beaver Creek plant, an operator and process engineer have recently come up with several ideas for improving their manufacturing processes, but are having difficulty convincing their boss, the production manager, to use their ideas for better process control—they cost too much, they are too risky, they require too much training, etc. Nearby, a similar situation has developed in the maintenance department where a technician and maintenance engineer have also come up with some ideas about how to reduce mechanical downtime. Likewise, their boss, the maintenance manager, believes they're too expensive and a bit "radical," and besides, he opines phrases like "if only people would just do what they're told, when they're told, everything would work just fine," or "if it ain't broke, don't fix it." Meanwhile, back in the design and capital projects department, they know that the plant was designed and installed properly, if only the plant people would operate and maintain it properly, everything would be just fine.

All the while, executives are following their traditional approach, intensifying the pressure for cost cutting in an effort to become more competitive. Simultaneously, they implore their staff to keep the plant running efficiently at all costs. Few, except for the people of the shop floor, have recognized the irony in this situation.

Challenges from global competition, challenges from within, challenges from seemingly every direction are all coming together to threaten the prosperity and perhaps the very existence of a long-standing, respected corporation.

The Players

Though based on actual companies and case histories, the above scenario is fictitious. There is no Beta International, or Beaver Creek plant, but it could very well describe the situation in many manufacturing companies today. Further, with some modifications, it could also reflect the situation in power utilities, automotive plants, paper plants, etc., and even in the government sector where a reduced tax base and pressure for cost cutting are creating intense pressure to improve performance. Beta International and its Beaver Creek plant, as well as other plants, are used in this book to illustrate real case histories that reflect the actual experience of various manufacturing plants, but the actual descriptions have been modified to mask the identity of the plants. Though based on real events, these case histories are not intended to describe any specific company's actual performance. Therefore, any correlation, real or imagined, between Beta and any other company is coincidental. Beta International is a composite of many different companies.

All businesses, and particularly manufacturers, are being called upon to do more with less. All are facing intense pressure, either directly or indirectly, from global competition, and all are behaving in very much the same way—cost cutting is a key corporate strategy. There is nothing inherently wrong with cost cutting, but it must be combined with a more strategic process for assuring manufacturing excellence. Cost cutting does little to improve the knowledge base that assures improvements in plant operation, in equipment and process reliability, and ultimately world-class performance.

So what are we to do? Well, most of us understand that if we don't grow our businesses, we just aren't going to be successful. We also understand that cost cutting typically reduces the effects of a growth strategy. Please do not misunderstand. Being prudent and frugal are hallmarks of good companies; and being the low-cost producer may be a necessity for long-term market leadership. However, too many companies focus on cost cutting almost to the aversion of growth, and/or the application of best practices, and over the long term may hurt their strategic position. Business excellence in most companies requires that the company do each of three things shown in Figure 1-1 exceptionally well—marketing, R&D, and manufacturing. Excellence

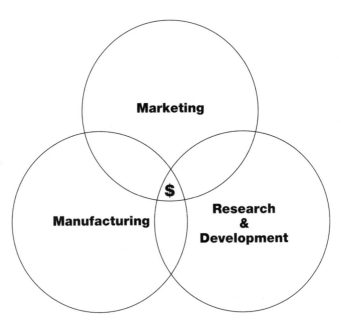

Figure 1-1. World-class business requires integration of key components.

in each is essential for long-term success, and each must be fully integrated with the other. Each must recognize certain overlapping areas where teamwork and cooperation are required, and that all areas must be fully integrated with a common sense of purpose—maximizing shareholders' financial return.

Each group must recognize mutual independence and dependence, but in the end, all groups must be synchronized to a common purpose and strategy that fosters a sense of trust—we all have a common understanding of where we're going and how we're going to get there.

It is common that a company at first will do a better job selling than it will understanding its markets and then developing a sales and distribution strategy to penetrate those markets. It is also common that considerable R&D may not be fully linked to the marketplace and customer requirements. Perhaps more to the point of this book, however, is that few companies do a good job integrating their marketing and R&D strategies with their manufacturing strategy, often treating manufacturing like a big reservoir from which sales "opens a spigot and fills their bucket with product" and then sells it. It's true of Beta International. While the thrust of this book is primarily manufacturing, it is critical that the manufacturing strategy be fully integrated with the marketing strategy. This is discussed in the following section and in additional depth in Chapter 3.

Integrating the Manufacturing and Marketing Strategy

There are several exceptional works about developing a manufacturing strategy and assuring its support for the marketing and overall business strategy.[1-5] These have apparently received insufficient attention until recently, but are now helping Beta to form its strategy, where manufacturing has historically been viewed by the marketing function as, in effect, "the place that makes the stuff we sell."

Beta understands well that all business starts with markets—some existing (basic chemicals, for example), some created from "whole cloth" (new process technology or unique instruments, for example). Beta was principally in mature markets, but of course was investing R&D into new product and process development. However, Beta was not actively positioning its products and its manufacturing strategy to assure an optimal position. Additional discussion on this, as well as a process for optimizing Beta's product mix is provided in Chapter 3, but for the time being, the discussion will be limited to the basis for integrating Beta's marketing and manufacturing strategy. What image does Beta want in its markets? What market share is wanted? What is the strategy for achieving this? Has Beta captured the essence of its business strategy in a simple, clear mission statement (or vision, or both, if you prefer)?

Using the model described in more detail in Chapter 3, Beta reviewed its 5-year historical sales for all its product lines, including an analysis of the factors for winning orders, Beta's market share, the gross margins for given products, and the anticipated total market demand for existing, and future products. Beta then reviewed its production capability, including each manufacturing plant's perceived capability for making a given product. More importantly, however, Beta's perception of manufacturing capability was balanced with a reality check through an analysis of historical delivery capability and trends for each plant's performance in measures like uptime and overall equipment effectiveness, or OEE (both defined below relative to ideal performance); unit costs of production for given products; on-time/in-full performance; quality performance; etc. They even took this one step further and looked into the future relative to new product manufacturing capability and manufacturing requirements for mature products to remain competitive. All this was folded into a more fully integrated strategy, one for which manufacturing was an integral part of the strategic business plan, and which included issues related to return on net assets, earnings and sales growth, etc.

Through this analysis, Beta found that it had many products that were not providing adequate return with existing market position and manufacturing practices, it lacked the capability to manufacture and deliver certain products (both mature and planned) in a cost-competitive way, and it could not meet corporate financial objectives without substantial changes in its marketing and manufacturing strategies. Further, it was found that additional investment would be required in R&D for validating the manufacturing capability for some new products; that additional capital investment would be required to restore certain assets to a condition that would assure being able to meet anticipated market demand; and finally, that unless greater process yields were achieved on certain products, and/or the cost of raw material was reduced, some products could not be made competitively. All in all, the exercise proved both frustrating and productive, and provided a much better understanding of manufacturing's impact on marketing capability, and vice versa.

Further, a surprising finding resulted from Beta's effort. Historically, Beta's efforts had focused on cost cutting, particularly in manufacturing, and within manufacturing, particularly in maintenance. However, as it turned out, this approach was not enlightened. Indeed, in many plants it had resulted in a deterioration of asset condition and capability to a point where there was little confidence in the plant's capability for achieving increased production to meet marketing's plan for increased sales. Other issues, such as poor performance in quality products at a lower cost/price, and less than sterling performance for on-time/in-full delivery to customers, only exacerbated the situation. After extensive review and intensive improvement efforts, manufacturing excellence became more than just a nice word. Measures associated with manufacturing excellence, *asset utilization rate* and *unit cost of production* became paramount, and the comprehensive integration of manufacturing, marketing, and research and development to achieving business success became better understood. For example, Beta began to adopt the philosophy stated by another major manufacturer:[6]

As a result of our global benchmarking efforts, we have shifted our focus from cost to equipment reliability and Uptime.

Through our push for Uptime, we want to increase our capital productivity 10%, from 80 to 90% in the next several years. We value this 10% improvement as equivalent to US$4.0 billion in new capital projects and replacement projects for global Chemicals and Specialties.

Maintenance's contribution to Uptime is worth 10 times the potential for cost reduction. Realizing this tremendous resource has helped make Uptime our driving focus for future competitiveness rather than merely cost reduction.

While prudently and properly saving money is a good thing, Beta is only now beginning to recognize that it will be difficult to save their way to prosperity; and that capital productivity must be included with labor productivity in their management measurements. Consider the following example.

Beta's Whamadyne plant had been "encouraged" to cut labor costs by some 10%, amounting to a "savings" of $2m per year. At the same time, Whamadyne was measured to be one of Beta's best plants, having an asset utilization rate of some 86%. (It was manufacturing 86% of the maximum theoretical amount it could make). Whamadyne management developed a plan to increase utilization rates to 92% by improving process and equipment reliability, without any major capital expenditure. Further, it was determined that this increase was worth an additional $20m in gross margin contribution, most of which would flow directly to operating income. It was also determined that requiring a force reduction would jeopardize this improvement. What would you do? What did they do? They took the risk and achieved much better performance in their plant, and therefore in the market place; and their maintenance costs came down more than the $2m sought; and they managed the need for fewer people over time through natural attrition, re-allocation of resources, fewer contractors. Genuine "cost cutting" comes through process excellence, not simply cutting budgets.

Becoming the Low-Cost Producer

So what are we to do again? In manufacturing, there is almost always greater supply than demand, requiring that a given plant focus on becoming the low-cost producer of its products. Granted, there are also other market differentiators, such as product quality, delivery performance, customer service, technology, etc., but a key business indicator is the ability to produce quality product at the lowest achievable cost for a given targeted market segment. This helps assure greater return on assets for further investment in R&D, marketing and distribution channels, etc., to further improve a company's business success.

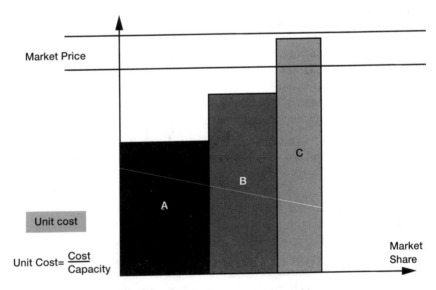

Figure 1-2. Market survivor profile.

Consider Figure 1-2, which represents three companies competing in a market where the market price is variable depending upon the state of the marketplace, the economy of a given region, etc. Each manufacturer makes its product(s) for a given unit cost of production that includes fixed costs, variable costs, capital costs, etc. For the purpose of this discussion, we've assumed that these are products of comparable quality for a given specification in the marketplace.

Company C is the high-cost producer. One year it may make money, the next year it may lose money, but all in all, it may not survive very long, because it is not generating enough working capital to sustain and grow the business. Given this scenario, it is bound to change, one way or another. It is typically fighting for its very survival, and therefore, it must embark on a course to improve its performance, typically by cutting its operating costs. It is also typically characterized by a reactive, crisis-driven manufacturing and corporate culture. It may even complain that its competitors "must be selling below cost." And, whether it stays in business is, in some measure, determined by competitors, which want prices high enough for good margins, but not too high to attract additional competition.

Company B is the mid-cost producer. Most years it makes money, and some years it makes considerably more money, but it is not viewed as the best in its industry. It tends to be complacent with its position, because it's typically been around for decades, it has almost always made money, and it is respected in its industry as a *good* company (but not the best). Sure, the management team recognizes that they have a few problems, but doesn't everyone? The compelling reasons for change seem more obscure, and are often taken less seriously. While perhaps less so than Company C, it too is often reactive in its management practices, and often driven by the "crisis" of the moment; or by the latest management fad, which it rarely executes well, because a kind of "this too will pass" attitude often prevails at the operating level.

Company A is the low-cost producer. It essentially always makes money, and in some years, it is very prosperous indeed. Notwithstanding market forces, it is in a better position to determine market price. It wants the price high enough to assure good margins, but not so high that new competitors are tempted to make major capital investments. It will work hard to assure that Company B and Company C are not overly aggressive in pricing, in either direction. It too is generally compelled to change, but for very different reasons from Company C. Its basic mode of operation requires, rather than prefers, the company to be the low-cost, high-quality producer with high market share. Company A has also done a good job integrating its marketing and manufacturing strategy by continuously balancing the drive for higher margins against market share. Its basic culture is one in which constancy of purpose and manufacturing excellence as determined by uptime, unit cost of production, delivery performance, and safety are a key focus throughout the organization. Manufacturing excellence, continuous improvement, and being the low-cost producer are inherent in its culture.

The unit cost of production in its simplest form can be characterized as the total cost of manufacturing divided by the total throughput (capacity). With this simple equation, there are three basic ways to lower the unit cost of production.

1. Cut costs while holding production capacity constant.
2. Increase production while holding costs constant.
3. Reduce cost and increase production simultaneously.

The difference between the best companies and the mediocre/poor ones in this model is the emphasis the best companies give to the denominator. That is, they want to assure that best practice is being employed so that they have the capacity when it is needed. The marketing and sales staff can then make decisions about applying this capacity, pricing and market share, based on manufacturing performance. On the other hand, the typical manufacturing company tends to focus on the numerator, that is, cost cutting, while hoping to hold throughput constant. The best companies focus on improving the reliability of their production operation, thereby improving performance for a given fixed asset, and assuring lower unit costs of production. Further, they get a bonus—by operating reliably, they aren't always "fixing things," nor routinely, and inopportunely, changing from one product to another to accommodate markets and customers. Good practice, reliable operation, reduces operating costs.

A key point is necessary here. The A's do not ignore costs. Quite the contrary, they are very cost sensitive, *expecting* to be the low-cost producer. They also expect that costs will continue to come down as they apply best practices. But their principle mode of operation is not to focus on cost cutting as a "strategy" in itself, but rather to focus on best processes and practices; whereas, the mediocre and poor companies use cost cutting as a principle means for success, while expecting that capacity will be available when it is needed. This approach can work, but it rests on the ability of the people at lower levels within the organization to somehow rise to the occasion in spite of what many of them perceive as poor leadership. The higher probability of success rests with focusing on best practice such that the capacity is available when necessary, and such that costs are lowered as a consequence. Strategically, this also lowers incremental capital requirements.

Company A, as the low-cost producer, is in a much better position to decide whether it wishes to pursue a strategy of increasing market share through lower prices and reliability of supply, yet still achieving good margins; or by holding market share relatively constant assuring very healthy profits, which would finance future investments. However, all three companies must consider that over the long term the price of most manufactured products tends to trend downward. Company A is in a better position relative to future developments, principally because it is driven to hold its position as low-cost producer. Companies B and C are at greater risk if prices do fall, and surprisingly Company B may be at particular risk, because it is likely to be more complacent than Company A and Company C, who are compelled to change, but both for different reasons.

Application of Increased Capacity

Of course, you can't simply make all the product possible, over-stock on inventories, drive up costs, etc. However, what strategy should you employ? If capacity could be increased, could all of the additional product be sold? At what price? At what volume would prices have to be lowered to sell any incremental volume. What capacity (asset utilization rate, uptime) is needed to assure competitive position? And so on.

Figure 1-3 provides an easy way to map manufacturing performance with market conditions and quickly judge its impact on financial performance. It plots return on net assets (= gross margin/profits) as a function of uptime (and/or unit costs) for given market prices. For this chart, the logic goes something like this. For a given plant, you could determine what your current asset utilization rate or uptime is. For that uptime, and when combined with current operating costs, you could also determine what your current **unit** cost of production is for a given product set. With a large number of products this may get a little more difficult, but some companies use the concept of equivalent product units (EU's) for this purpose. For a given unit cost, and in a given market condition (price) you could also determine gross profit, and subsequently return on net assets (RoNA). In fact, for a family of prices you could determine the uptime required to achieve a given RoNA.

Beta International's new CEO, Bob Neurath, has recently completed a review of a benchmarking effort centered on Beta's financial and manufacturing performance, and has concluded that Beta is resoundingly average. While there are a few pockets of excellence, over time a complacent culture has evolved within the company, where mediocrity is the standard, and where only a few are substantially above average. This evolution has only been exacerbated by the fact that when problems have arisen, the typical response has been to "engineer a solution" (and spend more capital), rather than stepping back to determine whether or not best practice has been applied and best performance has been expected. After all, "they've been around for decades and have been fairly profitable; sure they've got some problems, but doesn't everyone; they're a pretty good company."

Being "pretty good" and presuming the future is secure because the past has been successful are the beginning of the end for many companies. And at Beta this has become unhealthy, particularly in light of the increasing intensity of competition, and other ills of the company. Further, increasing global competition represents both threat and opportunity. Threat for those who are complacent, but opportunity for those who can aggressively capture those new markets. In any event, Mr. Neurath believes these issues represent opportunities, not

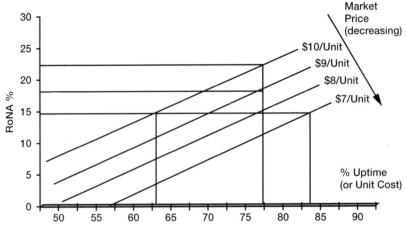

Figure 1-3. RoNA, market price, uptime chart.

problems, and that Beta International must view the global situation as opportunity. The challenge then is to establish new standards for performance and behavior. Beta must be the low-cost producer, among other factors, to assure market position and prosperity.

Beta's Beaver Creek Plant—RoNA vs. Uptime

Reviewing Beta's benchmarking data, we find from Figure 1-3 that Beta's Beaver Creek plant has been operating at an uptime of 63%, relatively poor, and likely leading to a position of no better than what could be characterized as mid-range—a low-end Company B. Because Beta believes that it can sell every unit of product it can make at Beaver Creek, for purposes of this discussion, uptime is defined as that percent of product a plant is making compared to that which it could make under ideal conditions—running 8,760 hours per year at 100% of peak demonstrated sustainable rate, making 100% quality product. However, it is believed that Beaver Creek could increase uptime from 63% to 77% in one year by taking the appropriate steps, and the marketing department has said that all the product could be sold at current market price. They grudgingly note that they are currently buying product from a competitor to meet customer delivery schedules. The value of this increased output translates into an increase in RoNA from just under 15% to 22% at a market price of $10/unit. After this analysis, the marketing department has also noted that even if market pressures forced the price down to $9/unit to sell additional product, or to construct a long-term alliance with key customers, RoNA still increases to over 18%. Note that Beta does not want to start a price war with its pricing, just improve its financial and marketing position, and its options. Further, under a more extreme scenario, RoNA would remain the same even if market price dropped to $7/unit, with a concurrent uptime of 83%. This kind of information is very useful in the thinking process and in creating a common theme for marketing and manufacturing. Chapter 3 describes a process for more fully integrating the marketing and manufacturing strategies.

A Model for Becoming the Low-Cost Producer

Bob Neurath has concluded that all Beta's plants must develop this type of information, which will in turn be used in creating a long-term business strategy that links marketing and manufacturing into an understanding of the sensitivities for a given level of performance. Indeed, the data indicate that uptime and RoNA are mediocre at best. Further, once understood, this information can be used to position the company strategically with certain key customers in key markets. One marketing strategy is to strategically position with key customers and offer to reduce prices modestly over the coming years, in return for a minimum level of business, recognizing that manufacturing performance must also improve to provide a reliable supply to those customers, and concurrently improve RoNA. This approach is expected to create a strategic alliance between Beta and its customers, which will assure both market share, as well as an adequate return on assets. This information can in turn be used to help Beta to understand the profits/RoNA at which it can operate for a given market price and manufacturing level of performance, and then adjust business objectives consistent with current and strategic capability. Put more simply, Mr. Neurath has directed the operating units to:

1. Determine the unit cost of production needed to assure market share leadership (among other factors).
2. Determine the uptime, or overall equipment effectiveness, required to support this unit cost.
3. Determine any additional fixed or variable cost reductions necessary to achieve this targeted unit cost.
4. Validate the feasibility of achieving the targets.
5. Determine the key steps required to achieve that uptime and those key cost factors.
6. Presume success (presumptive market positioning) in achieving that level of uptime, unit cost of production, and market share. Proceed accordingly, and in parallel. Marketing and plant operations must work as a team to drive the improvement process.
7. Allow people within operating units considerable freedom to do the job right and assure maximum reliability and uptime, and plant operational success.
8. Measure and manage along the way.

Some plants will not be able to achieve a unit cost of better than about 110–120% of the recognized lowest-cost producer. Current technology, physical limitations, raw material costs, etc. limit the ability of these plants, even in the best of circumstances from being the lost-cost producer. This in itself is useful information in that it provides an understanding of what is possible with existing assets, and how the company may need to strategically re-think the business and its long-term fit into corporate objectives. Short term it also supports greater understanding and teamwork between marketing and manufacturing.

Further, Mr. Neurath has reluctantly accepted that it will probably take 2–4 years to achieve substantially improved manufacturing performance, and perhaps even longer to achieve world-class performance at most of Beta's plants, given their current condition and level of performance. That said, he is pressing very hard for implementing the processes to achieve this level of performance.

Steps to Manufacturing Excellence

But how will Beta's operating managers determine the key next steps for what each of the operating plants are specifically to do?

- The first step in the improvement process is to determine where you are as compared to the best. How do you compare to world-class companies, in uptime, in unit cost, in on-time/in-full measures, for example? How do you compare to typical companies? To do this, you must do some benchmarking. This generally creates some cognitive dissonance, or positive tension, because it creates an awareness of just how big the gaps are between typical and world-class performance. When properly applied, this knowledge can lead to improved performance. More on that in the next chapter.
- Next, you must determine where your losses are as compared to ideal circumstances. This requires a system that allows you to track every hour in which you are not operating at the ideal rate, and assign a reason for the failure to perform at the ideal rate. This can then be used for analysis of key losses and key steps for eliminating those losses, and is discussed in the following. While putting this system in place, if you don't have one yet, you can identify the major causes of losses using the technique described in Chapter 3.
- Finally, you must compare your practices to best practices. Note that this differs from benchmarks, or numbers. Practices are what you do, not how you measure. The best manufacturing companies position themselves to *design, buy, store, install, operate, and maintain their assets for maximum uptime and reliability—reliability of production process and reliability of equipment.* Best practices in each of these areas are described in detail in chapters 4–13. Further, the best plants integrate their manufacturing strategy with their marketing strategy and plan, as described in Chapter 3. Consider Figure 1-4, the reliability process for manufacturing excellence.[7]

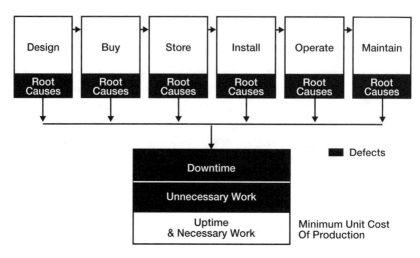

Figure 1-4. The reliability process.

Beta International must position itself to do all these things exceptionally well. Doing poorly in one of these areas introduces defects into the processes. These defects flow down into our manufacturing plants, resulting in lost capacity and higher costs. Further, if a mistake is made upstream in the reliability process for manufacturing excellence, it tends to be compounded downstream as people try to compensate for the mistakes within their organization. Beta must be able to use the knowledge base reflected by best practice and from within the operations and maintenance departments to provide feedback into the design, procurement, storage, and installation efforts, as well as into the operating and maintenance functions, to help minimize the number of defects being created. Beta must use this knowledge base to eliminate these defects and losses in its drive for excellence in manufacturing. More on the details of exactly how this is done as we continue.

To eliminate defects and losses from ideal, we must understand what ideal is, and measure all our losses against ideal. For example, if in an ideal world you could operate your plant 8,760 hours per year (that's all there are except for leap year when you get an extra 24 hours), making 100% quality product, at 100% of your maximum demonstrated sustainable rate, with an optimal product mix (no downtime for anything—changeovers, planned, unplanned, etc.), how much could you make? Certainly this would be ideal, and it is recognized that no one will ever be able to achieve this. The more important issue, however, is how close can we get to this, and sustain it? Let's measure our losses from ideal, and then manage them. If we don't have sufficient market demand, why? If we have extensive unplanned mechanical downtime, why? And so on—measure it, manage it, eliminate or minimize the losses from ideal. Moreover, we may also find that some assets must be rationalized, that is we can produce at market demand requirements with substantially fewer capital assets, necessitating that some be decommissioned or even scrapped. While this may be a painful thought, given the original capital investment, it may be better to stop spending money to retain a non-productive asset, than to continue to spend money ineffectively.

Measuring Losses from Ideal

Figure 1-5 illustrates a general definition for uptime, overall equipment effectiveness (OEE), or asset utilization and the losses related thereto. The terms in Figure 1-5 are defined as follows:[6]

- **Asset utilization rate**—That percentage of ideal rate at which a plant operates in a given time period. The time period recommended is 8,760 hours per year, but this can be defined as any period, depending on how market losses are treated.
- **Uptime or Overall Equipment Effectiveness (OEE)**—That percentage of ideal rate at which a plant operates in a given time period, plus the time for no-market-demand losses.
- **Quality Utilization**—That percentage of ideal rate at which a plant operates in a given time period, plus market demand losses, and changeover and transition losses.
- **Potential Rate Utilization**—That percentage of ideal rate at which a plant operates in a given time period, plus market demand losses, changeover and transition losses, and quality losses.
- **Availability**—That period of time the plant is available to run at any rate.

These terms can be confusing, depending upon any individual's experience base—hence the effort to define them. For example, many people refer to uptime as any time a line or plant is up and running. For them, this does not mean that it is being run in an ideal way, just that it's up and running, regardless of rate, quality, or other losses from ideal. Further, it may be necessary to introduce other categories, depending on the nature of the business and the losses. For example, utility downtime may be a critical category for loss accounting. Production paperwork for the FDA in the food and pharmaceutical industries may represent key losses. The point is to develop a model that accounts for all losses from ideal, and then use that model to manage and minimize those losses, all things considered. The goal with this methodology is to assure that "there's no place to hide" any losses from ideal. Once we account for those, then we can truly begin to manage them in an integrated way. Indeed, we may find that some so-called "losses" are entirely appropriate, and assure optimal performance over the long term. For example, planned maintenance "losses," product changeover "losses," etc. are an integral part of business excellence when *properly done.*

Beta's continuous plants have adopted the term uptime, while the batch and discrete plants have adopted the term OEE. All plants apply asset utilization—tactically as a measure of day-to-day performance, and strategically as a measure of the effective use of capital. Further, *sustainable peak rate* is, as the name implies, that maximum rate demonstrated to be sustainable for an extended period. Many of Beta's plants have used their best 3-day performance ever; others have used their best production run ever, etc. The point is to use a rate that represents a serious challenge, but is not totally unrealistic. Realism comes when you compare your actual rate to the best you've ever done.

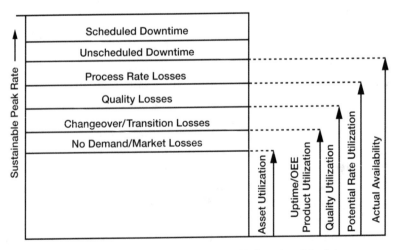

Figure 1-5. Uptime/OEE/Asset Utilization Model.

Scheduled and Unscheduled Downtime. These are normally considered the responsibility of maintenance. Unscheduled downtime is typically for breakdown or reactive maintenance. Scheduled downtime is typically for preventive maintenance or PM. In supporting business excellence measurements, we generally want to eliminate, or at least minimize, unscheduled downtime; and we want to optimize (minimize for a given effect or goal) scheduled downtime using a PM optimization process (Chapters 9 and 10) that combines preventive, predictive, and proactive methods with equipment histories and knowledge of current condition to assure doing only what is necessary, when it is necessary. Subtracting these times yields *actual availability*.

With this in mind, it has been Beta's experience that much of the unscheduled downtime for equipment maintenance has a root cause associated with poor operational practice, e.g., pump failures being caused by running pumps dry and burning up the seals (a root cause review at one of Beta's plants found 39 of 48 seal failures were due to operational error); by running conveyers without operators routinely adjusting the tracking; by poor operator TLC (tightening, lubricating, and cleaning using so-called TPM principles discussed in Chapter 13), etc. Hence, it is important that operations and maintenance work as a team (see Chapter 15) to identify the root cause of unscheduled downtime, and minimize it. Minimizing scheduled downtime also requires teamwork, particularly in integrating the production and maintenance schedules so that PM can be performed as scheduled, minimizing perturbations in the maintenance planning and scheduling effort, and assuring proper parts, resources, testing, etc. Properly done these losses can be minimized and support cost reduction in manufacturing costs, poor delivery performance and time delays due to equipment failures, and improved inventory planning through increased reliability.

Process Rate Losses. Generally, these are losses that occur when the process is not running in an ideal manner, e.g., production process rates at less than ideal, cycle times beyond the ideal time, yields at less than ideal, etc. These too can be caused by either operational or maintenance errors, e.g., if a machine or piece of equipment has been poorly installed, resulting in the inability to operate it at peak rate, then it's likely that a design or maintenance problem exists; or fouling in a heat exchanger could be due to improper gasket installation by maintenance, poor process control by operations, poor piping design, or some combination. Measuring the losses from the ideal is the first step in motivating the drive to identify the root cause. Subtracting these losses results in *potential rate utilization*.

Quality Losses. These are usually losses due to product quality not meeting specification, resulting in scrap or rework being necessary. It too can be the result of poor design, operational or maintenance practices, or some combination. In some cases specific measures are put in place for the cost of various drivers of quality non-conformance. However, these quality losses are generally a small fraction of the total losses from ideal. One concept is to use the overall uptime/OEE and related losses as a measurement of the Cost of *process quality* non-conformance. In any event, subtracting the straight quality losses such as scrap and rework, a measure of *product* non-conformance, results in quality utilization.

Changeover/Transition Losses. These include downtime losses, derate losses, and/or, product quality losses that occur during a changeover or transition to a new product, both the shutdown losses for the existing product, as well as the startup losses for the new product. Minimizing the changeover and transition losses will help minimize manufacturing costs. Changeovers, as we'll see in Chapter 3, can represent a huge potential for losses, particularly when product mix, marketing and manufacturing issues are not well integrated. Subtracting changeover/transition Losses results in uptime/OEE, or product utilization rate.

At this point, after subtracting all these losses from ideal, we have reached a measurement of uptime or OEE as defined in Figure 1-5, and which takes credit for the no-demand and market losses. If our market losses are near zero, then uptime/OEE and asset utilization rates are the same. However, if, for example, we only run a 5-day, 2-shift operation, then our market losses are quite high—we're only operating 10 of the 21 shifts available for a given asset. Alternatively, we could measure OEE only for the time run—e.g., 5-day, 2-shift operation—excluding market losses from consideration. In other words, we can characterize OEE as the sum of asset utilization plus no-demand and market losses, which is more common in continuous process plants; or we can characterize it as the operating efficiency for a given period of time such as a 5-day, 2-shift operation and ignore market losses. Either model works as an improvement facilitator, but identifying all losses, including market losses, and using asset utilization as a key performance indicator is more likely to drive senior management in the improvement process. It will also help senior management identify tactical operating performance, as well as strategic capital requirements.

Other issues relative to losses from ideal. We could include any number of categories in addition to those shown, e.g., break times, wherein machines are shut down during breaks, and might not otherwise be down, if the scheduling of resources accommodated not shutting the equipment down. We might also detail losses due to utility interruptions for steam, electricity, compressed gases, which we want to account separately. We might want to break out unscheduled downtime into categories associated with maintenance errors and operational errors. The model in Figure 1-5 is simply a *tool* we use to determine our losses from ideal, and how close we can come to ideal performance as we have defined it, and to managing and minimizing those losses. A few points need to be highlighted:

1. We frequently make legitimate business decisions that these losses from ideal are acceptable, in light of current business goals, product mix, technology, staffing, union agreements, etc. The point is that we want to measure these losses and then make a thoughtful business decision about their acceptability and reasonableness.

2. It is important to distinguish between industrial standards, such as 150 units per minute on, say, a production line, and ideal standards, such as 200 units per minute in the ideal world. The first is used for production planning and recognizes current performance for management purposes. The second is a measure of ideal performance against which we judge ourselves for making process improvements toward this ideal.

3. As we de-bottleneck and make our improvements, we often find that equipment can run under ideal circumstances at higher rates, e.g., 220 units per minute. We then adjust our industrial production planning standards, as well as our ideal standards upward to accommodate the measurement still being against ideal performance. *Uptime or OEE is a tool, not an end, for performance improvement.* We use industrial standard rates for production planning, we use "perfection" rates for OEE measurement as an improvement facilitator, and we use measures such as unit costs of production as a measure of the desired outcome.

No-Demand and Market Losses. These generally refer to those losses associated with a lack of market demand. The manufacturing staff has little short-term influence on market demand. However, it is critical to the long-term success of the business to highlight this equipment and process availability for strategic decision making regarding gaining additional market share, new capital requirements and/or for capacity rationalization.

Tactically, uptime or OEE is a measure of the daily operating effectiveness of the manufacturing function. It seeks to minimize all losses from ideal and to reach a point where the losses are acceptable from a business perspective; and where production rates are sustainable at a minimal cost of goods sold, all things considered.

Strategically, asset utilization represents the opportunity to strategically position corporate assets toward new products and/or greater market share (and minimal unit cost), or to decommission certain assets that are no longer needed, and the cost of which is not justified in light of current performance. It is understood that certain lines may not be decommissioned in the short term because of company qualification standards for which a given production line may be *uniquely* qualified. But, this should at least highlight the need to do a trade-off analysis for sound business planning, and for not incurring any unnecessary operating and maintenance costs.

Tactically and strategically then, uptime/OEE and asset utilization rates support decisions related to the following, assuring maximum return on capital:

1. Additional production capability for the sale of new products.
2. Additional production capability for the sale of existing products.
3. Daily operating performance.
4. Contract manufacturing for other companies.
5. Reduction in the number of production shifts and costs at a given facility.
6. Mothballing of appropriate production lines for appropriate periods to reduce costs.

On which processes should we be measuring uptime or OEE? The answer to this question is more problematic. Because of plant configuration, product mix, etc., it may not be possible to measure uptime/OEE or asset utilization on all processes. The logistics may just be too difficult, and/or most staff may not be trained to even think in terms of uptime or OEE. At Beta, the approach being used for those difficult situations is to map key processes and select those that (1) are bottlenecks to many finished products; (2) have the highest volume; (3) have the highest gross margin contribution; (4) have the largest quality losses; (5) are considered representative of a number of products or processes; or (6) are some combination or other criteria. Using this approach to narrow your focus will help alleviate getting too bogged down in the logistics of the improvement process, and allow focus on the critical production processes and issues.

Sample Calculation of Batch Plant OEE

Continuous plants tend to be relatively straightforward for setting up an uptime measurement. With some minor modification to the model of Figure 1-5, losses can generally be routinely accounted. Measuring OEE in batch and discrete plants, however, is often more difficult, partly because they generally have more discrete manufacturing steps, some of which feed multiple finished products, partly because they generally produce a larger number of products, partly because the logistics of doing the calculations is just more complex. Using the technique previously described will help to focus the measurement effort, but to illustrate the method, let's take an example from Beta's Hemp Hill plant, a batch operation, which had been measuring the following performance indicators at one of its plants for one of its key production lines:

1. Availability. Although the term being used was uptime, or any time the line was up and running, availability is a more accurate characterization using our model, because it did not include the effects of rate, quality, or other losses. And, because downtime was accounted separately, this number also excludes scheduled downtime.
2. Downtime. This is the time when the equipment is down unexpectedly, and is synonymous with unscheduled downtime losses in the model.
3. Changeover time. This is the time for product changeovers. In the model this was part of the changeover and transition losses.

4. Clear/clean/material changes. This is the time for clearing, cleaning, and setups. This also could be part of the changeover and transition losses.
5. No-demand time. This is the time during which the equipment is not in use for production and can be used to help determine asset utilization rate. It also apparently included scheduled downtime for the following:

(a) Scheduled PM and repairs. This time would normally be characterized as scheduled downtime in the model, and subtracts from no-demand time.
(b) Special and planned projects. This time is not considered by the model shown, but could easily be made a part of the model as a separate category.

6. Quality losses. This was broken into several categories, one of which was product quality losses due to equipment failures.
7. Process rate losses. This was available, but there was some confusion about the industrial engineering standards being applied, as compared to ideal rates that required additional analysis.
8. Other. There were also other losses that did not directly fit into these categories, but needed an accounting, e.g., break times, utility failures, startup losses, etc. These losses may be acceptable under the current business structure, but should be identified separately.

Note: Convincing everyone to account for every hour the line was not operating at peak rate, and the related causes, for loss accounting, was a difficult process. Excuses were numerous, thwarting the effort to assure that there's "no place to hide" poor performance. Ultimately, the value in the measurement was seen, and a measurement system put in place to make sure production lines were being used effectively; and that additional information was available to make tactical and strategic decisions for process improvement.

The calculation in Table 1-1 was applied to a line that essentially operated on a 5-day, 1-shift basis, with the following information being "normalized" to a 24-hour day. The basis for the calculation included:

1. No-demand time was reported at 63%, but this also included scheduled downtime for PM, repairs, and projects. This was reported to average 1 hour/day, although the work was actually performed in much larger blocks of time.
2. Quality losses were reported at 1%.
3. Process rate losses were estimated at about 10%. The peak demonstrated sustainable rate was reported at 200 units per minute, but the line was reported as typically running at 150 units per minute, or a 25% "loss" from ideal. However, this required further review with industrial engineering. A nominal loss of 10% loss was used.
4. Changeover, cleaning, setup, etc., losses were reported at an average of 31%.
5. Breaks were reported at 40 minutes per run. Note: No one is suggesting that people shouldn't be allowed to take breaks. The model accounts for all time related to all production activity. Once the losses are accounted, then business decisions are made as to their acceptability.

Using these data, an average day was broken into two parts—63% of 24 hours for "no-demand" and 37% for production activities, including maintenance, or 15.1 hours for no-demand, and 8.9 hours for production. However, because an average of 1 hour/day was reported for PM/repair/project activities, we subtracted 1 hour from no-demand and added it to production activities, making the average production time (including maintenance) 9.9 hours, and no-demand 14.1 hours.

Nakajima, who developed total productive maintenance (TPM) principles that include the measurement of OEE, might disagree with this approach, because he apparently allows for an indeterminate time period for scheduled maintenance. In this example, we're following a more restrictive application of OEE principles, which accounts for every hour of every day, and improving all business activities associated with the entire production function, including maintenance. Every production function must make these kinds of decisions, and then use the measurement tool for improving its processes, and not necessarily as an end in itself. This approach gives the calculations shown in Table 1-1, and depicted graphically in Figure 1-6.

Table 1-1
Sample OEE Calculation

	Reported	Estimated Hours	% of 9.9 hrs	% of 24 hrs
Scheduled downtime	1 hr	1.0 hrs	10.1%	4.2%
Unscheduled downtime	16%	1.4 hrs	14.4%	5.8%
Changeover/transition losses	31%	2.8 hrs	27.9%	11.5%
Scheduled breaks	⅔ hr	0.7 hrs	6.7%	2.8%
No demand	na	14.1 hrs	na	58.8%
Total non-running hours/%		20.0 hrs		83.1%
Process Rate Losses	10%	—	0.4 hrs	1.7%
Quality Losses	1%	—	0.04 hrs	0.2%
Quality Production at Peak Rate (~Asset Utilization Rate)			3.56 hrs	14.9%

Note: This leaves us with 4 hours during the day when we are actually running the process, but only at 90% of its peak sustainable rate, and with 99% quality:

Using different scenarios for OEE and asset utilization calculations gives:

$$
\begin{aligned}
\text{OEE(@9.9 hrs)} \quad &= \quad \text{Availability} \times \text{Rate} \times \text{Quality} \\
&= \quad (100\% - (10.1\% + 14.4\% + 27.9\% + 6.7\%)) \\
&\quad \times 90\% \times 99\% \\
&= \quad (100\% - 59.1\%) \times 90\% \times 99\% \\
&= \quad 36.4\% \\
\text{OEE (@24 hrs)} \quad &= \quad \text{Market losses} + \text{Asset utilization} \\
&= \quad 58.8\% + 14.9\% \\
&= \quad 73.7\% \\
\text{Asset utilization} \quad &= \quad 16.7\% \times 90\% \times 99\% \\
&= \quad 14.9\%
\end{aligned}
$$

Further, at Beta's Fleming plant, also a batch operation, which supplies material for the line previously described, some additional difficulty was being experienced in developing an OEE measurement, primarily because the plant used a fermentation process as part of the production process. How do you measure peak sustainable rate on a fermentation process? Rather than do this per se, after reviewing historical production data, Beta found that for the key process, which had already been mapped, a cycle time of some 100 hours (e.g., the average

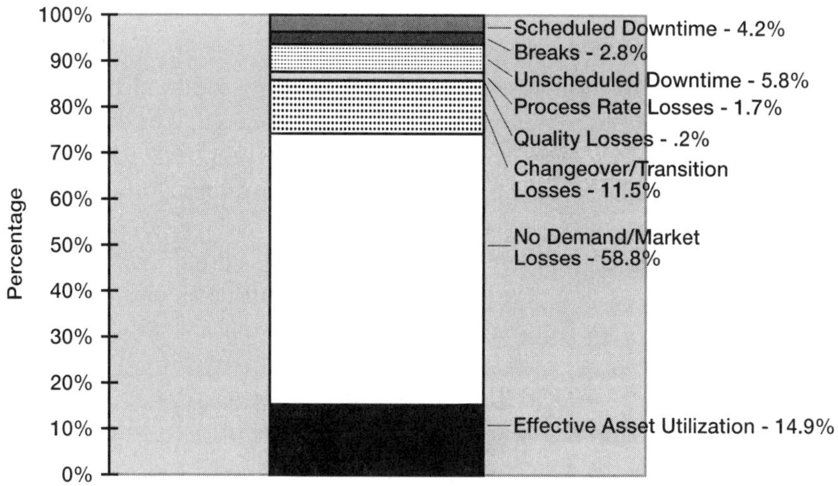

Figure 1-6. Sample uptime/OEE calculation.

of the three best runs) was an ideal run for the fermentation process. We also found from the data that a peak yield of 92% was achievable. With this information the OEE measurement was remodeled:

$$\text{OEE} = \frac{(\text{Ideal cycle time} + \text{Ideal setup / cleanup / PM})}{(\text{Actual cycle time} + \text{Actual setup / cleanup / PM})} \times \frac{\text{Actual yield}}{\text{Ideal yield}} \times \%\text{Quality}$$

so, for example, one run of the process yielded the following:

$$\text{OEE} = \frac{(100+20)}{(160+40)} \times \frac{85\%}{95\%} \times 100\% = 55\%$$

					Losses
Loss accounting:	Cycle time	=	200 – 120	=	80 hours
	yield	=	92% – 85%	=	7%

In this example, the production process ran at 55% of the ideal. If 85% is considered a "world-class level of performance," then the estimated loss is 30%. This could in turn be assigned a $ value for the production process and product, and a value estimated for the losses from the ideal. Some observations on this method:

1. It requires that maintenance and production work as a team to define more clearly the losses from ideal. For example, the 80 hours could be because of poor practices for setup, cleanup, PM, production, etc.; likewise for yield performance. The key here is to identify the losses from ideal, and to work hard to eliminate them. We might also find that in a given circumstance 55% is actually reasonably good.
2. This process could be used to calculate a weighted average for all production using this process stream, and could be combined with other production processes to calculate an aggregate weighted average of manufacturing performance.
3. A quality rate of 100% was assumed in this example, or alternatively that quality was included in the yield determination. In this process the batch was either good, or not, and in the latter case the quality was 0%.
4. The calculation does not include the effects of low (or high) asset utilization. For example, if this process was only used during 50% of the month, then the effective asset utilization rate would be 50% of 55%, or 27.5%. Both measures are useful in that one gives a measure of the effectiveness of the production process itself; the other a measure of the business use of available production capacity. Both measure the prospective business opportunity associated with the product being made.

Discussion of Sample Measurement

The previous discussion suggests substantial opportunity for production process improvement, or market share improvement, or production line rationalization, or some combination. However, the decision making process is subject to additional discussion, because not all factors that lead to business decisions at Beta or in any given organization are included in this approach. For example, if Beta decided to rationalize production lines at Hemp Hill (mothballing, decommissioning, etc.), it would also have to consider whether or not the remaining lines were capable and/or qualified under current regulatory, corporate, and engineering requirements to run the products that would otherwise run on the decommissioned line. Qualifications of operators, anticipated products, etc. would also have to be considered.

In the short term Beta used the given information to make tactical decisions about improving production practices. If Beta could eliminate unscheduled downtime, and reduce scheduled downtime for PM and repair (without deleterious impact on the equipment) by half, and if changeover and transition times could be cut in half, then on average production times could be reduced by 33%. Additional improvements could also be made in assuring running the process at peak rate during a production run, and assuring minimal quality losses. After considerable review, it was finally concluded that about the best OEE achievable under present circumstances for the Hemp Hill plant was 50–55%. At the present time, nine people are operating this line per shift. Theoretically then, the same quantity of product could be produced with 6 people. At a nominal cost of $50K per year per person, this reduces costs per year by $150K. It is understood that theory rarely equals reality, and making linear assumptions is not always valid, because systems tend to be non-linear, but at least Beta now has a basis for making decisions about production planning and rationalization of existing capacity.

Strategically, Beta will use this information to rationalize production capacity. As certain plants improve performance, production requirements will be transferred there, assuring maximum performance. If markets materialize as expected, production capacity will be brought to bear using existing capital assets. If markets do not materialize, then certain production facilities will be decommissioned, at least until they are needed again.

A Special Case—Beta's Dwale Plant

At Beta's Dwale plant, a continuous process plant, they had developed an understanding from a benchmarking effort that 95% uptime was a world-class level of performance for their type of plant. They determined their peak demonstrated sustainable production rate based on their output during their best-ever 3-day continuous performance. However, on further review, they found that there were non-linear variables for fixed and variable costs that would influence their decision about what the optimal targeted uptime should be. They found that variable costs in the form of energy and certain feed material increased sharply above about 87%, leveling off thereafter, but then increasing again above 95% (see Figure 1-7). They also found that maintenance costs increased sharply between about 90% and 95% of peak demonstrated rate, primarily due to fouling and choking of the process. This fouling also affected their ability to keep the

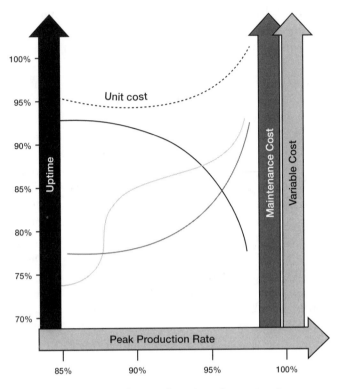

Figure 1-7. Optimal uptime determination.

process on line, reducing their uptime due to additional maintenance. After some analysis, they concluded that their best sustainable performance would be running the plant between 90 and 95% of peak demonstrated rate. Operating the plant at this rate, they felt they could achieve an uptime of 90%, which was considered to be their best achievable and sustainable production rate. It was just not realistic, nor cost effective, to try to run the plant at 100% of its demonstrated rate and still expect to achieve an uptime in the range of 95% without significant additional engineering and capital investment.

Some sites, particularly large, integrated process sites with multiple plants may have structural constraints imposed upon any given plant. For example, environmental discharge constraints may limit one or more plants' ability to operate at peak rate. Business constraints and/or feed stock supplies from upstream plants may force a downstream plant to operate in a less than optimal mode. For example, at one of Beta's downstream plants, some chemical reactor vessels were operated to take feed stock of one kind, while the other vessels were operated to take feed stock of another kind, a kind of buffer for fluctuations in site operation. However, no one ever reduced the peak demonstrated rate to account for this, or counted this as a loss attributed to the site operation. Structural constraints imposed by business or operating conditions must also be accounted in the measurement of uptime or OEE.

Hiding Behind Excess Capacity (The Hidden Plant)

Many managers take the position that they couldn't sell all that they could make. Whether this is true or not is problematic. For example, if they could reduce their unit costs and improve delivery performance, they might be able to immediately gain market share, and sell all they could make. In a strategic sense, however, those underutilized assets represent opportunities such as increased business volume, and return on net assets, but it may be in the rationalization of assets. Hence the previous model.

Many managers use excess capacity as an excuse for poor or sloppy practice. For example, if a plant is operating at 60% asset utilization rate, when world class is 90%, the plant may have another 30% of sales opportunity, at a lower unit cost of production; or could potentially make the product for substantially lower costs, improving profits, and without incremental capital investment. Some managers have been known to use this 30% "reserve" to make sure they can meet delivery schedule, incurring additional costs associated with work-in-process buffer stocks, higher levels of staffing, overtime, scrap product, higher operating and maintenance costs, etc.

Using excess capacity as a "reserve" is the wrong way to do business. It almost always assures no better than mediocre performance, and sometimes worse. Costs incurred are excessive, often extraordinary. Excess capacity often masks poor practices, which increases unit costs, reduces profits and market share, and can result in capital expansion for needed capacity, rather than optimal use of existing assets. These things make companies less competitive, and can ultimately lead to their demise. For example, suppose a company is operating a 5-day, 3-shift operation. With this in mind, our asset utilization rate can be no better than $15 \div 21 = 71\%$. Further suppose that when we measure our uptime or OEE during the 15-shift period, we find that we're operating at 57%, a fairly typical rate when all losses from ideal are accounted. If we could get this rate to 85% or better, this would represent a 50% improvement. We would find that we could produce the same product during a 5-day, 2-shift operation. In the short term we save a great deal of money. In the long term, we have incremental capacity without incremental capital investment.

When excess capacity does exist, it should be viewed as opportunity waiting, and used strategically to increase market share, and over the long haul to maximize return on assets and profits. It should not be used as an excuse for sloppy practice. At Beta's Salyersville plant, a large, continuous process plant, the following conversation occurred with the maintenance manager:

Benchmarking Consultant: "How much does downtime cost you?"

Maintenance Manager: "Nothing, we have 8 lines, we only need 5 to meet current market demand, so when one line shuts down, we start up one of the spares, and keep on producing. So it doesn't cost us anything."

Benchmarking Consultant: "So you're carrying sufficient staff to operate and maintain 8 lines, or at least more than 5?"

Maintenance Manager: Pausing, "Well, probably more than 5."

Benchmarking Consultant: "How about spare parts, are they sufficient for more than 5 lines?"

Maintenance Manager: "Well, probably more than 5."

Benchmarking Consultant: "How about overtime, do you spend considerable overtime to make repairs, or switch over the lines? These failures don't usually occur at a convenient time do they?"

Maintenance Manager: "Well, no they don't, and we probably spend more overtime than we should."

Benchmarking Consultant: "How about colateral damage, do you ever have any because of running a machine to failure, rather than catching it long before it gets so bad it becomes a crisis?"

Maintenance Manager: "Well, probably . . . well, yes we have, on line 3 last week we had a heck of a mess because of a catastrophic failure."

Benchmarking Consultant: "How about scrapped product, or reduced quality, does that occur when you have to switch lines and lose product in process?"

Maintenance Manager:	"Well . . ., almost always."
Benchmarking Consultant:	"How about inter-process flows, does the downtime on the failed line result in delays or disruptions in upstream or downstream processes, requiring considerable effort to re-align the plant?"
Maintenance Manager:	"Well . . ., usually." (At this point, the wind was clearly out of his sails. He was even a bit agitated.)
Benchmarking Consultant:	"How about management attention? Don't events that require a switch-over result in distracting management attention away from other issues that could add more value to the corporation?"
Maintenance Manager:	"Probably."
Benchmarking Consultant:	"Look, I'm not trying to be hard on you, or anyone for that matter. I try to help people see things from a different perspective, to help them identify opportunities for improvement, so they can make more money."
Maintenance Manager:	"I think we have several *opportunities* here, don't we?
Benchmarking Consultant:	"It sure seems that way, but we've just taken the first step in capitalizing on those opportunities. Let's look at how improved processes and practices can help eliminate some of these costs." (We went on to review a strategy to help change the plant's culture from being repair focused to being reliability focused.)

If we have 8 lines, but only need 5, why not operate the plant as if we have only 5, using staff, spares, overtime, etc. at world-class levels of performance to maximize profitability for those 5 lines. Alternatively, why not operate a production line at a world-class level using a 5-day, 2-shift operation, vs. a 5-day, 3-shift operation. What about the "excess capacity"? Strategically, those represent increased market share and improved profits (not excess capacity per se; or, it represents the opportunity to rationalize assets). Once we get the plant to operating reliably at superior levels of performance for 5 lines—striving to be the low-cost producer in the market—then we can position our products to increase market share, while still making a healthy profit, expanding our marketing and distribution efforts, and bringing those additional lines on as we need the product for our newly gained customers. In doing so, we maximize return on assets, profits, and share price.

Differences Between Batch and Continuous Manufacturers

Many have noted that there are substantial differences between the way in which batch and continuous manufacturing plants are operated, most observing that you really cannot expect a batch or discrete plant to be operated like a continuous plant. Agreed. However, these differences should not be used as an excuse for sloppy practice. One of the fundamental questions still remains—What is ideal performance, and how far is my plant from ideal? This is regardless of the type of plant.

Data collected from some 300 manufacturing plants—batch/discrete, continuous, and combination—show the differences in performance, as viewed by the people who operate the plants, are striking. As described in the next chapter on benchmarking, people who work in continuous manufacturing plants report that their practices, when compared to a best practices standard (one that results in higher uptimes, lower unit costs, and better safety) are almost always better than the practices in a typical batch or discrete plant. The reasons for this are uncertain, but it is theorized that the batch manufacturers always believe they can make up for lost production with the next batch, not recognizing that time lost is lost forever. Whereas the continuous manufacturer's mistakes are almost always highly visible, principally because of the very nature of the plant—there are fewer places to hide when a continuous plant suffers lost production. When a batch plant does, this appears not to be the case. More detail on this issue, as well as key success factors, and the differences between batch and discrete plants is provided in Chapter 2 and Appendix A.

Focused Factories, Agile and Lean Manufacturing

In a related area, it has become popular that focused factories represent the seeming best approach for manufacturing plants.[8] While the concept of focused factories has been well received and has shown considerable improvement at some of Beta's plants, it should be emphasized that this has typically been at their batch and discrete plants, with the concepts being more difficult to apply at their continuous plants. Further, even at their batch and discrete plants, what has often resulted within the maintenance function is that "the firefighters have only moved closer to the fires, and little is done to eliminate the cause of the fires." Improved equipment reliability and performance rarely results from this approach, nor is it expected to adequately support related strategies such as agile and lean manufacturing, which require high reliability and performance. *It's hard to be agile or lean when you're broken.* Further, improving production flows and minimizing floor space can lead to substantial production improvement, but has also led to inadequate pull space, lay-down area, etc., for maintaining equipment, at times resulting in increased costs and longer downtime. Certainly plant layout and production flow is critical, but it must fully consider reliability, maintenance, and operating requirements.

The view by some focused factory advocates that having backup machinery and equipment is a solution to capacity and production problems does not appear to be well founded. Additional equipment is not normally the solution to poor maintenance practice, as it increases the need for additional capital, as well as operating and maintenance expense, etc. Getting to the root cause of equipment failures and improving maintenance practices is a much better approach. Beta has found that properly applied, maintenance management systems are not a burden, but a key tool for equipment reliability, and that work orders are an essential element for planning, managing, and generally minimizing maintenance work requirements. They have also found that most often a hybrid organization of some decentralized (focused resources), and centralized resources works best at most of their operations.

Finally, Beta has also found that supervisors, by whatever name they may be called, e.g., team leaders, coaches, facilitators, etc., are in fact needed. Teams that have no inherent natural leadership as a part of them and/or that have limited guidelines for their role have often failed to achieve the desired results at Beta. Leadership and management are still a requirement in most of Beta's plants regardless of the name given the function. Most of us have played on athletic teams, and most of us have had team captains and coaches. Few of us ever disagreed with the coach, whose direction was almost always abundantly clear. Many of us have forgotten that using a team concept for management, as great it is, still requires clear leaders and managers (perhaps disguised as coaches or captains). We may have also forgotten that the goal for a team is clear—beat the opposition; it is not to have a "feel good" experience in and of itself.

Summary

As best practices are implemented at Beta International, fewer people will be required to achieve the same production goals. However, Beta decided to show loyalty to its employees and to work hard to avoid downsizing, and has pledged that it will use the following techniques to minimize that possibility:

1. Not replacing workers lost through attrition: resignations, retirement, etc.
2. Reduced contract labor, using employees even when retraining is required.
3. Reduced overtime. A smaller paycheck is better than no job.
4. Voluntary reductions in staffing.
5. Termination of poor performers.
6. Reallocation of employees for new, or different jobs, including any retraining.
7. Finally, and by no means least, reallocation of resources to handle expanded business volume.

World-class business performance requires excellence in and the integration of marketing, manufacturing, and R&D, and that we know what excellence is by measuring it; it requires that we know what it means to be the low-cost producer of our products, and how to achieve and sustain that position; it requires that we understand how our manufacturing performance relates to our return on net assets and general corporate performance; it requires that we understand our losses from ideal and manage them; it requires that we put in place a reliability process for manufacturing that assures that we design, buy, store, install, operate, and maintain our manufacturing assets in a superb way. Finally, it requires that we integrate our marketing and manufacturing strategy in a comprehensive way, focused on world-class performance.

Each of us sees light (and information) according to where he stands relative to the prism. Beta, like most major manufacturing companies, tends to operate each business function as if each one were the only "color" in the rainbow, and works hard to optimize each function, missing the continuous, interrelated nature of all the issues. Because of this, they only "see" things from one distorted perspective. Because of this, they have tried to optimize their processes, always optimizing at the sub-optimal level. If Beta is ever to find the proverbial gold at the end of the business rainbow, they must recognize that this continuum of issues must be fully integrated and each recognized for its contribution, and interrelationship. Bob Neurath must instill a common sense of purpose for world-class performance among all within Beta International—world-class performance and the gold at the end of the business rainbow. This involves focusing on reliability and capacity improvement for the existing assets, understanding and integrating manufacturing with markets and their sensitivities, measurement of uptime and losses from ideal, and understanding and applying best practices in an integrated way in the design, buy, store, install, operate, and maintain continuum for manufacturing excellence.

References

1. Skinner, W. "Manufacturing—The Missing Link in Corporate Strategy," *Harvard Business Review,* May/June, 1969.

2. Hayes, R. H. and Wheelwright, S. C. "Restoring Our Competitive Edge: Competing Through Manufacturing," *The Free Press,* 1984.

3. Hayes, R. H. and Pisano, G. P. "Beyond World Class: The New Manufacturing Strategy," *Harvard Business Review,* January/February, 1994.

4. Hill, T. *Manufacturing Strategy—Strategic Management of The Manufacturing Function,* MacMillan Press Ltd., 1993.

5. Turner, S. An Investigation of The Explicit and Implicit Manufacturing Strategies of a South African Chemical Company, master's thesis, The Graduate School of Business, University of Cape Town, S.A. December, 1994.

6. Flynn, V. J. "The Evolution of Maintenance Excellence in DuPont," a presentation sponsored by E.I. duPont de Nemours & Co., Inc., by arrangement with the Strategic Industry Research Foundation, Melbourne, Australia, August, 1996.

7. Fraser, A. ICI Manufacturing Technology, Runcorn, Cheshire, England, 1997.

8. Harmon, R. L. "Reinventing the Factory II," *The Free Press,* New York, NY, 1992.

Benchmarks, Bottlenecks, and Best Practices

For the man who knows not what harbor he sails, no wind is the right wind.

Sienna

Benchmarking, according to Jack Grayson, involves "seeking out another organization that does a process better than yours and learning from them, adapting and improving your own process. . . ."[1] Benchmarks, on the other hand, have come to be recognized as those specific measures that reflect a best-in-class standard. Best practices, as the name implies, are those practices best for a given process, environment, etc., and that allow a company to achieve a benchmark level of performance in a given category. Benchmarking, then, involves emulating the best practices of others to improve your processes so that you can achieve a superior level of performance as measured against benchmarks, or best in class. Benchmarking is a continuous process, requiring constant attention to the latest improvement opportunities, and the achievements of others. Further, as Joseph Juran said, "If you don't measure it, you don't manage it." So benchmarks represent those measures we choose to manage to improve performance.

This chapter explores Beta's use of benchmarking, which revealed they were thoroughly average, and represented the beginning of their journey to understanding and implementing the best practices discussed later. We will also review the dynamic nature of bottlenecks, which can help prioritize resources for applying best practices and minimizing key losses, ultimately leading to improved performance. But first, let's review the benchmarking process itself.

Benchmarking—Finding Benchmarks and Best Performers

The first step in benchmarking is to define those processes for which benchmark metrics are desired, and which are believed to reflect the performance objectives of the company. While this may seem simple, it can often be quite complicated. You must first answer the questions "What processes are of concern, e.g., those that support business goals and strategy?" and "What measures best reflect my company's performance for those processes?" Then you must answer the question "What measures best reflect my division or department's performance which in turn supports corporate objectives?" and so on. These decisions will vary from corporation to corporation and from industry to industry, but let's suppose we have an overall objective to improve corporate financial performance, and in particular, manufacturing performance.

Some suggestions at the strategic level are as follows:

Category
Return on net assets
Return on equity
Earnings growth
Profit as a % of sales
Market share
Safety record, etc.

Beta ultimately chose as corporate key performance indicators (KPI's) the principle measures of return on net assets, earnings growth, and safety.

At the strategic operational level, we might see:

- Return on net assets
- Product unit cost
- Percent plant capacity utilization (or uptime, overall equipment effectiveness)
- On-time/in-full deliveries
- Inventory turns
- First-pass/first-quality product
- Training time per employee
- OSHA accidents per 200,000 labor hours
- Customer satisfaction

At the business unit level, Beta chose as its KPI's return on net assets, uptime, unit cost of production, on-time/in-full, customer safety and safety.

Certainly there are other measures within a business unit that must be monitored and used to support the business. Indeed, it is likely that any given business would choose different measures, or measures unique to its industry, and you are encouraged to develop your own analysis in this regard. In any event, these were chosen as encompassing Beta's other supporting and subordinate measures.

At the operational and departmental level, and supporting key business measures were a variety of measures:

- Uptime, or OEE
- First-pass quality yield, cycle times, defect rate, equipment/process capability (statistical)
- Maintenance cost as a % of plant replacement value
- Percent downtime, planned and unplanned
- O&M cost as a % of total costs and per unit of product
- Percent overtime
- Average life, mean time between repairs for critical machinery

Beta's principle plant measures were generally uptime/OEE (and losses thereto per Figure 1-5), maintenance cost as a percent of plant replacement value, unit cost of production, inventory turns, on-time/in-full deliveries, and safety. Each department understood this, and chose other measures within their department that supported the plant's measures.

Within a given industry, we might see industry-specific metrics, such as cost per equivalent distillate capacity (refining), equivalent availability or forced outage rate (electric utility), labor hours per vehicle (automotive), and so on. No industry-specific measures were used for Beta, but may be used in the future at specific plants. A more detailed listing of performance measures that may facilitate additional consideration and discussion in the selection process is provided in Reference 2.

The key for Beta, as it is for most companies, is to select those measures that reflect the performance objectives of the corporation, or for a given process within the corporation, and then subsequently to determine how the company compares to other companies, generally, though not necessarily, in their industry, especially those in the upper quartile. In general no more than 10 key metrics, and preferably 5 or so, should be selected in each category of interest, and they should relate to each other in a supportive, integrated relationship.

Before going to the next step, a strong word of caution is advised at this point. Benchmarking is part of *beginning* the process for continuous change, and is not a conclusion. Too many executives, after going through a benchmarking exercise, forget that the true definition of benchmarking is *finding another organization that does a process better than yours (not just doing the numbers), and essentially emulating what they do.* Being good executives and decision makers, they tend to get the benchmarks—the numbers, not the practices or processes—and then make arbitrary decisions on the numbers, before the processes are deployed.

For example, a world-class measure of inventory turns on maintenance stores at a manufacturing plant is typically viewed as greater than 2. A typical organization has a turns ratio on spare parts of 1, or sometimes even less. Knowing this, the good executive might then decree that half of the spare parts inventory should be eliminated, without recognizing that their organization is a highly "reactive" operation with high breakdown losses, and *needs* additional spare parts to support this mode of operation. The executive has failed to recognize that superior practices in operations, maintenance, and stores resulted in high turns, not arbitrary decisions.

Benchmark data tend to have a very high level of "scatter," and discerning what is "best" for a given organization in a given business situation can be an enormous effort. Further, a given plant may have inherent design or operational capability that either enhances, or limits its capability to achieve a world-class level of performance for a given measure. Finally, other corporate issues such as product mix

(Chapter 3) can have a very big impact on operational performance, even in an exceptionally well-run manufacturing plant.

The key is to use benchmark data as the beginning of a process for change (which never stops), and to use the information to make changes to your practices and business decisions that will improve the performance indicators. It is *not* to be used for *arbitrary* decision making or cost cutting by executives. This was and continues to be a difficult issue for the executives at Beta, as it often is for most companies who are seeking rapid improvement. The key is to understand processes that lead to superior performance, not to arbitrarily cut budgets with the hope that everything will turn out all right.

Making the Comparison

Comparing your company to other companies is the next step. Having selected the key metrics, you must now make sure that you are properly measuring these metrics within your company, that you understand the basis for the numbers being generated, and that you can equitably apply the same rationale to other information received. Now, to develop comparable data from other companies may be somewhat difficult. You may have several choices:

1. Seek publicly available information through research.
2. Set up an internal benchmarking group that will survey multiple plants within a corporation, assuring fair and equitable treatment of the data. Benchmarks will then be defined in the context of the corporation.
3. Seek the assistance of an outside company to survey multiple plants, usually including your corporation, but also expanded to other companies within the company's industry.
4. Seek the assistance of an outside company to survey multiple plants, many of which may be outside your industry, in related, or even unrelated fields.
5. Some combination of the above, or other alternative.

If you choose to do benchmarking, a couple of points are worth mentioning. It is recommended that a standard such as the Benchmarking Code of Conduct[3] be followed. This assures that issues related to confidentiality, fairness, etc. are followed. For benchmarking outside the company, particularly within your industry, it is recommended that you use an outside firm, to help avoid any problems with statutes related to unfair trade practices, price fixing, etc. Properly used, benchmarking is an excellent tool to assure improved performance.

Benchmarking has become associated with "marks," as opposed to finding someone who does something better than you do and doing what they do, which may more accurately be called best practices. Notwithstanding the semantics, benchmarking and application of best practices are powerful *tools, not solutions,* to help improve operational and financial performance. The ultimate benchmark is consistently making money, at substantially better than industry average, over the long term. Applying benchmarking and best practices can help assure that position.

Let's consider some prospective world-class levels of performance, e.g., the "benchmarks" developed by Beta International shown in Table 2-1. Note these are nominal in that they represent a composite of several sources, and specific "benchmarks" may vary depending on plant design, process design, industry, product mix, business objectives, etc., and may change with time as companies improve. However, they do represent a good cross section from Beta's experience.

Be cautious about using benchmarks. First, there is considerable scatter in the data used in benchmarking. Second, benchmark data are constantly changing as plants improve their processes. Third, no single benchmark should be used to make any decisions; rather, all the data must be considered in light of the company's overall business goals. Fourth, variables related to product mix, processes, etc., will affect benchmarks. For example, while the data in Table 2-1 are relatively good as guidance, we could review the paper products industry and find that a world-class level for uptime in a tissue plant might be 95%+, in a newsprint plant 90%+, in a coated paper plant 85%+, depending on any number of factors. Likewise, in the petrochemical industry, we might find that a world-class olefines plant would operate at 95%+, and that plastics and elastomers plants would only operate at 85%+.

To further illustrate the point about being cautious when using benchmark data, let's consider maintenance costs as a percent of plant replacement value. This number is commonly used in manufacturing plants to "normalize" the maintenance costs for a given plant asset. However, it's important to understand how these data vary with circumstances. For example, the two variables to develop the measurement are themselves highly variable—maintenance costs in the numer-

Table 2-1
Comparative Data: World-Class and Typical Performance[5-16]

Performance Measure	Nominal World-Class	Typical
Manufacturing Performance		
On-time/in-full	99%	80–90%
Uptime (continuous process plants)	90–95%	70–80%
Overall equipment effectiveness (discrete)	80–85%	50–70%
Quality - Cpk	>2	>1.33
Defect rate	50–100 ppm	500–5,000 ppm
Waste/scrap as % of manufacturing costs	0.1–0.2%	1–3%
Customer returns	<0.01%	<0.1%
Critical equipment/processes "capable"	95%	30–70%
OSHA injuries per 200k hrs		
Recordables	<0.5	5–10
Lost time accidents	<0.05	0.2–0.5
Maintenance Performance		
Maintenance costs as a % of PRV*	1–3%	3–6%
Breakdown production losses	<1–2%	5–10%
Planned maintenance	>90%	50–70%
Reactive maintenance	<10%	45–55%
PRV $ per mechanic	>$6–8M	$2–4M
% Maintenance rework	<1%	>10%
Overtime	<5%	10–20%
Stores/spare parts management		
Parts stockout rate	<1%	4–6%
Stores value as a % of PRV*	0.25–0.5%	1–2%
Parts inventory turns	>2	1
Line items/store employee/hr	10–12	4–5
Stores value/store employee	$1–1.5M	$0.5–1.0M
Disbursements/store employee/yr	$1.5–2M	$0.5–1.0M
Human Resources		
Training ($/yr)	$2–3K	1–1.5K
(Hrs/yr)	40	20 hrs
Employee turnover rate	<2–4%	5–15%
Absentee rate	<1–2%	4–8%
Injury rate	—See Above Data—	

PRV is plant replacement value, simple in concept, but more difficult in practice. For example, if you had to rebuild the plant today, what would it cost? Alternatively, if it is insured for replacement value, what is that? Or, what price would the plant bring on the open market? Or, what is its original capitalization, adjusted for inflation? Or, some combination of the above.

ator and plant replacement value in the denominator—and require understanding of each's genesis, discussed in the following.

The Numerator

Maintenance costs may have to be normalized to a labor base and some "equivalent value" for labor. For example, at Beta's plant, located in Asia Pacific, this ratio was only 0.75%. However, when reviewed more fully, it turned out that their actual labor rates were very low, less than half of what you might expect if the work were performed by European or American workers. When we took the actual labor hours, and multiplied by US labor and overhead rates, the ratio came up to ~1.25%. Secondly, this particular plant, while well managed, may have been "saving" maintenance costs at the expense of the long-term reliability of the equipment and not spending enough to maintain the equipment and the plant infrastructure on a life cycle basis. However, this second point is more of a judgment call. Further, some of the "maintenance expenses," particularly for upgrades of major capital items were being capitalized (vs. expensed). While this is a legitimate accounting choice, it can skew benchmark data somewhat, depending on how you treat these items. Other issues to consider include reviewing 1) the historical maintenance costs for a given set of plants and their general trend, and 2) the actual condition of the assets—has it deteriorated over the past few years? As always, maintenance costs will depend to some degree on the type of plant. For example, a paint pigment plant is likely to incur higher maintenance costs as a percent of replacement value than an electronics plant. Finally, maintenance costs at a given time may not be the key factor in overall business excellence, and extra money spent to produce higher uptimes may be appropriate in some circumstances.

The Denominator

How was the plant replacement value determined? For example:

1. Was it the plant's insured replacement value? At full value?
2. Was it the initial capital value, plus inflation; plus added capital plus inflation on the added capital?
3. Was it a professionally assessed value based on selling the asset?
4. Was it based on similar assets with similar output in similar products that have recently been sold?

5. Were there other unique circumstances that resulted in a higher-than-normal asset valuation. For example, at one of Beta's plants, the effluent treatment requirements substantially increased the plant replacement value, but did not add a commensurate amount to the maintenance costs. At another, the reverse was true.

There are probably other factors in the numerator and denominator that may be considered to assure that "like-to-like" comparisons are made, but these are ones that come to mind immediately. Benchmarking is a good process to help begin to understand how to improve performance, but *don't use any single benchmark measure to make any decisions or reach any conclusions about anything.* The data must be used in the aggregate, and the processes and practices that yield improved performance must drive behavior and business decisions.

For example, it could be that a plant has low maintenance costs and low uptime, possibly meaning that the high downtimes are because of poor maintenance practices—not enough maintenance; or that they have high uptimes and high maintenance costs as a percent of PRV because they have lots of in-line spares and lots of breakdown maintenance, contributing to higher unit costs of production; or, in the best cases, they have high uptimes and low maintenance costs because they're doing the right things right.

All these must be considered. In the case of Beta's Asian plant, it was actually recommended that they spend more money on maintenance, not less, because that was likely to produce higher uptime, as well as slightly higher unit costs of production. But, the gross margin on their product was so high that the incremental financial gain made on the incremental production was well worth the additional expense, in spite of the slightly higher unit cost of production! Much depends on your business objective.

As you might expect from this discussion, asset utilization rate is, if not the most important measure to a manufacturer, among the most important measures. Two measures that help capture this are overall equipment effectiveness (OEE),[4] and uptime, a measure generally attributed to DuPont in its creation, and understood to have been developed from the OEE concept. At Beta, OEE is generally used in discrete and batch manufacturers and is further discussed in following sections. Uptime, or a variant thereto, is generally used in continuous process industries, e.g., refinery, chemical and petrochemical, pulp and paper, primary metals, etc.

Beta International ultimately decided to use the following model as an integral part of the improvement process:

- What is the plant's uptime or asset utilization rate?
- What are the causes of lost utilization, e.g., no demand, production changeovers, planned downtime, unplanned downtime, reduced rate, reduced yield, reduced quality, poor utilities, etc.? Note: this means you must measure the causes of every hour of lost utilization. A sample of the causes of losses is provided in Table 2-2, Sample Uptime/OEE Measurement and Related Losses.
- What is being done to eliminate the causes of these losses?
- What is the plant's unit cost of production?
- What is my personal responsibility (at all levels) in eliminating these causes?

Table 2-2
Sample OEE Measurement and Related Losses
for a Batch Manufacturer

Peak Sustainable Rate	100%
Minus Losses:	
No demand	10%
Changeovers	12%
Reduced rate/cycle times	5%
Quality rejects	1%
Planned downtime	5%
Unplanned downtime	5%
Other losses	2%
Total losses	40%
Net output	60%

Additional discussion is provided later in this chapter under "Manufacturing Uptime Optimization," regarding methods for creating a common sense of purpose, and for determining and measuring the cause of major losses.

One interesting statistic that Beta found in doing some comparative analysis is provided in Figure 2-1. This correlates uptime as a function of reactive maintenance. What was found was that on average, for every 10% observed increase in reactive maintenance, an approximate

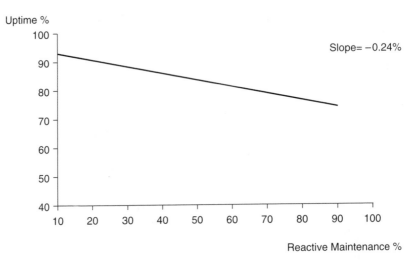

Figure 2-1. Uptime vs. reactive maintenance.

2% reduction in uptime was realized. Reactive maintenance is defined as that portion which is run-to-failure, breakdown, or emergency. In other words, it's all the work that you do during a week that wasn't anticipated at the beginning of the week. These data imply that highly reactive organizations experience loss of output because of the reactive processes they have in place. It could also be further implied that high reactive maintenance levels also result in high maintenance costs, because the general literature reports that reactive maintenance typically costs twice or more that of planned maintenance.

Beta also put forth considerable effort to determine what factors would affect the improvement process as they strove for world-class performance. These efforts included perceptions within rank and file, as well as management, on issues such as management support and plant culture, organization and communication, performance measures, training, operations and maintenance practices, stores practices, and overhaul practices. These self-assessments indicated that one of the critical parameters in Beta's case, when compared to plants with substantially better performance, was the issue of management support and plant culture. Management support and plant culture reflect the degree to which management is perceived to be supportive of manufacturing excellence, basic reliability principles and practices, and the extent to which management has created a proactive, team-based, process-oriented culture. Beta was generally within the typical range in their scores in most areas, except for this one, where it ranked some 5–10% below average. Coincidentally, Beta's average uptime or OEE was below an average industrial manufacturing plant. Beta was apparently so focused on cost cutting they had created a workforce afraid to take the risks associated with changing their processes, and who had greater focus on cost cutting and delivering a budget than on delivering manufacturing excellence.

Table 2-3 is a summary of typical and world-class measures from these self-assessments. Appendix A provides additional detail, including statistical correlations of the key success factors, or "drivers" for best practices and improved performance. This analysis shows *uptime is positively correlated with all leadership/management practices, and*

(text continued on page 50)

Table 2-3
Reliability and Maintenance Practices Assessment

Management Practices	Max	Characteristic/Score -Average Scores- Batch	Continuous	Typical World Class
Mgmt support/plant culture	100%	51%	57%	>75%
Organization/communication	100%	50%	59%	>75%
Performance measures	100%	44%	60%	>75%
Training	100%	48%	50%	>75%
Operational practices	100%	50%	57%	>75%
Reactive maintenance	100%	53%	46%	<10%
Preventive maintenance	100%	47%	57%	>75%
Stores practices	100%	36%	47%	>75%
Shutdown/overhaul practices	100%	50%	68%	>75%
Predictive maintenance (Vibration)	100%	18%	60%	>75%
Predictive maintenance (Oil, IR, UT, etc.)	100%	35%	55%	>75%
Proactive maintenance	100%	25%	40%	>75%

Notes:
1. These data have been compiled from a database of some 300 manufacturing plants who participated in the self-audit. A detailed discussion of these parameters is provided in Appendix A. The scores have been normalized to percentages and do not reflect the weighting given to different areas, which is also discussed in Appendix A.
2. A world-class plant is viewed as one that sustains an OEE or uptime of some 85–95%, and concurrently reports scores in the upper quartile in essentially all categories shown, with one crucial exception, and that is having a reactive maintenance of less than 10%.

with all operating/maintenance practices, that is, the higher the score in best practice, the higher the uptime. Conversely, in this same study, *when reactive maintenance levels were high, all leadership/management practices, as well as all operating and maintenance practices, were poorer.* Nor was any one practice, or success factor, the "magic bullet," but rather all had to be done in an integrated and comprehensive way. The conclusion is that in a reactive culture, practices tend to be poorer, uptime lower, and costs higher—processes are not in control and practices are less than optimal. In a reliability-focused culture, uptime is higher, costs lower, and process and practices are in control. As David Ormandy said, "If you do all the little things right, the big bad things don't happen."

The concept of uptime, typically used for continuous manufacturing plants, and OEE, typically used for batch and discrete plants, while a fairly simple one, was difficult for the management of Beta to embrace initially. They had become so accustomed to managing to budgets, and to manufacturing a targeted quantity of product based on historical experience, some fairly fundamental principles of manufacturing were being ignored at many plants. These are reviewed in the following section in a different light.

From total productive maintenance (TPM[4]) principles, we understand that all production processes are limited (1) by the amount of time the equipment can actually run, its availability; (2) by the yields it provides when it is available, its process rate and efficiency; and (3) by the sellable product produced, its quality. The product of these parameters defines maximum output through so-called overall equipment effectiveness, or OEE as previously noted. This overall equipment effectiveness parameter will in large measure be driven by its reliability, which can in turn, drive asset utilization, unit cost, and ultimately market share, profits, and return on assets. Consider the data in Table 2-4.

Even with the level of performance shown, the plant can only produce 85% of its maximum capacity. But, plant overall equipment effectiveness (OEE) levels of 85% are generally accepted as "world-class" for discrete manufacturers.[5] Additional discussion of TPM is provided in Chapter 13.

This example illustrates the compounding effect of availability, production rate/yield, and quality, which is further compounded when multiple production steps are involved in the production process, cre-

Table 2-4
Overall Equipment Effectiveness

Measure	Definition	Nominal World Class
% Availability	Available time/max available time	>95%
% Performance efficiency	Actual yield or throughput/max throughput	>95%
% Quality rate	Quality production/total production	>95%
% Overall equipment Effectiveness (OEE) =	Availability × performance efficiency × quality	>85%

ating dynamically variable bottlenecks in the daily production process. This is discussed in the following section.

Bottlenecks—A Dynamic View

In *The Goal*,[17] Goldratt explains bottlenecks in a manufacturing process and how to manage bottlenecks, which will always exist in any manufacturing plant. However, Goldratt doesn't emphasize the fact that bottlenecks are quite dynamic, and can change daily. For example, on a given day a lack of raw material may be the production bottleneck; on another day unplanned downtime in one area; on another day rate reduction in another area; and so on. Beta generally understood where its design bottlenecks were. Indeed, at any given plant, plant management could almost always identify the bottleneck in the production process. Often, however, this was not the limiting factor of production on a given day. It was dependent on which equipment was down, or which process was difficult to control, or the quality of the raw material, or the most recent production requirement from sales, or any number of factors.

In this section, we will review some exemplary data concerning how equipment and process reliability, or the lack thereof, can dramatically affect production capacity and therefore profitability; and by inference the dynamic nature of bottlenecks. We've seen the TPM principle of overall equipment effectiveness (OEE = Availability × Process rate/Yield/Efficiency × Quality), and how it can lead to a measure of a plant's actual output compared to its theoretical output. We've also seen how these effects are cumulative and compounding in their ability to substantially reduce output.

This effect is only further compounded when one process feeds another in a manufacturing plant. Studies have shown that downtime events can dramatically reduce capacity of a given manufacturing plant. Consider the following Beta plant where process A feeds process B, which feeds process C, which yields the finished product:

Current rated capacities
  A @ 100 units/hr
  B @ 110 units/hr
  C @ 120 units/hr

If each step is operated at capacity, producing 100% quality product, then the maximum throughput would be 876,000 units per year, and would be limited by process A, the bottleneck. Suppose further that we've collected data from each production area and found the processes typically operating as follows:

	Planned Downtime	Unplanned Downtime	Process Rates	Quality Rate
A	10%	5%	95%	98%
B	10%	10%	90%	95%
C	10%	15%	90%	90%

Then, production rate (or OEE) for each manufacturing step will be the product of availability × production rate × quality, or:

	OEE	Equivalent Capacity
A	79.1% × 100 = (85% × 98% × 95%)	79.1 units/hr
B	68.4% × 110 =	75.2 units/hr
C	60.7% × 120 =	72.9 units/hr

Now, plant capacity is limited by Process C, and equals

	Availability	×	Process Rate	×	Quality
=	(75% × 8,760)	×	(120 × 90%)	×	90%
=	638,604 units/yr		(72.9% of max)		

Or does it?

Suppose planned downtime occurs at the same time for each process, because we have considerable control of this factor. But, as luck would have it, unplanned downtime is such a random variable that it rarely occurs at the same time for each process. Suppose further, that we are in a manufacturing environment with a just-in-time philosophy, keeping inventory and work in process to an absolute minimum. Then, we have the following:

	Availability	×	Process rate	×	Quality
Process A yields	(8,760 × 85%)	×	(100 × 95%)	×	98%
	= 693,223 units/yr				

From the information above, processes B and C have

	B	C
Non-coincident downtime	10%	15%
Quality	95%	90%
Rates	90%	90%

Process B's output is

= A's output × B's production rate
= 693,223 × (100% − 10%) × ((110% ÷ 100%) × 90%) × 95%
= 586,779 units/yr

Similarly Process C's output, and therefore, the plant's annual output is

= 485,797 units/yr

which is only 55.3% of maximum theoretical capacity. Simply eliminating unplanned downtime in each process, that is, maximizing process and equipment reliability, and recalculating the output yields an annual output of 627,570 units/yr, or 72% of maximum, a 30% increase in output. In effect, they could find a plant within their plant by eliminating unplanned downtime. Further, eliminating unplanned downtime and improving process reliability through a comprehensive improvement strategy also provides additional gains:

1. Product quality increases. Increased process reliability assures equipment is running as it should and yielding maximum-quality product. Further, fewer breakdowns reduce scrap, rework, and transition losses. In effect, quality is improved.
2. Process efficiencies and rates increase. Considerable process inefficiency can occur as equipment is failing, or when being restarted after repair. This is particularly true when a commissioning process is not in place to assure adequate and proper repair. For example, according to the Electric Power Research Institute, over 50% of the failures in fossil power plants occur within one week of startup and last for one week. This reduces availability and rates (yields, efficiency, etc.).
3. Planned downtime decreases. As process and equipment reliability increases, fewer overhauls are necessary. Further, more planning and work are done prior to the overhaul effort, so that minimum planned downtime is necessary for overhauls. Better application of resources is inevitable.

Consider the potential effect of these three inherent improvements that result from a good reliability-based strategy. For example, suppose we could reduce planned downtime for each process from 10% to 8%, that we could improve quality by 2% in processes B and C, and that we could improve process yields by 2% in each process. These are relatively minor improvements. However, working through the math yields a total output of 683,674 units/yr, another 9% in increased output, and now at 81% of maximum, nearing a world-class level of >85%. Alternatively, if market demand is substantially below running the plant 24 hours a day, 7 days a week, then this same approach allows for reducing a 5-day, 3-shift operation to a 5-day, 2¼-shift operation, saving tens of thousands, if not millions per year.

We've covered several key benchmarks, touched briefly on the dynamic nature of bottlenecks, and looked at best practices and how they can bring us to a world-class level of performance. However, one of the most difficult issues is getting started. The next section describes how one of Beta's plants initiated its improvement process and created a common sense of purpose and teamwork in the effort.

Manufacturing Uptime Improvement Model

As Beta has found, simple cost cutting may not be the most effective solution for improving manufacturing performance. Indeed, in some cases cost cutting has resulted in a deterioration of assets such that manufacturing performance has suffered substantially. Nor are cost cutting and arbitrary decision making likely to result in benchmark levels of performance. Improved productivity, improved output using existing assets, lower unit costs of production, etc. are a natural consequence of good processes and best practices applied to the manufacturing environment. But, where do we begin with the improvement process? We can't focus on everything at once, so how do we apply our limited resources to provide the greatest improvement? How do we sustain the improvement process? The following is one model that has worked well at many of Beta's plants.

We'll begin with the assumption that manufacturing uptime as previously defined is a key measure of the success of a manufacturing plant. Indeed, in the best plants in the world, OEE is typically in the range of 85%+ for batch and discrete plants, whereas an average batch plant operates in the range of 60%; and uptime is typically in the range of 90–95% for continuous process plants, whereas the average plant operates in the range of 75–80%.

If we ask: What is my uptime or OEE? What are the causes of lost uptime? This is sort of a "Where am I and why am I here?" set of questions. Next we must ask, "What am I doing to eliminate the causes of lost uptime?" Here's where things begin to get more complicated. The first two questions may be difficult enough for many manufacturers, considering determination of their real and imagined bottlenecks, their product mix effects, process flow effects, etc. However, most can usually come up with a reasonable estimate of theoretical capacity and resultant uptime, and of some key causes of lost uptime. Typically, these are at the strategic level, and perhaps a best guess, or both. So how do we refine this, and more importantly, how do we decide what the root causes are, and what to do next? The following outlines a process that several of Beta's plants have used to "jump start" the improvement process.

At the Beaver Creek plant, the technique of failure modes and effects analysis (FMEA) was used to begin the process for establishing priorities, with the plant being viewed as a system, a system that frequently experienced functional failures. *A functional failure was defined as anything that resulted in substantial loss of production capacity, or that resulted in extraordinary costs, or that created a major safety hazard.* The first step was to have a team of people use a production process block diagram to verify (or determine) the specific peak production rates of each step of the production process. They didn't have the complicating effect of having to consider too many products, but if that happens, select a key one or typical one, use it, and then use the process to normalize other products relative to product demand. This process will allow you to determine your "design" bottleneck(s) in the production process. Recall that an improvement in the throughput at the bottleneck results in an improvement of the throughput of the entire plant. In any event, set up a block diagram of your production process. For example, the following one shows where process A feeds process B, which feeds process C. Other processes also feed into the final product, e.g., process D:

D →→
   ↓

A→ B→ C (Finished product)

Next, create a set of cross-functional teams, one from each major production step, to define and analyze "losses" at each step in the production process, and to offer suggestions regarding reducing these losses. As noted, for purpose of the review and analysis, a functional failure of the system is defined as *anything* that results in substantial loss of production capacity, or substantial unnecessary costs, or a major safety hazard.

Each cross-functional team from the various production steps should typically consist of an operator, a production supervisor, a mechanic and/or electrician, and a maintenance supervisor. These should be people who are peer leaders within their areas of the plant, and who feel the freedom to express their considered opinions. Other people could be involved as part of these teams, and this decision should be left to those leading the effort. The key is to have a team of people who understand where the plant's problems are, and who are willing to work as a team to help resolve those problems. Finally, there should also be a group of support staff who represent another team for the review process. This is likely to consist of a plant engineer, a member of the purchasing staff, a member of the human resources staff, a store person, someone from utilities, and perhaps others who can contribute to problem resolution as the review evolves.

This will result in teams of nominally 4–5 people from each of the production areas, people who are most familiar with the production and maintenance practices, plus one or two teams of people from other plant support areas, such as purchasing (spare parts and raw material), stores, capital projects, contractor support, project engineering, utilities, and human resources. Some may argue that all this is unnecessarily tying up too many people, and some of that criticism may be warranted, but you just can't tell *a priori* whether it is or not. It's been Beta's experience that once you get a group like this together, all focused on plant success through solving problems. It's surprising, even fascinating, what is revealed in the review process. Team building takes place without focusing on what team building is, because everyone is focused on problem solving for the good of the plant. More examples of that below.

As noted, once the group is together, we define a functional failure of the production process as *anything* happening in the plant that results in lost uptime, or extraordinary cost, or a safety hazard. Once a functional failure has been identified in a given area, we also ask how often these failures occur, and what are their effects (principally financial as to lost uptime or extra costs).

Next, using a facilitator (a must) we "walk through" the production process with the team assembled, defining functional failures associated with each step in the production process. We begin with the first step in the production process, e.g., process A, but once we've finished with finding all the functional failures, their frequencies and effects, in process A, we also look downstream and ask the questions: "Are failures in process B causing any failures in process A? Are failures in any of the support functions, e.g., utilities, purchasing, human resources, capital projects, etc., causing any failures in process A?" And so on. Next we go to the team in process B and ask the same series of questions, then looking upstream and downstream, and at the support team to identify functional failures of the system. Using this same method, we walk through each step in the production process looking for functional failures in the system. Finally, we also make sure that all the support functions are encouraged to communicate with the production functions regarding how production could help the support functions more effectively perform their job. This process is *not* used per se as a problem-*solving* exercise, only as a problem-*identification* exercise, including a general order of magnitude to their relative size and importance.

For example, at one of Beta's plants, step A in the production process, we found that:

1. One particular piece of equipment was frequently failing, resulting in most production losses. Further review of this equipment was held in abeyance until root cause analysis could be applied.
2. Raw material quality was a major contributor to lost uptime, lost quality, poor process yields, etc. (As opposed to the ability of the operator to run, or the mechanic to repair a given set of production equipment.)
3. Gearbox (or pump, or motor, or compressor, etc.) failures were a major contributor to mechanical failures. (However, the gearbox was purchased without the proper service factor, and has been run at higher-than-design rates, so it's not likely a "maintenance" problem per se, but rather more likely a design/procurement problem.)
4. Operator inexperience and lack of training is a major contributor to poor process yield. (Operators had been asking for additional training for some time.)
5. Market demand was highly variable, both in product mix and quantity, resulting in frequent downtime. (Marketing had tried to "reduce overhead allocation" by selling anything the plant could make, resulting in 200 different products, but only 5 made up 75% of production demand; the opportunity cost of downtime for changeovers, and the cost of equipment reliability had not been considered; marketing must target its niches more effectively.)
6. Spare parts were frequently not available, or of poor suitability or quality. (Purchasing had no real specifications or understanding of the need—low bid was the criterion, lacking specifications.)
7. Inherent design features (or lack thereof) made maintenance a difficult and time-consuming effort, e.g., insufficient isolation valves, insufficient lay down space, skid-mounted pumps, etc. Lowest installed cost was the only real criterion for capital projects (vs. lowest life cycle cost).
8. Poor power quality was resulting in frequent electronic problems, and was believed to be causing reduced electrical equip-

ment life. (Power quality hadn't been considered by the engineers as a factor in equipment and process reliability.)

9. Lubrication practices for mechanical equipment needed substantial improvement. (The lubricators, who weren't well-trained to begin with, were let go some time ago in a cost-cutting move. Would you deliberately choose NOT to lubricate your automobile regularly, or have 10 different people with 10 different skill levels and backgrounds to do your lubrication?)

10. Mechanics were in need of training on critical equipment and/or precision mechanical skills. A few needed a fresh (or refresh) course in bearing handling and installation. (Reducing training expenses was another cost-cutting move to "save" money. Someone once said: "You think education is expensive—try ignorance!")

And so on. Next, we repeated this process for each step in the Beaver Creek production process, gathering estimations and potential causes for the losses in uptime and/or extraordinary costs. A point worth mentioning is that this may be a very imprecise process, bordering on controlled chaos. Further, in a forum such as this, we're not likely to be able to accurately calculate the losses; we're estimating, perhaps even "guesstimating." As such, these estimates will require validation at some later time. However, these estimates are being made by those who should be in a position to know best. Perhaps more importantly, an additional benefit is that we have our staff working as a team to understand each other's issues, and using this information to focus on common goals—improving process and equipment reliability, reducing costs, improving uptime, and in the final analysis improving Beaver Creek and Beta's financial performance.

After we complete this process on each of the steps in the production process, we step away from the individual process analyses and began to judge the overall plant operation, that is, how our bottlenecks might shift, depending on the nature of what we've found in the review; how our previous impressions may now have changed; how cost reduction efforts may now focus on different issues; how we may be seeing systematic effects at every step; how one process can have a dramatic effect on downstream processes; etc. Further, at Beaver Creek we made an estimate of how each affected production capacity, costs, or safety, so that we could prioritize how to apply resources to areas where we could achieve the most benefit with the available resources. Before jumping to any premature conclusions, and by reviewing the causes and solutions to each, we considered carefully the areas where the most benefit was to be gained.

For Beaver Creek, we found that most quantifiable production losses or major costs were caused by no more than three problems or issues, and sometimes by only one key problem. Such was the case in step A, wherein a single piece of equipment was causing most of the production losses, followed by poor raw material quality, followed by gear box problems, the sum of which accounted for over 90% of production losses. But, we also found several systematic issues prevalent throughout the organization, e.g., lack of training for operators, mechanics, and electricians, spare parts quality and availability, product mix and production planning, lubrication practices, design practices—particularly getting input from the plant on operational and maintenance issues, etc. These systematic issues had to be resolved at a plant level or higher, while in parallel solving equipment specific issues at the area level.

As we went through this analysis, we also began to determine where to best apply certain technologies and practices. For example, if the gearboxes were causing extraordinary downtime and costs, we could in the short term use vibration analysis (a so-called predictive technology) to anticipate problems and be prepared to respond to them in a planned, organized way. In the long term, the engineers had to look for more constructive solutions by improving the basic design (a more proactive approach). If raw material was a problem, in the short term we could monitor the quality of raw materials more frequently and mitigate these effects. In the long term, we could work more closely with suppliers to eliminate the root cause. If a given piece of equipment was the problem, we could set up a detailed root cause failure analysis process to eliminate this problem.

Further, we considered how best to prioritize our production and maintenance planning efforts, anticipating where resources were best applied. What also came from the analysis was that we were doing a great deal of preventive maintenance to little effect—either over-doing it on some equipment and achieving little uptime improvement, or under-doing it on other equipment and experiencing unplanned equipment downtime. We can begin to consider how to optimize our PM practices. More on that later in Chapter 10. We could go on, but the point is that if you don't understand where the major opportunities are, then it is much more difficult to apply the appropriate technologies and methods to improve your performance in a rational way. This method facilitates defining major problems and issues and, perhaps more importantly, creates a team-based approach to resolve those problems.

Some other obvious but easy-to-fix problems came up during the review. For example, the Beaver Creek plant had numerous steam, air, and gas leaks at their plant—an easy economical thing to correct with an almost immediate payback. At Beaver Creek, a typical manufacturing plant, some 30% of their steam traps were bad—a tremendous energy loss, unnecessarily costing some $50,000 per year. They also had four 250-horsepower compressors. Only two were needed for most production requirements. Three operated routinely. Conservatively speaking, their savings in getting their air leaks fixed was also $50,000 per year (250 hp × 6,000 hours/year × $0.05/kwh). Nitrogen leaks were also present and substantially more expensive. Finally, a point that should be emphasized—having lots of air and steam leaks at Beta's Beaver Creek plant sent a clear message—these leaks aren't important to management and how we view our plant. Getting them fixed sent another clear message—we care about our plant and we want it operated right.

Further, at Beaver Creek they did not do precision alignment and balancing of their rotating equipment, in spite of numerous studies that indicate equipment life and plant uptime can be substantially improved with precision alignment and balancing. They also found that when they began to truly measure equipment performance, some surprises resulted. At Beaver Creek, pump failures were "keeping them up at night," and when they began to measure their mean time between repairs, their pumps were only running some 4–5 months between repairs. Thus, they began a pump improvement program that helped them focus on improving pump reliability and uptime. A bonus was the fact that they reduced costs and improved safety because they weren't routinely repairing things. Their new "model" for behavior was "fixed forever" as opposed to "forever fixing."

They also found that it was vital to their success to begin to do critical equipment histories, to plan and schedule maintenance, and to be far more proactive in eliminating defects from the operation, regardless whether they were rooted in process or people issues. This was all done with the view of not seeking to place blame, but seeking to eliminate defects. All problems were viewed as opportunities for improvement, not searches for the guilty. Beta's Beaver Creek plant had nothing but opportunities when we started the process for improvement. They are now well on their way to substantially improved performance.

Finally, this same process is now being applied at other Beta plants for identifying major opportunities, creating a sense of teamwork, and creating a common sense of purpose related to uptime improvement. At the same time, however, this review process revealed several systematic issues about Beta International and its corporate wide practices, which required considerable improvement in the way Beta designed, bought, stored, installed, operated, and maintained its plants. These are discussed in the following chapters, but not before we address the critical issue of integrating the marketing and manufacturing function, and a process for rationalizing product mix in the next chapter.

References

1. Grayson, J. National Center for Manufacturing Science Newsletter, Ann Arbor, MI, November 1991.

2. Maskell, B. H. *Performance Measurement for World Class Manufacturing*, Productivity Press, Cambridge, MA, 1991.

3. *The Benchmarking Management Guide*, Productivity Press, Cambridge, MA, 1993.

4. Nakajima, S. *Total Productive Maintenance*, Productivity Press, Cambridge, MA, 1993.

5. "Calculating Process Overall Equipment Effectiveness," *Maintenance Technology*, Barrington, IL, June 1994.

6. Mendelbaum, G. and Mizuno, R. *Maintenance Practices and Technologies*, Deloitte & Touche, Toronto, Ontario, Canada, 1991.

7. Jones, E. "The Japanese Approach to Facilities Maintenance," *Maintenance Technology*, Barrington, IL, August 1991.

8. Kelly, K. and Burrows, P. "Motorola: Training for the Millennium," *Business Week*, March 1994.

9. Moore, R., Pardue, F., Pride, A., and Wilson, J. "The Reliability-Based Maintenance Strategy: A Vision for Improving Industrial Productivity," Industry Report, Computational Systems, Inc., Knoxville, TN, September 1993.

10. Ashton, J. "Key Maintenance Performance Measures," Dofasco Steel-Industry Survey, 1993.

11. Jones, K. *Maintenance Best Practices Manual*, PE - Inc., Newark, DE.

12. Hartoonian, G. "Maintenance Stores and Parts Management," *Maintenance Journal*, Volume 8, No. 1, Mornington, Australia, January/February 1995.

13. HR Benchmarking Study, European Process Industries Competitiveness Center Newsletter, Cleveland, Middlesbrough, UK, Autumn 1997.

14. Wireman, T. *World-Class Maintenance Management*, Industrial Press, New York, NY, 1990.

15. Author's benchmarking.

16. Liker, J. K. *Becoming Lean*, Productivity Press, Portland, OR, 1997.

17. Goldratt, E. *The Goal*, North River Press, Croton-on-Hudson, NY, 1992.

3

Integrating the Marketing and Manufacturing Strategies

Bein' all things to all people is like bein' nothin' to nobody.

Anonymous

Businesses should clearly understand their targeted market(s), and within those markets their profile customer(s). This allows a business to better focus on its strategic business strengths and target markets and customers more effectively. For example, an instrumentation and control company might define its targeted markets as those that represent heavy industrial manufacturers, e.g., chemical and petrochemical, pulp and paper, refining, power generation, automotive, primary metals, textiles. These would typically be those industries where their products provide the greatest benefit for precision process control, and therefore greater production output and reduced cost. Others, such as food and general manufacturing, might simply not be targeted and therefore would not receive any priority relative to resources for promotion, new product development, design modifications, etc. Of course, the company would sell its products to these industries, but wouldn't spend significant money to try to gain their business. Further, within these "targeted market" industries, for example, a profile customer might have sales of >$100M per year, operate in a continuous or 24-hour/day mode, and have production losses due to poor control valued at >$10K per hour. These plants would place a very high value on process control, and would have the financial resources to buy and implement the technology.

With this in mind, the company would focus its design and new product development, marketing and sales, advertising, manufacturing capability, distribution channels, customer support, etc. on the needs of these targeted markets, and more importantly on making the profile customers within these markets knowledgeable of, and successful in, using its products. This customer success translates into the company's success. As we'll see, Beta generally has a very good sales organization, but is generally less mature in understanding its markets, particularly as it relates to fully integrating its marketing and manufacturing strategies to achieve a much more successful business strategy.

Several exceptional works have been written regarding the development of a manufacturing strategy and integrating this fully into the marketing and overall business strategy.[1-3] Yet, these and similar works have received little attention at Beta, where manufacturing has historically been viewed by the sales function as "the place where we get the stuff we sell," a kind of spigot from which to fill our buckets for selling at the local market. Only recently has Beta begun to use the approaches described in these works and this chapter to form its strategy.

Beta's Pracor Division

Beta understands that all businesses start with markets, some existing (basic chemicals, for example); some created from "whole cloth" (new drug technology, for example). This company is currently primarily in existing, mature markets, but of course is investing R&D into new product and process development. Beta has a strong desire for its Pracor Division, which sells into the industrial market, to expand into the moderate and rapid growth areas where its newer, higher margin products have already established a modest position. However, Beta has not spent adequate effort to strategically position its products for gaining market share, nor for assuring that its manufacturing capability and strategy could support those marketing targets and its strategic business objectives.

For example, products and product mix have often been created through happenstance—a sales person would promise something that the plants then had to deliver. The most difficult questions asked were "Can you make it? On time? At a reasonable gross margin?" Product specifications have sometimes been created to meet a specific sales order versus having done the market analysis to create the products that would serve key customers. Granted, there must always be the give and take necessary to understand the customer's needs as they evolve, but these needs should be under regular review, and market analysis should adapt to those changing needs and *anticipate* them. It is understood that being flexible and agile is important, and that being consistent and rigorous is also important. The best companies balance both well, understanding that simply reacting moment to moment to every potential sales order is not likely to lead to superior performance. Additional discussion on optimizing product mix at one of Beta's plants is provided later, so for the time being, the discussion focuses on the development of Beta's integrated marketing and manufacturing strategy for its Pracor Division. Where does it want to position itself in its markets? What market share does it want? What is its strategy for achieving this? Has this strategy been communicated to the shop floor level so that all have a clear sense about how to get there? Let's have a look at one model for addressing some of these issues.

Market/Product Success Factors

The mission of Beta's Pracor Division was to create a common sense of purpose within the organization, "To be the preferred supplier" to its customers. Lots of issues are embodied in this simple statement, and properly "lived" it could (unlike most mission statements) provide a genuine common sense of purpose throughout the organization. Just a quick note—mission statements should create this common sense of purpose. Most mission statements are long drawn out "corporate speak," which albeit important for senior management to articulate, do *not* create a common sense of purpose that drives the organization. Few people at Beta International know its corporate mission statement. More on this issue is provided in Chapter 15, Organizational Behavior and Structure. In any event, what does being the preferred supplier mean in practice, and how will we achieve this? One way to answer this question would be to answer Turner's question,[3] "What wins orders?" If you can win the order, then you are the preferred supplier by definition. After considerable thought, noting their products applied to different markets, and that different markets and customers had different expectations, Beta developed the preliminary profile in Table 3-1 to answer the question, "What wins orders?" in its three markets (A, B, and C) for its five principal product lines (1–5):

Table 3-1
Rating of Market/Product Success Factors

	A/1	A/2	A/3	B/1	B/4	C/5
Price	5	5	4	3	2	1
Quality Specs	3	3	4	4	4	5
On Time Delivery	3	3	4	5	4	5
Packaging	4	2	3	3	3	5
Technical Support	1	2	3	2	3	4

In Table 3-1 a score of 1 means the customer is relatively indifferent to this factor, so long as it is within a reasonable range, while a score of 5 means they are highly sensitive. These sensitivity factors can in turn be interpreted into actual marketing and manufacturing requirements, thus facilitating a higher rate for "winning orders." It should also be noted that quality per a given specification is a requirement, that is, if you can't meet the customer's specification on the order 99% of the time or better, you're not going to get many orders. The sensitivity relates to the need to meet increasingly difficult customer specifications.

For Beta, market A and products 1–3 (A/1–3) represent Beta's historical strength, but in a business that is changing substantially. The products are mature, e.g., commodities, showing slow steady growth, and becoming highly price sensitive, which is increasingly cutting into Beta's historically good margins. To Beta's chagrin, certain customers for A/3 are demanding an even higher quality at a lower price, though not as intensely price competitive as A/1–2. Even this is likely to change in time, as demands for steadily increasing quality and performance are common expectations in most all industries today. Likewise, these same customers are demanding more reliable delivery, e.g., just in time, 100% on time/in full, and increasing their packaging flexibility requirements. Fortunately, technical support requirements were only minimal in A/1–2, but showing an increase in A/3.

Sales in market A have historically been most of Beta's business (some 60%). Increasing price sensitivity has lead to cost-cutting exercises over the past several years, reducing Beta's operating and maintenance budgets for its manufacturing infrastructure. This has resulted in deterioration of some of its assets, and exacerbated its ability to deliver quality product in a timely manner—the plants just aren't as reliable, particularly in packaging capability. This has begun to erode customer satisfaction and market position, though it hasn't become a critical issue, yet. Finally, A/3 represents the same product, but in several new market applications requiring additional technical support. For some years now, Beta has provided only minimal support in most markets, providing that effort on a case basis only for those who demanded it. Staffing and capability are therefore limited. This has also limited its ability to support those new customers in A/3, and increasingly, in markets B and C. The customer support function will require a significant investment in the future.

In market B the customer is less sensitive to price, generally more sensitive to quality and delivery, as well as packaging and technical support requirements. However, again because of the lack of reliability in Beta's plants, quality and delivery performance have suffered, leaving it at risk in these markets, which make up some 25% of its business. This market is also expected to grow moderately in the coming years, and is a "must" part of Beta's growth plans.

Market C and particularly product 5 represent a major, new growth opportunity that will allow Beta to assert itself in an area with relatively high margins. However, though relatively price insensitive, stringent requirements in quality, delivery, packaging, and technical support, when combined with manufacturing problems in these areas, could result in Beta's failure to capitalize on these markets. Also, these markets will require additional capital projects at the plants to fully support product manufacturing, including associated packaging requirements. Also, substantial technical support is required, something which Beta, as noted, is not accustomed to supplying. All this requires substantial investment and training for a market that short term has low volume and high margins, and a net small return. Long term, Beta believes this is a market in which the company needs to be a major player. It could ultimately constitute over 30% of its business. Given Beta's desire to increase its volume of business in markets B and C, it is essential that these issues be addressed as quickly as possible.

Finally, there are many products, 6–30, that are typically sold into other markets D–Z, as well as A–C, but which only constitute 5% of business volume at this division of Beta. In other words, over 80% of Beta's products make up 5% of its sales in this division, while 3% of its products (product 1) make up over 35% of its sales. These low-volume products are generally those sold to certain customers with the sales force forecasting large potential, little of which has materialized; and/or with R&D coming up with the latest "gee-whiz" product, which likewise has not fully materialized. Make no mistake, these types of risks must be taken, but these same risks often result in offering too many products, especially when markets and product mix are not regularly scrutinized. How else will we truly know about a new product's potential, unless we try it? That said, however, a rigorous process must be established so that it's common practice to review markets, product mix, sales histories, anticipated demand, etc., for continuing modification and rationalization of products and mix.

Volume and Market Growth Analysis

Using this information, and other market and customer data, Beta has made the *preliminary* observations shown in Table 3-2.

Table 3-2
Markets/Products History and Forecast

Market	Products & Current Average Price/Unit	Position	Current Volume/ Market Share	5-Year History	5-Year Forecast	Goal— Volume/ Market Share
A	1-$2,000 2-$2,000 3-$2,050	Leader	58%/ ~30%	Slow, steady growth @~2%/yr	Slow, steady growth @~2%/yr	~45%/ ~35%
B	1-$2,100 4-$2,200	Follower, Moderate Supplier	25% / ~15%	Moderate Growth @~5%/yr	Moderate Growth @~5%/yr	~30%/ ~20%
C	5-$2,350	Developing	11% / ~10%	Rapid Growth @~15%/yr	Rapid Growth @~15%/yr	~25%/ ~20%
D–Z	6-30 Avg~$2,250	Uncertain	6%/ NA	Limited	Uncertain	3%/—

Table 3-2 shows that in general Beta would like to change its business mix from being as dependent on its historical mature market to more specialized products, which will allow for greater product differentiation, growth, and profits. For example, in market A, it would like to reduce its percent of business volume from nearly 60% to 45%, and yet modestly increase market share, from 30–35%, in a market which is growing at only 2% per year. To do this will require an increase in total volume of 10–15% over a 3- to 5-year period, depending on market price and other factors. If this is to be, Beta must capture more market share in market A, and simultaneously expand quickly into other markets that are growing more rapidly.

In market B, which is expected to grow at 5% per year, Beta would like to modestly increase its percent of total business, as well as market share. This will require a growth in total volume of 40–60%, depending on price, supported by moderate improvements in quality and on time deliveries, and very modest improvements in customer support and packaging.

Finally, in market C, which is growing at 15% per year, Beta would like to substantially increase its business volume, as well as market share. Similarly, this will require a growth in total volume of 250–350%, or roughly triple its current volume. Keeping in mind its drive "to be the preferred supplier" and achieve these goals, this now requires additional analysis. What production capability—volume, cost, quality—are necessary to support these goals? What is Beta's strategy for making all this happen? What wins orders? Beta must gain more than its historical share in all markets, and must be able to support these gains with its manufacturing capability.

Beta's strategy must also assure meeting the following minimum goals, which, in turn, are required to support return on equity and earnings per share growth:

Sales growth:	10% per year, consistent with market growth objectives
Return on net assets:	20% per year minimum
Profit after tax:	Consistent with RoNA objectives

Manufacturing Capability for Supporting Market/Volume Goals

Beta next undertook an analysis of its operational and manufacturing practices to determine if they supported key marketing and corporate business objectives. Note: While all this is proceeding, the sales department continues to berate manufacturing, demanding that they "do more, and do it better," despite the fact that their production requirements for manufacturing are often late, wrong, and can change frequently during any month. Production planning is often an oxymoron. The marketing function has taken a back seat to the sales department in an effort to "Make money, now!" But this reactive approach to selling is only exacerbating the ability of the manufacturing plant to deliver on its customer requirements. All things considered, the Pracor Division is in a bit of a conundrum. In any event, let's consider their historical manufacturing capability and performance to meet the demand of the marketing and sales departments, which is summarized in Table 3-3:

Table 3-3
Demonstrated Manufacturing Capability

Location	Capacity Peak, K units/yr	Production Output, Actual	Uptime (Figure 1-5)	Principal Products Capability	Average Unit Cost
Plant 1	40	27.2	68%	1–4	$1,600/unit
Plant 2	30	24.6	82%	1–4	$1,450/unit
Plant 3	25	18.2	73%	1–5, 6–30	$1,550/unit
Plant 4	25	19.2	77%	1–5, 6–30	$1,500/unit
Plant 5	20	15.0	75%	3–5, 6–30	$1,550/unit

All things considered, this performance is no better than average. Uptime is about five points below average for this type plant, and unit costs are about $50/unit more than what is believed to be an industry average for these products. Other plant performance indicators such as on-time deliveries, stock turns, first-pass quality, etc., are also in the average range. These parameters are important in an integrated analysis, but for present purposes, they will not be reviewed. You are encouraged, however, to bring this or other information into your analysis as appropriate.

Finally, all plants can theoretically produce all products. However, because of operator training, plant configuration, market areas, etc., it is quite difficult as a practical matter to do so. The plants are currently configured to produce as shown. In an emergency any plant could be reconfigured and staffed to produce any product necessary, but at considerable additional cost.

Performance by Plant and by Product Line

Beta further undertook an analysis by plant and by product line of each plant's actual performance as it relates to output and gross margins, using the unit prices and unit costs shown. The results of this are provided in Table 3-4. Summarizing this, Beta is achieving a gross margin of some $58.6M, which after costs associated with R&D, marketing and sales, administration, interest, and taxes, leaves some $8.5M in profit after tax, or just under 4% profit on sales. This also translates to a return on net assets of about 8%, with net assets of $110M for this business. This performance, while not terrible, is not particularly good, and is troubling in light of the trend that appears to be going in the wrong direction. Nor does it support the business volume and market share goals described in Table 3-2.

Let's consider the plant's operating performance—uptime, unit costs, and gross margin contribution (Tables 3-3 and 3-4)—in light of its stated market direction, growth requirements, and success factors—"What wins orders" (Tables 3-1 and 3-2).

First, as we've seen, Beta has done some manufacturing benchmarking and concluded that its uptime and cost performance are no better than average. Uptime for these plants ranges from 68–82%, with a weighted average of about 75%. According to the data available, this is 5% below average for this industry, and at least 15% below so-called world-class levels of 90%+. Further, unit costs are above average, and at least 10% above the best plants.

Particularly troublesome is the fact that the largest plant, which should have the best performance, has the poorest performance. It is a large plant that produces mostly high-volume, commodity-type products, and that should have the lowest unit cost of production. Quite the opposite is true. It has the highest cost of production, and its uptime and reliability are the poorest, making it increasingly difficult to assure customer satisfaction. If Beta is to (1) gain market share in market A, (2) achieve higher profits, and (3) achieve other key corporate objectives, plant 1 must improve its performance. For example, price performance is critical to Beta's success in market A, as well as packaging in product no. 1. If Beta is to succeed in this market, pricing must come down, and costs must come down *proportionally more* to support Beta's goals for increased market share, and concurrent improved financial performance.

Plant 2 seems to be doing reasonably well, but could still support improved performance in markets A and B. Key to this is moderately improved uptime and unit costs, and improved technical support.

Plant 3 is only slightly better than plant 1, and plant 4 only moderately better in terms of uptime and unit costs. However, it appears that these plants are trying to be all things to all people, and apparently trying to act as "swing plants" in the event plant 1 or 2 fails to meet delivery schedules, as well as address markets B and C, and D–Z. While plant 4 seems to be doing a better job at this, a clearer focus needs to be established.

Plant 5 is relatively well focused on higher margin, higher quality products, but is also producing lots of small order products for markets D–Z. While these appear to have relatively high margins, these margins

Table 3-4
Plant Performance by Product/Market—
Output and Gross Margin

Market/ Product Plant No.	A/1 KUnits, GM $K	A/2	A/3	B/1	B/4	C/5	D–Z 6-30	Totals
1	13.1 $5.24K	8.7 $3.48K	2.8 $1.26K	1.1 $0.55K	1.5 $0.90K	0	0	27.2 $11.43K
2	9.1 $5.00K	5.7 $3.14K	4.8 $2.88K	3.1 $2.02K	1.9 $1.42K	0	0	24.6 $14.46K
3	3.6 $1.62K	4.6 $2.07K	1.8 $0.90K	2.5 $1.38K	2.1 $1.36K	2.1 $1.68K	1.5 $1.05K	18.2 $10.06K
4	2.5 $1.25K	1.3 $0.65K	1.2 $0.66K	5.8 $3.48K	3.4 $2.38K	3.8 $3.23K	1.2 $0.90K	19.2 $12.55K
5	0 0	0 0	3.2 $1.6K	0 0	4.0 $2.60K	4.5 $3.60K	3.3 $2.31K	15.0 $10.11K
Totals	28.3 $13.11K	20.3 $9.34K	13.8 $7.30K	12.5 $7.43K	12.9 $8.66K	10.4 $8.51K	6.0 $4.26K	104.2 $58.61K
GM $/unit	0.46	0.46	0.53	0.59	0.67	0.82	0.71	0.56
Total Sales, $M	$56.60	$40.60	$28.29	$26.25	$28.38	$24.44	$13.50	$218.06
Total Costs, $M	$43.49	$31.26	$20.99	$18.82	$19.72	$15.93	$9.24	$159.45
Avg Cost, $/unit	1,537	1,540	1,521	1,506	1,529	1,532	1,540	1,530

have not included the effect of downtime on principal products and markets, which appears to be disrupting production plans routinely, especially for key strategic markets. With this in mind, Beta must answer the question—what *value* should be placed on the *opportunity cost of lost production when making product for non-key markets?*

The Plan

Beta's Pracor Division has no choice but to support its market share and business volume goals detailed in Table 3-2. The strategy for doing this begins with winning orders using the market/product success factors in Table 3-1. Specifically, it must lower prices in market A, improve quality and delivery overall, particularly in markets B and C, and improve packaging and technical support for markets A, B, and C. All this must be done, while improving margins and return on net assets. Therefore, the following must be done:

- **Improve uptime and manufacturing performance to near world class.**
  Using a reliability-driven strategy, described in Chapters 4–17, improve the uptime at all its plants, including specific targets which are near world class of 90%. Lower uptimes would be acceptable in plants running a larger number of products. Further, quality and on-time delivery requirements in the newer, faster growing markets are critical to the success of the business. Having mediocre performance in manufacturing reliability could be the death knell for the business in light of these requirements.
- **Review product mix and rationalize those products that offer little strategic return.**
  The tentative conclusion was that business volume in Markets D–Z for non-core products should be cut in half, and most of that remaining business should be focused at plant 4, which had demonstrated its ability to effectively manage changeovers, and still maintain relatively high uptimes. It's likely that there is considerable business in these markets that Beta just doesn't want, at least not at the current price. A more detailed model and case history for product mix rationalization is provided in the next section.
- **Set higher standards for new products being promoted by R&D, and/or marketing and sales.**
  Link the manufacturing function more fully into the decision-making process concerning the impact of new products and/or "difficult" products.

• **Increase market share in the more mature businesses.**
Increasing market share requires substantially improved manufacturing performance, especially in mature businesses. To support concurrent financial performance is a must. This requires much higher uptimes, and much better cost performance. Some of this cost performance would come about as a result of improved uptime, but additional reductions in fixed and variable costs also must to be realized to support the marketing plan. These cost reductions should be a consequence of best practice, not arbitrary cost cutting.

• **Reduce prices in some products/markets.**
To support certain pricing sensitivities, particularly in market A, Beta concluded that it had to reduce its pricing by at least 7%. Further, it also anticipated that increased competition, and increased pricing pressures, would result as others recognized the increased opportunity in markets B and C.

• **Expand its technical support capability.**
This is a must to assure customer satisfaction, especially in the more attractive markets. This includes not just telephone support, but also training seminars in product applications and use, frequent joint sessions with customers to understand needs, complaints, etc. Annual surveys, with follow up discussion, to assure understanding of needs. Note that these training seminars would also be used internally for marketing, manufacturing, and R&D staff.

• **Improve packaging capability.**
Short term this is a must, and may require modest capital expenditure short term. This may also result in excess packaging capability as reliability improvements are made. Beta is willing to make this investment to assure customer satisfaction and market share, in spite of the potential of excess packaging capability later. While this will have a negative impact on RoNA short term, Beta may have little choice. A packaging team has been established to determine whether the need for additional packaging can be avoided through rapid deployment of reliability practices.

Revised Pricing Strategy

As a result, Beta has concluded that it will likely be necessary to modify its pricing structure as shown in Table 3-5, consistent with success factors related to "what wins orders."

Table 3-5
Planned Pricing Structure

Market/ Product	Current Price, $/unit	Planned Price, $/unit	Success Factor Comments/Rationale
A/1	2,000	1,850	Packaging premium on pricing
A/2	2,000	1,800	Rock bottom pricing
A/3	2,050	1,950	Quality/delivery premium
B/1	2,100	1,950	Quality/on-time delivery premium
B/4	2,200	2,100	Relative price insensitivity; quality/delivery premium
C/5	2,350	2,250	Relative price insensitivity, but increasing competition; premium on high standards for all requirements
D–Z/all*	2,200	2,200	No price concessions; selectively increase prices; reduce demand 50%

Note that in Markets D–Z, no price concessions will be offered, and that prices will selectively be increased.

With all this in mind, Beta will now approach key customers in each market with the goal of establishing long-term contracts (3–5 years) for minimum volumes, in return for achieving their specific objectives, e.g., lower pricing and better packaging in market A; superior quality, delivery, and technical support in markets B and C, etc. These discussions will be targeted and backed by a specific plan of action that outlines how *each* customer's requirements (in each market) will be met to support the customer's business. For example, over the next 3–5 years, Beta might discount its product in market A by 5–10%, prorated over the time period, and allowing for raw material cost adjustments. In each case, Beta will strive for a strategic alliance for assuring mutual success. However, Beta will still use pricing modifications as appropriate to assure that all pricing is market sensitive, maximizing profits as needed, and protecting market share as needed.

Plant Performance Requirements

To support this plan, Beta also concluded that the plant performance must improve dramatically, from just under 75% to nearly 87%, and unit costs must come down by at least $180 per unit. A target value of $200 per unit will be established. Details are shown in Table 3-6 and are necessary as a minimum to support market share and financial objectives.

Table 3-6
Plant Performance Data—Unit Cost and Uptime

Plant	Current Cost, $/unit	Planned Cost, $/unit	Current Uptime	Planned Uptime
1	1,600	1,350	68%	90%
2	1,450	1,300	82%	90%
3	1,550	1,350	73%	85%
4	1,500	1,450	77%	80%
5	1,550	1,350	75%	85%

Improved uptime will support achieving these unit cost objectives, but in and of itself is not sufficient. Best practices must be put in place that assure that costs are not unnecessarily incurred, particularly in maintenance, where equipment downtime and repair costs have been a key contributor to excess costs and/or lost production.

For example, plant 1, where raw material costs are 50% of the total cost of manufactured goods, must improve its uptime from 68% to 90%, *and* reduce operating and maintenance costs by an additional $1M/yr to achieve a unit cost of less than $1,350/unit. The other plants found a similar situation, particularly plant 4, where unit costs were only anticipated to be reduced by $50/unit. However, it was also anticipated that additional costs would be incurred because Beta was making plant 4 the plant that would become good at product changes, and at handling rapid responses to market and sales conditions. Note from Table 3-7 that plant 4 will handle 66% of products for markets D–Z, and that the total volume for these markets has been cut in half. This approach will necessarily reduce its uptime to a maximum estimated at about 80%. Plants 3 and 5, likewise would also be limited to about 85% for similar reasons, and would act as backup for certain situations, but would not be anticipated to be as agile. Plants 1 and 2 would focus on being the low cost, high volume producer.

Other Actions Required

On further review, Beta found that plants were not fully capable of determining their product costs by product line, or to do so-called activity-based accounting. Hence, the unit cost of production had to be aggregated for each plant. In the future, each plant will formulate and implement the basis for tracking the cost of given product lines more specifically. This in turn will allow greater refinement in the cost and pricing strategy for given products. This effort will also include making a determination of the opportunity cost of lost production.

The Expected Results

Beta was convinced that applying a manufacturing reliability strategy for increasing uptimes and lowering production costs would also further reduce "out-of-pocket" costs. This would support its pricing strategy, while providing adequate margins to assure meeting financial objectives.

As shown in Table 3-7, gross margin contribution from the plants will increase from $58.6M to $71.2M, or some $12.6M. Beta anticipates that about $1M may be necessary to improve packaging capability, both in terms of equipment and training, and to do some minor de-bottlenecking in certain production areas. This will only be spent if necessary after the packaging team's review. It is also anticipated that an additional $1M will be spent to develop and implement practices at each of the plants to assure best practice for achieving the desired objectives, and represents less than 1% of plant replacement value. Finally, it is anticipated that over $0.5M will be required for administration, additional commissions on sales, etc. This brings the net operating income increase to some $10M, which in turn results in about $7M in increased net income. This represents an 80% increase in profits and return on net assets. However, RoNA is still only 14%, and other goals related to business mix and market share are still not being achieved, even with this substantially improved performance.

On further review, Beta also concluded that it must:

- Achieve an additional unit cost reduction of some $50/unit.
  This will bring its average unit cost to about $1,300/unit, and/or additional equivalent output commensurate with financial goals. This will result in achieving a 20%+ RoNA.
- Perform additional de-bottlenecking reviews of all its plants.
  Bottlenecks that could be increased in capacity without major capital investment represent additional opportunity for gaining market share with existing assets using the reliability strategy described herein. This

Table 3-7
Pro Forma Plant Performance by Product/Market—
Output and Gross Margin

Plant No.	Market/Product A/1 KUnits Gross Margin	A/2	A/3	B/1	B/4	C/5	D–Z 6–30	Totals
1	17.3	11.5	3.7	1.5	2.0	0	0	36.0
	$8.65K	$5.17K	$2.22K	$0.90K	$1.50K	0	0	$18.44K
2	9.1	5.7	4.8	4.7	2.7	0	0	27.0
	$5.00K	$2.85K	$3.12K	$3.06K	$2.16K	0	0	$16.19K
3	3.6	4.6	1.8	3.6	3.1	4.2	0.3	21.2
	$1.80K	$2.07K	$1.08K	$2.16K	$2.33K	$3.78	$0.25K	$13.47K
4	2.5	1.3	1.2	5.8	3.4	3.8	2.0	20.0
	$1.00K	$0.45K	$0.60K	$2.90K	$2.21K	$3.04K	$1.50K	$11.70K
5	0	0	3.2	0	4.0	6.5	0.7	17.0
	0	0	$1.92K	0	$3.00K	$5.85K	$0.59K	$11.36K
Totals	32.5	23.1	14.7	15.6	15.2	14.5	3.0	118.6
	$16.45	$10.54	$8.94	$9.02	$11.20	$12.67	$2.34	$71.16
GM $/unit	0.51	0.46	0.61	0.58	0.74	0.87	0.78	0.60
Total Sales, $M	$60.12	$41.58	$28.67	$30.42	$31.92	$32.62	$6.60	$231.93
Total Costs, $M	$43.67	$31.04	$19.73	$21.40	$20.72	$19.95	$4.26	$160.77
Avg Unit Cost, $	1,344	1,344	1,342	1,372	1,363	1,376	1,420	1,356

may also support deferring capital investment to meet expected increases in volume. Note that bottlenecks are not just "design," and tend to be dynamic and variable, depending on plant equipment performance on a given day. Indeed, the design bottleneck may rarely be the actual bottleneck, principally because it gets so much attention to assure its operational reliability. The real bottleneck then tends to "bounce around" depending on what isn't operating properly on a given day. This dictates that the entire plant be highly reliable.

• **Build one or two additional plants, depending on plant size and location.**

These plants would be focused on producing products for markets B and C, because plants 1 and 2 can, with the improvements indicated, provide the additional capacity needed in market A. It is anticipated that 10–15K units per year of products 1 and 4 will be required for market B, and 20–25K units of product 5 will be required for market C to support anticipated growth. Given the plant is performing at 85% uptime, this necessitates one plant rated at nominally 40K units per year, or two small units each at about half this.

• **Approach its key suppliers to assure they are applying manufacturing excellence principles.**

Raw material costs represent about half of Beta's manufacturing costs. Beta will work with them to assure excellence such that at least some of the benefit flows through to Beta, allowing it to further reduce its manufacturing costs. Note for example, that a 5% reduction in raw material costs could be the equivalent of cutting energy costs in half. Beta intends to work with key suppliers to develop strategic relationships to assure they have manufacturing excellence that will in turn assure they receive the lowest possible cost at the highest possible reliability of supply.

• **Reduce waste in raw material use.**

Because raw materials represent half of manufacturing costs, small improvements are equivalent to larger ones in other areas. Beta will investigate ways to improve processing yields. This will be done not so much in the process itself, as it will with the minimization of waste and scrap. An example of simple waste reduction that comes to mind is that of a refining company participating in the benchmarking with Beta. To make a long story short, this refiner was experiencing some 1%+ loss in yield conversion from crude stocks. This was reduced to 0.25% after a new sight glass/design and appropriate PM was introduced to allow operators to view the water purging process more effectively, so they did not do excessive purges. Beta will seek the help of its operators and maintenance to help reduce waste.

R&D has also expressed that it is currently working on several process improvements that could improve yields and reduce raw material requirements. These will be incorporated into the strategic plan.

• **Establish a process for cross training manufacturing and marketing/sales personnel.**
Beta had also found that in this business unit, its sales manager had previously worked in manufacturing as a production supervisor. This individual understood the production process and the plant's capability. He also understood the general sensitivities as to costs, production capability, etc., and could readily relate his role as sales manager to his old position as production supervisor. This proved invaluable in terms of his ability to integrate customer requirements and manufacturing capability. Beta is currently considering making it a requirement to have key sales staff spend at least a year in a production supervisory role, facilitating the practical requirements of integrating manufacturing and marketing strategies.

• **Assure that supply chain issues are integrated into the plan.**
At Beta much attention had been previously given to improving supply chain performance, yet without addressing the fundamental requirement for manufacturing excellence. Supply chain objectives will be very difficult to meet if manufacturing excellence, reliability of supply, etc., are not integrated into the supply chain analysis and plan. Reducing work in process and inventories, increasing stock turns, assuring 99% on time deliveries, assuring 99%+ first pass quality, etc., requires manufacturing excellence.

• **Integrate other issues such as capital spending, asset condition and expected life.**
While not addressed specifically as part of this analysis, Beta is also addressing and integrating other issues such as capital spending, asset condition and expected life, specific operating and maintenance requirements for each plant, etc. This is being done using the reliability process discussed briefly in Chapters 1–3 and as detailed in the next chapters.

• **Beta will also be applying this methodology to its R&D efforts in the future.**
Using a "what wins orders" approach, Beta will more actively assure that most R&D is tied to improving product specifications and manufacturing performance related to winning orders. Further, a review will be undertaken to determine which R&D conducted over the past 5 years or so has lead to what sales volume and/or

improved gross margin contribution. What did we think then, and have our expectations been realized? This analysis will be used to more actively manage the R&D activities. One note of caution on this, and that is that some R&D still needs to be truly cutting edge and experimental, even recognizing that there is a relatively high probability this will not result in a return on the investment. The next discovery will never be made unless some freedom is permitted in the research process.

With this effort, Beta's Pracor Division is well on its way to more fully integrating its marketing and manufacturing strategy, but as with most things, this process is iterative and requires continuing attention and adaptation. Next we'll consider how they more effectively rationalized product mix, and then we'll get into the details of how manufacturing excellence is being established throughout Beta International.

Effect of Product Mix on Manufacturing Performance

Manufacturers, including Beta International, are increasingly called upon to be the low-cost producer of their products, and simultaneously to assure maximum flexibility for meeting varying customer needs—the customer is king. Customer responsiveness, customer demands, flexible (agile, cell, etc.) manufacturing, are strategies often used to satisfy the customer demands and to assure maximum market share, market penetration, asset utilization, and, ultimately, profits.

However, is this the proper strategy? Does it lead to higher profits? Treacy[4] makes this point when suggesting you should "choose your customers, narrow your focus, dominate your market." More recently a major consumer products company is paring down its products to assure greater profitability and market focus.[5] By inference, one of the thrusts of the book is that we must strategically select our customers, target our markets, and not try to be everything to everyone. This section deals with one issue related to this strategy—product mix, and its effect on the ability of a given manufacturer to achieve maximum market share and profits. It represents a case history for one of Beta International's plants.

Beta's Sparta Plant—Rationalizing Product Mix

Beyond the issues described at the beginning of this book, Beta's Sparta operation is a mid-sized manufacturing plant located in middle America. The plant employs over 400 people, and is highly regarded as a supplier of high-quality products. They have recently seen substantive changes in their markets and in competitive pressures thereto. These changes are partly related to changes brought about by GATT and NAFTA, partly related to changes in customer demographics, and partly due to internal pressures forcing modernization of an older plant—in both equipment and work habits. Moreover, Beta has included flexible manufacturing as part of their basic manufacturing strategy, the intent being to assure maximum responsiveness to meeting customer needs; and ultimately maximum market share and profits.

Sparta's plant management is feeling the pressure from Beta's senior management to improve performance—merely maintaining the status quo will not assure survival, let alone prosperity. Moreover, Bob Neurath sees the changes brought about by NAFTA and GATT as more of an opportunity than a threat—if they can improve performance and penetrate those new markets, particularly in foreign countries, improved growth and greater profits are clearly available. This is particularly true in light of the new banner product that Sparta is to manufacture. They want to capitalize on these markets using existing manufacturing assets (no additional capital expense), of course, while maximizing continuing customer satisfaction. They have advised the management of the Sparta plant that based on their analysis, improvements are necessary to assure the plant's competitive position in current, as well as new markets. Beta is intent on expanding its markets, investing its capital, and manufacturing its products where, all things considered, it could make the most profits.

Benchmarking Audit

The Sparta plant had recently gone through a benchmarking audit to determine where it stood relative to world-class performance. The results of the audit were both discouraging and encouraging—Sparta was typically in the average range for the major audit categories, considerably below world class. At the same time, the analysis showed that world-class performance should:

1. Allow the company to manufacture an additional 1,000,000 units per year of its products with the same assets (they had been struggling to make 4,000,000 per year).
2. Reduce operating and maintenance costs of some $1,000,000 per year.

The total value of this improved performance was estimated at $5,500,000 in increased net operating income.

Strategically, the audit demonstrated that if they could accomplish the objective of being world class, product unit costs would improve, thereby allowing more strategic pricing and customer alliances, and greater market share and profits. Further, they could apply the same principles to other manufacturing facilities in the company to assure long-term prosperity for the company.

The specific results of the benchmarking audit indicated:

1. Asset utilization, as compared to theoretical maximum, was running near 70%, better than the average plant. However, world-class plants operated at 85% or better.
2. Plant unplanned downtime was quite high, running near 10%, and well below a world-class standard of less than 1–2%.
3. The process thought to be the production bottleneck was not. It was running at 98% availability. The process thought to have over 100% excess capacity was in fact the limiting factor in production because of unplanned downtime, raw material quality, and other operational issues.
4. Twenty products produced 90% of total sales. Another 180 products yielded the balance of sales, and represented some 50% of the total *number* of purchase orders. Indeed, some 50 products yielded just 2% of sales.

While these issues are fairly complex, we'll simplify the first three by summarizing their plan of action:

1. The company began the process for improving equipment and process reliability by applying an integrated process for operations and maintenance excellence, including a balance of preventive, predictive, and proactive methodologies. This resulted in lower unplanned (and planned) downtime for maintenance, and in general making their maintenance department a reliability-

focused function, as opposed to its historical role of rapid repair (and unfortunately often poor quality work).

2. They also set up work teams (maintenance, production, engineering, purchasing and personnel as appropriate) for improving process and operator effectiveness.

3. They spent a great deal of effort in getting operators much more active in equipment ownership, routine care and minor PM's, and in precision process control. These practices are described in chapters 4–17. And, to the point of this section, they began the process for "product rationalization," discussed in the following.

Product Mix

As previously noted, 20 of their 200 products (or stock keeping units, SKU's), produced 90% of their sales; the balance of 180 products produced the remaining 10% of their sales; interestingly, 50 produced only 2% of sales. At the same time, all products were typically offered on the same delivery schedule. The result of this policy was frequent stops of a production run to insert a small order, in large measure because they were highly responsive to customer demands, and had a commitment to on-time delivery of quality products. Historically, they had also developed a culture among the sales staff of "not losing an order." When combined with the current strategy of flexible or agile manufacturing, this led to the following:

1. Frequent changeovers
2. Reduced process stability (and statistical process capability)
3. Reduced equipment reliability
4. Increased downtime
5. Increased production and handling costs
6. Reduced production capacity

At this point the decision was made to critically analyze their key markets and key customer characteristics, e.g., those that brought 80–90% of their business, and to strategically assess what markets, and therefore products, they truly wanted to pursue.

They concluded that their key markets were in two major areas, and that they did not dominate those markets—they had some 10% of worldwide business volume. They also concluded that portions of their business were not as valuable as previously considered. For example, historically they had assumed that a 50% gross margin (almost twice normal) was adequate for some of the low volume products to assure good profit margins. However, when they factored in the opportunity cost of lost production for supplying key markets, the value of downtime, the handling costs, etc., they found that their "linear thinking" had led them to the wrong conclusion, and that using this set of assumptions they were actually losing money on the so-called "high-margin," but low-volume products. For example, upon analysis they found that on average one hour of downtime was worth nearly $3,000 in *net operating income* on their 20 key products. When considered in terms of gross sales volume, the figure was even more dramatic at $10,000. When they factored the lost production opportunity into the small order cost, they found that they actually lost money on most of orders for fewer than about 10,000 units of product. Further, when they factored in the cost of handling the larger quantities of small orders associated with the small volume, the costs were even higher. Effectively, they found that if they truly allocated costs to the production of the product, and opportunity cost to the lost production, they were losing substantial money on small quantity orders. And it gets worse.

Equipment reliability was suffering substantially (resulting in unplanned downtime) during the frequent starts, stops, changeovers, setup modifications, etc. While the statistics were difficult to determine (because they didn't have good equipment histories or adequate statistical process control data), they estimated that their equipment reliability was poor at least in part because of starting and stopping on a frequent basis—much like starting and stopping a car on a mail route, as opposed to running it for hours on the interstate, the car just won't last as long, or be as reliable on the mail route.

Process capability, that is the statistical variation in product quality, was also suffering substantially. When shutdowns occurred, process stability deteriorated, resulting in poorer quality product. Cpk was less than 1, a poor showing. The company had few "commissioning" standards or tests for verifying that the new setups were properly done before they restarted the equipment. They ran the product, checked it after the fact, and then made adjustments until the quality was acceptable. The frequent starts, stops, and changeovers led to greater scrap and reject rates for their core products, as well as the many small-quantity products.

Product Mix Optimization Process

The next step in the process was to review all current products, quantities sold, setup times, changeover downtime, unplanned equipment downtime, planned downtime, etc. They also reviewed the design specifications of their small volume products and found that many had very small differences between them, leading to an effort to consolidate products with very similar characteristics. In some cases this was a marketing opportunity—they could tout a higher quality product for the same price, and with reduced overall costs of production, actually make more money. Considering the value of reduced downtime and reduced order handling, they found improved profits (or reduced losses) even on the smaller volume orders. Other issues also had to be considered. For example, making small quantity orders for key customers as part of a trial run was key to product and market development. Similarly, small runs had to be made for R&D and engineering to test new products, and to advance production process capabilities, etc.

Out of all this came a process for rationalizing their product mix. Consideration was given to:

1. Consolidating products with very similar characteristics, with a focus of assuring that the highest value product was offered.
2. Subcontracting production for some small orders to companies that were more suited to small quantities, and then marking the product up to assure making money on those orders. This should also give an indication of true market price and production costs.
3. Setting up an internal production line which did nothing but small order products, and then managing that line to meet customer needs for small orders—optimizing small production processes.
4. Very selectively taking those products which have no margin, or strategic value, and transferring those products to a nominal competitor, in cooperation with the customer, so as to maintain the relationship with the customer.
5. Pressing the marketing department to make better forecasts for the small order products, and then making larger quantities of those small orders in anticipation of the orders coming in later in the year. Note that because the orders were generally small, even making ten times a normal historical quantity may not substantially affect inventory and related carrying costs.

6. Negotiating with customers for improved lead times for smaller quantities (so that quantities could be consolidated), and better production planning could be accomplished.
7. Implementing rapid changeover methods and training of staff in rapid changeover techniques, including a commissioning process for both equipment and product reliability.
8. Dropping some products that did not meet the minimum profit requirement, or a strategic need for new product development or key customer alliances.

This is not suggesting that Beta should not make small-volume products, or that Beta shouldn't be flexible or agile, nor is it suggesting that Beta should arbitrarily eliminate certain products below a certain profit level. For example, it is understood that if your best customer requests a small-quantity order for a test market effort, you're very likely to take the order; or if R&D asks for a small production order to test a new product, you're very likely to make the product; or if a good customer requires a product mix that includes low-margin and (mostly) high-margin products that you will make the low-margin ones, etc. Rather, it is suggesting that we consider all things on balance and make decisions accordingly; that we have strategic business reasons for these products; and that we understand our key markets and customers, and our real costs of production. If we do so, we will be more likely to rationalize and optimize our production efforts to our key markets, increasing the probability of our success.

The combination of these methods lead the company to a better process for positioning itself for reduced production costs, better market and product positioning, greater market share, and greater profitability.

Summary

Beta has renewed its effort to be more effective in integrating its marketing, manufacturing, and R&D efforts to achieve its mission to "Be the preferred supplier." The process for this, like most things, is relatively simple in concept, but more difficult in practice:

1. Define and rank critical success factors in key markets/products—what wins orders?
2. Establish key market/business goals for each market/product.

3. Review historical performance in marketing and manufacturing to determine how they can support the key success factors and business goals. Assure communication and teamwork. The Pracor Division will use Figure 1-3, which links manufacturing performance to market pricing in achieving RoNA objectives, as a tool for assuring common goals and expectations.
4. Understand what the gap is relative to achieve key business goals and establish a plan for eliminating those gaps.
5. Rationalize product mix.
6. Execute the plan. Execute the plan. Execute the plan. Well, you get the picture!

In physics we learned that for every action there is an equal and opposite reaction. Seemingly, for every business strategy, there is probably an equal and opposite strategy—economies of scale for mass production vs. cells for flexible manufacturing; out-sourcing vs. loyal employees for improved productivity; niche markets vs. all markets and customers; centralized vs. de-centralized management, and so on. These strategies are often contradictory and add credibility to what someone once said, "There are no solutions, only consequences." Therefore, Beta must consider the consequences of its marketing and manufacturing strategies in a comprehensive and balanced way, and make every effort for strategic optimization, in its markets, such that it will maximize profits and return on net assets.

Integrating the marketing and manufacturing strategies and effectively rationalizing product mix can have a substantial impact on business performance, market share, unit costs, production capacity, operating costs, on equipment reliability, and ultimately on profits. Several options exist to position companies to optimize their strategic market and profit position in the marketplace. At Beta, these options are being reviewed and exercised as appropriate to assure competitive position.

Let's explore next how Beta is putting the right practices in place to assure world-class manufacturing performance for supporting marketing and sales performance. In particular let's review how they are assuring manufacturing excellence in how they design, buy, store, install, operate, and maintain their plants for optimal performance.

References

1. Skinner, W. "Manufacturing—Missing Link in Corporate Strategy," *Harvard Business Review*, May-June, 1969.

2. Hayes, R. H. and Pisano, G. "Beyond World-Class: The New Manufacturing Strategy," *Harvard Business Review*, January-February, 1994.

3. Turner, S. "An Investigation of the Explicit and Implicit Manufacturing Strategies of a South African Chemical Company," master's thesis, The Graduate School of Business, University of Capetown, South Africa, December, 1994.

4. Treacy, M. and Wiersman, F. *The Discipline of Market Leaders,* Addison-Wesley Publishing, Reading, MA, 1994.

5. Schiller, Z. "Make It Simple, Proctor & Gamble's New Marketing Mantra," *Business Week,* New York, NY, September 9, 1996.

Plant Design and Capital Project Practices

4

> Your system is perfectly designed to give you the results that you get.
>
> *W. Edwards Deming*

After going through an audit of design and capital project practices, it became clear that when implementing new capital projects, including the construction of new plants, Beta International typically did not adequately apply historical experience, particularly of the maintenance and operations departments, to help assure highly reliable plant equipment. While not an excuse, Beta is fairly typical. According to the Society for Maintenance and Reliability Professionals (SMRP), 86% of manufacturers surveyed do not use a life-cycle cost model when designing new capital equipment projects.[1] Indeed, at Beta, the design and installation philosophy appeared to be one of lowest installed cost and minimum adequate design (MAD). While minimum adequacy may be appropriate, the problem for Beta was that the basis for minimum adequacy was often poorly defined, and was often driven by constrained capital budgets, rather than lowest life-cycle cost. This approach to design and capital projects typically did not lead to the lowest life-cycle cost, nor to the lowest unit cost of production for manufacturing.

Further, the economic importance of addressing reliability and life-cycle cost during the planning, design, and procurement phases should not be underestimated, and a characteristic graph of the implications of life-cycle cost is shown in Figure 4-1. According to Blanchard,[2] while expenditures for plant and equipment occur later in the acquisition process, most of the life-cycle cost is committed at preliminary stages of the design and acquisition process. The subsequent design and construction phases (which include the detailed specifications) determine an additional 29% of the life-cycle cost, leaving approximately 5% of the life-cycle cost to be determined by maintenance and operations. Further, it was also reported[3] that some 60–75% of the life-cycle cost is associated with maintenance and support, with the balance of 25–40% being the initial acquisition of the asset. While this same pattern may not occur for specific operating plants, the point is well taken that design and installation efforts can have a dramatic effect on life-cycle cost, something known intuitively to most of us. What should this mean in terms of our practices? Clearly, preliminary design efforts should include *all* the project costs, *not just the initial costs.*

More recent benchmarking efforts, which surveyed some 60 major corporations and 2,000 large capital projects, have reached similar conclusions[4] regarding typical performance:

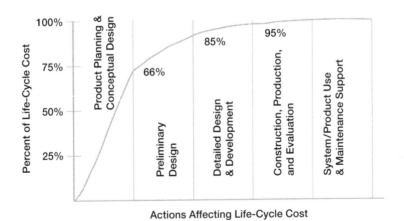

Figure 4-1. Phases of life-cycle cost commitment.

1. Start-up and operability of new assets has not improved in the past 20 years, despite the ample scope for improvement.
2. More than two-thirds of major projects built by process industries in the US in the past five years failed to meet one or more of the key objectives laid out in the authorization.
3. Outsourcing for contractor led projects has grown from less than 10% to nearly 40% between 1975 and 1995. The hope that outsourcing of engineering projects would result in lower engineering costs has not been met. Engineering costs as a percent of total installed costs have climbed from 12% to 21% in the same period.
4. All-contractor projects were the worst on every performance metric.

The survey goes on to say of the *best* projects:

1. Instead of viewing the capital projects as the line responsibility of the engineering department, they view projects as the principal means by which the corporation's capital asset base is created. They view technology and engineering as elements in the supply chain that results in competitive products, not as nonintegrated functions.
2. The importance of the FEL (front-end loading for business, facility and project planning integration) was hard to overstate. While fewer than one project in three meets all its authorization business objectives, 49 out of 50 projects that achieved a best practical FEL index score also met all objectives.
3. An excellent project system consists of business, technical, and manufacturing functions working together to create uniquely effective capital assets.
4. The best projects were functionally integrated teams, which consisted of owner functions such as engineering, business, operations and maintenance, and outside engineering and construction contractors. Even vendors were included in many of the most effective teams.
5. The best-in-class all maintained some form of central organization that was responsible for providing the organization of the work process for front-end loading, a skilled resource pool in several core competencies, and provided the organizational and interpersonal "glue" that bound operations, business, engineering, and outside resources into an effective project process.

Clearly, the decision to address reliability and life-cycle cost is best made during the planning and design phase. As decisions regarding these issues are made later in the life cycle, the return on investment decreases as plant problems reduce equipment availability and product capacity.

The other concept often underestimated during the purchasing process is the role that "infant mortality," or early-life failures, plays in equipment life-cycle cost. According to some studies discussed in Chapter 9, Maintenance Practices, these early life failures can account for 68% of equipment failures.

Because of this, specifications must be verified by performing post installation checks at a minimum. For major equipment, the vendor should test the equipment prior to shipment and provide the required documentation. The equipment should be retested following installation to ensure the equipment was properly installed and not damaged during shipment. These same requirements apply to contractors as well as employees.

Beta is currently in the process of modifying its design and capital projects methods to help assure maximum asset reliability and utilization, lowest life-cycle cost, and lowest unit cost of production. This is described in the following case study.

The Design Process

Beta's Stone Coal Creek plant was experiencing significant maintenance downtime. As you would expect, maintenance costs were also extraordinarily high. Maintenance was considered "the bad guy"— why couldn't they just fix the equipment right, and fast, and cheap? An idealistic objective perhaps, but not very realistic under the circumstances.

On reviewing the plant, several issues arose. The piping and pressure vessels were made principally of carbon steel, several heat exchangers were graphite or other brittle material. Most pumps (typically configured as a primary and an in-line spare) had been skid mounted for ease of fabrication and reduced expense, but from a vibration perspective had not been isolated from one another. As a consequence the primary pump (because it had not been properly aligned or balanced—too expensive) typically "beat the backup pump to death." Some pumps were even "free-standing" for ease of repair when failure occurred.

Reviewing process control practices indicated that very often the plant experienced transients of varying forms—transients in moisture content of the process stream, which formed acids that attacked the carbon steel, fouled the reactor, and dissolved the piping itself; and physical transients in the form of hammer, which wreaked havoc with brittle components. Finally, in the rush to get the plant back on line, maintenance would frequently not "dry" the piping they had replaced, or align the pumps, or fit gaskets properly, or do many of the things that they knew were the right things to do; but under the pressure for production, they did the best they could. Some or all of this may sound all too familiar.

So where does the root cause for the problems of the Stone Coal Creek plant lie? Maintenance would advise that operators are running the plant into the ground. Operations would advise that mechanics just never seem to do things right the first time. The design and capital projects staff would be long gone, not caring much about any operating problems—everything looked pretty good when they left. After all, they got the plant installed on time and within budget. Most of us standing on the outside would conclude from the limited information provided that all three were at the root cause of poor plant reliability. What follows is a process, a model, and case histories on how plant design and capital projects can work more effectively with operations and maintenance to assure world-class manufacturing, short and long term.

Design Objectives

As any good design engineer would tell you, one of the first things you must do is determine your design objectives. All too often, this effort does not include adequate reliability or maintainability objectives; nor does the installation effort include a process for verifying the quality of the installation effort (beyond the typical verification of process capability at a brief moment in time). A fundamental objective of every manufacturer should be to become the low-cost producer of their products, or at least as low as reasonably achievable. To do so, life-cycle costing must be considered, and as previously noted from the SMRP data,[1] in the vast majority of cases, it is not. There's much more to plant design and world-class manufacturing than process flows, process chemistry, and standard design methods. This is not to diminish their importance, but rather to recognize other issues that are often ignored, but of equal importance.

In the Stone Coal Creek plant, design engineers had come under considerable pressure to get the plant designed, installed, and running to meet expanded market demand as quickly as possible. Concurrently, capital budgets were very constrained. With these constraints, they used less expensive material. To justify this, they had to assume that few, if any, transients, either chemical or physical, would be experienced during the operation of the plant (a boss of many years ago taught me how to spell "assume" with three syllables, after I had made a major, and incorrect, assumption on a project). In other words, they assumed that the process would always be in complete control. This was difficult, however, because they also put in place inexpensive instruments for process control, which were frequently operated near their design limits. This was only exacerbated by operators who were not particularly well trained (not in the budget), and who rarely used control charts or statistical process control (not in the budget, or part of their culture). Even more difficult was the fact that feed stocks often contained water and other contaminants, and were not frequently verified as to quality, because the laboratory was poorly equipped (not in the budget), and understaffed, for the task at hand (not in the budget).

All these constraints and problems were typically ignored until a series of crises literally shut down or severely curtailed operation, incurring extraordinary maintenance costs and production losses. These costs were not in the budget either, and yet were far greater than what it would have cost to properly design and install the plant. As pressures grew for "production" to meet growing market demand, maintenance requirements were almost always sacrificed for present production, at the expense of future production. In the end, Stone Coal Creek plant reached a stage where the business was near abandonment. After much effort, pain, and anguish, they are just now returning to some level of control. As a footnote, it was remarkable that the chief of engineering and the project manager were actually praised for the "good job" they had done in bringing the plant into operation below budget and on schedule. Clearly, new standards were needed for determining excellence in a design or capital project effort.

Key Questions

First, all parties should have a common understanding of reliability and maintainability:[5]

Reliability relates to the level to which operational stability is achieved because equipment does not fail—the equipment is available at rated capacity whenever it is needed, and it yields the same results on repeated operation. It could also be defined as the probability that plant or equipment will perfom a required function without failure under stated conditions for a stated period of time. Reliability is an inherent characteristic of the system, and therefore very much a part of the design. Typical plant equipment includes:

Rotating equipment
    Centrifuges
    Compressors
    Conveyors
    Fans
    Motors
    Pumps
    Turbines

Instrumentation
    Electrical
    Electronic
    Pneumatic
    DCS/process control

Stationary equipment
    Piping
    Pressure vessels
    Tanks
    Heat exchangers
    Valves
    Ventilation

Electrical equipment
    Switchgear
    Motor controllers
    Transformers
    Motors

Maintainability relates to those issues that facilitate equipment repair—minimal time, effort, and skill, and specified material to return it to reliable operation as quickly as possible.

Some key questions related to reliability and maintainability should have been asked during the design, and before the capital authorization, to help define requirements for manufacturing excellence and assure business success:

• What are my reliability objectives for this plant related to availability and uptime, e.g., 95% availability, operating at 98% rate/yield, and 98% quality, i.e., 91%+ uptime?
• What are similar plants experiencing? Why?
• Are these similar plants measuring losses from ideal using uptime or OEE metrics?
• What losses are being experienced due to poor equipment maintainability and reliability?

- How will we acquire equipment histories, and operating and maintenance experience prior to the design effort?
- What are the key design parameters that will assure high (or low) reliability?
- What are the current procedures, practices, and standards for this type plant/equipment?
- What are the assumptions being made regarding reliability of process control, e.g., zero process chemistry and physical transients? What are the sensitivities or the equipment and processes to the foreseeable transients? What are the inherent control parameters, limits, and capabilities?
- What kind of maintainability requirements should be included? For example,

Access and lay-down space
Handling—lifting, installing, removing
On-line and routine inspection capability, including condition monitoring and PDM
Tagging or labeling of valves, pumps, and components
Color coding of piping
Industrial hygiene requirements, e.g., lighting, toxic exposure limits, ventilation requirements, noise limitations
Protective coating requirements
Documentation, procedures and drawings requirements
Special handling, tools, etc.

- What are/should be the training requirements for operators, for mechanics, technicians? How and when will this be accomplished? Should operators and mechanics participate in the startup and commissioning process?
- Are there specific ergonomic issues for this operation that must be addressed?
- Are standard suppliers already in place? How will standardization of equipment design be assured? What are the existing guidelines or supplier alliances?
- Are suppliers of major equipment required to include a detailed bill of material for their equipment, including a magnetic disk in a specific format?
- When is the design going to be presented *in detail* to operations and maintenance staff for their input? What is the methodology for this?

Note: "Drawings over the wall on Thursday, pm, and expecting comments by Monday, am" is NOT a review process.

- Will a senior operator and maintainer be on the project team?
- How will spares and PM requirements be determined? Will the supplier(s) perform an RCM or FMEA analysis to support definitive requirements?
- Will contractors be used for the installation effort? Have specific validation criteria been established for the quality of their work? Will they deliver "an effect" or a set of equipment?
- What commissioning standards have been set for the equipment (and the process)? For example:

Equipment:
    Vibration levels at specific frequencies and bands are below
       certain levels.
    Lubricants validated as to specification, quantity, and quality.
    Electric power of high quality, e.g., no harmonics, surges, sags,
       or ground loops.
    Motors have proper starting current, low cross-phase
       impedance, proper capacitance, and resistance to ground.
    Infrared scan shows no hot spots, e.g, good electrical
       connections, motor controllers, transformers, quality
       lagging, quality steam traps, etc.
    Leak detection shows no air, nitrogen, compressed gas, or
       vacuum leaks.
Process:
    Proper temperatures, pressures, flows for key processes.
    Process is sustainable for weeks at proper yields, conversion
       rates, cycle times, etc.
    Control charts for key process variables are within defined limits
       during sustained periods.
    Operators demonstrate ability to properly operate pumps,
       valves, and other equipment.
    Limited transients occur in both physical process and/or
       chemical process.
    Process control is readily apparent for all key process variables.

- When and how will purchasing participate in the design effort? What is their role?
- When and how will stores participate in the design or installation effort? Storing for reliability during the construction phase is very

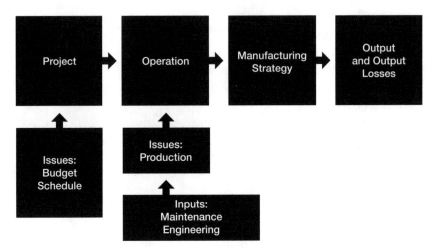

Figure 4-2. Traditional design and capital projects process.

important, and assuring stores capability for installation support is also very important.

• What is the philosophy or methodology for resolving conflict—lowest installed cost or lowest life-cycle cost?
• Are we willing to accept incrementally higher engineering costs for a longer, yet more comprehensive design process?

The old method for design used to develop the Stone Coal Creek plant is shown in Figure 4-2. A better model, which captures these issues is shown in Figure 4-3. Granted, the proposed model will require more time, more communication, more teamwork, etc., but when most manufacturers typically operate a plant for 30+ years, wouldn't an extra 6 months be worth the effort and expense? Certainly, it would have been for the Stone Coal Creek plant, and for Beta International as a whole.

Additional suggestions and case histories follow to illustrate these points.

Operations and Maintenance Input

In the ideal world, comprehensive loss accounting would be routinely available to define the causes of major losses and to lend itself to better design efforts. Root cause failure analysis would be common and much would have been learned regarding how to better design

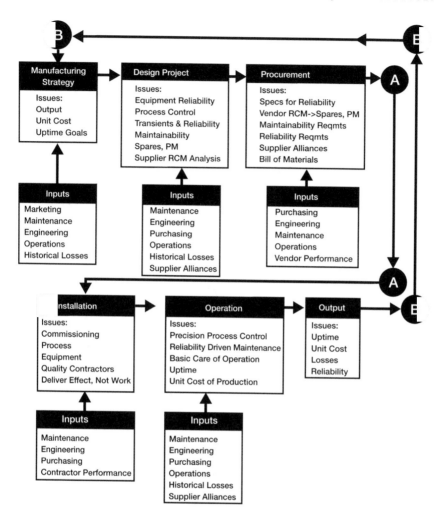

Figure 4-3. Design and capital projects process flow model.

future equipment and processes. Comprehensive equipment histories would be routinely used to determine where the major problems (and losses) were and also to support better design. Unfortunately, this is rare, and equipment histories are typically limited. So, how do we get operations and maintenance input from the beginning of a design effort. Beta International has now implemented the process shown in Figure 4-3, and described in the following.

The project lead should contact leaders in the operations and maintenance department and inquire about major losses and the principle reasons for them as they relate to design. Three or more case histories should be identified and briefly documented to help facilitate the thinking process for improvement.

A focus group consisting of maintenance personnel (mechanics and engineers), operations (operators and production supervisors), purchasing and stores personnel, and design/capital project engineers should be convened. After an introduction as to the purpose of the focus group—getting operations and maintenance input for the coming design, these case histories should then be presented to the focus group to start the group thinking about where the potential opportunities are and what might be done to capture them. The goal is to identify major opportunities for improving plant reliability through "designing out" current problems in existing operating plants, and thereby reducing life-cycle cost (as opposed to installed cost). As a bonus, you also get higher uptime, and lower unit cost of production, and the opportunity for higher market share and operating profits.

Once these opportunities are identified, then the group should work with design to help develop a process for resolving major issues. Input points should be identified by the group for continuing review of the design, linking key deficiency areas to solutions and various stages of the design and installation effort. A formal design review plan should be developed for each major opportunity (previously know as losses). Finally, a formal review process should be defined for providing the details that were only outlined by the plan. A good comprehensive design review process would not simply be dropping the drawings off to operations and maintenance on a Thursday afternoon, and expecting feedback on Monday morning. The project engineer should be required to explain in detail the overall design, as well as the basis for selecting each major piece of equipment. Feedback should be provided by those impacted by the design, and this information should be used to resolve potential conflict, and to develop detailed requirements for maintainability and reliability.

Estimating Life-Cycle Costs

Often, a tedious job, estimating life cycle costs should not be viewed as a trivial task. Panko[6] provides a model for this effort, which essentially requires developing a spread sheet and estimates for the following parameters:

Project title

Project life, years
Depreciation life, years: Year 0, Year 1, Year 2, Year 3, Year 4, etc.

Initial investment cost
  Design and start-up
  Training
  Equipment
  Material
  Installation
  Commissioning

Total initial investment

Operating costs
  Operating cost
  Maintenance cost
  Utility cost (power, fuel, air, water, hvac, other)
  Spare parts inventory increase

Historical production losses

Rebuild/replacement

Salvage/residual value

Other expenses

Tax savings on depreciation

Cash flow
Discount factor
Discounted cash flow
Cumulative present value
Present value

Estimates should not be limited to only these parameters, which demonstrate the principle and serve as a model for use. As is demonstrated in this chapter, the input of maintenance and operations in providing historical experience and information for developing these estimates is critical, especially production losses.

Additional examples of the impact of poor design practices on operating and maintenance costs at other Beta plants follow. Perhaps these will trigger ideas that will help in your design efforts for assuring lowest life-cycle cost, maximum uptime, lowest unit cost of production, and maximum profits.

Additional Case Histories

Turkey Creek Plant. This plant had historically used carbon steel heat exchangers in a process that was fairly corrosive. At one point they had considered using titanium, but the initial cost was approximately six times that of the carbon steel. For as many heat exchangers as they had, replacing all heat exchangers would cost some $10M, and was considered prohibitive.

At the same time, the Turkey Creek plant seemed to be constantly plugging tubes, or replacing or repairing heat exchangers, in one way or another. One of the engineers had run some calculations on the high maintenance costs, and had concluded that if the maintenance costs were added to the initial costs for the exchangers, titanium was still a better choice, but it would have taken several years to reap the return. Given limited capital budgets, they struggled along with carbon steel.

However, the engineer had neglected a key cost component in the analysis. On reviewing the system, it turned out that deterioration in the heat exchanger performance was routinely resulting in minor derates in the production process. These occurred when heat exchangers were taken off line briefly for tube plugging, when plugged tubes reached a level where full rate could no longer be sustained, and when exchangers were simply off line for replacement. These losses seemed relatively minor and tolerable, until a full accounting was taken over a year-long period. It turned out that when the value of these production losses accumulated over a year and were included, titanium heat exchangers would have paid for themselves within the first year of installation through improved production alone. The reduced maintenance costs would be a bonus, and the ability to reallocate resources to more productive efforts would also be a bonus. The Turkey Creek plant replaced the carbon steel heat exchangers with titanium ones.

Warco Plant. Warco was a relatively new production plant, but after two years was still having difficulty achieving its output on which the plant was justified for investment purposes. In fact total production losses from the plant were valued at some $5M, making its return on net assets poor.

On reviewing the plant, it was found that insufficient isolation valves had been provided to be able to isolate specific portions of the production line without having to shut down the entire line. As a consequence, on more than one occasion, the entire line had to be shut down for maintenance resulting in substantial loss of production. Further, very limited analysis was performed regarding equipment criticality and the development of a critical bill of material (maintenance and operations were not involved in this "analysis"), and as a consequence, insufficient spares were purchased as part of the capital project. This resulted in the unavailability of spares and loss of production capacity, as well as incremental maintenance costs. Further, instrumentation was difficult to access for routine maintenance and calibration, and the instrumentation was considered to be marginally acceptable for the application. As a consequence of difficult calibration of marginally acceptable instruments, the process was often not in control, resulting in production losses from the cost of poor quality, and over the long term accelerating corrosion of stationary equipment. While no major losses have yet occurred from the corrosion, they can be expected in the future.

A $1,000,000 improvement project was initiated to successfully eliminate these design defects, but the $5M already lost will never be recovered.

Stamper Branch Plant. This plant had been operating for approximately one year at a level well below expectations. Production losses from poor performance were estimated in excess of $3M, not to mention extraordinary maintenance costs, which were running over 6% of plant replacement value.

On reviewing the plant, it was determined that the pumps were of a new design from a new company with no demonstrated reliability record, but were quite inexpensive from an initial cost perspective. The pumps "contributed" significantly to lost production, as well as increased maintenance costs. The plant compressor was also selected on the basis of low bid, over the objection of the corporate compressor specialist. Likewise its unreliability "contributed" to major maintenance costs and plant downtime. The bulk storage area for the finished product also had several wrong and/or incompatible materials, resulting in extraordinary maintenance costs, and a higher injury rate from more frequent exposure to a hazardous environment. Isolation valves were also insufficient in number and design to allow for on-line inspections of critical equipment, resulting in a run-to-failure mode of operation for portions of the plant.

The specifications for the pumps were changed, and a small upgrade project totaling some $60K eliminated or mitigated most of the problems.

Summary

These experiences are not unusual, and at Beta International pressures related to budget and schedule for major capital projects had historically outweighed issues related to designing for uptime, reliability, unit cost of production, and lowest life-cycle cost. Lowest installed cost and minimum adequate design (without effectively defining adequacy) reflected the dominant management method for capital projects. However, it did not provide the best business position for maximizing profits long term. New standards, and a new culture is being implemented at Beta and must be nurtured so that it focuses on lowest life-cycle cost, maximum reliability, and uptime. These processes will help assure maximum output, minimum unit cost of production, maximum profits and return on net assets. However, simply improving the design and capital project process will not be sufficient. We still must have good procurement, stores, installation, operation and maintenance practices. Those are discussed in the next chapters.

References

1. Society for Maintenance and Reliability Professionals, Spring '96 Newsletter, Barrington, IL.

2. Blanchard, B. S. *Design and Manage to Life-Cycle Cost,* MA Press, Forest Grove, OR, 1978.

3. Blanchard, B. S. *Maintainability—A Key to Effective Serviceability and Maintenance Management,* John Wiley and Sons, New York, NY, 1995.

4. The Business Stake in Effective Project Systems, Independent Project Analysis, Inc., Presentation to The Business Roundtable of Western Michigan, Grand Rapids, MI, 1997.

5. Society for Maintenance and Reliability Professionals, Fall '95 Newsletter, Barrington, IL.

6. Panko, D. "Life-Cycle Cost Analysis Determines Cost Benefits," Society for Maintenance and Reliability Professionals Summer '97 Newsletter, Barrington, IL.

Procurement Practices

5

The quality of our offerings will be the sum total of the excellence
of each player on our supply team . . .

Robert W. Galvin

Some time ago, Beta International began an intensive effort to
review and improve supply chain performance. This effort addressed
the entire supply chain from raw material to delivery of finished
product to the customer, but particular attention was given to consolidation of the number of suppliers and getting better pricing from
those suppliers, to improved production planning and turns on finished product, and to a more limited extent, turns on stores/spares.

Beta's management had come to understand that good supply chain
management required excellence in manufacturing. Plants had to be
operated in a reliable, readily predictable manner to produce high-
quality product that could be easily integrated into the supply chain
and distribution strategy being developed. Plants that could not operate in this manner would make it extraordinarily difficult to meet the
challenges of the global supply chain strategy being developed. Most
of Beta International's manufacturing plant performance as measured
by weekly production rates, uptime, unit costs, etc. were in need of
substantial improvement. Some business units were even purchasing a

considerable amount of product from competitors to make up for plant production shortfalls and meet contracted customer demand.

Further, as already noted, a benchmarking effort indicated that Beta's aggregate plant asset utilization rate was typically no better than the average range of 60–80%, as compared to a world-class level of 85–95%. On-time delivery performance for customer deliveries was typically 85–90%, as compared to a world-class level of 99%+. Reactive maintenance was typically over 50%, as compared to a world-class level of less than 10%, indicative of a highly reactive, and often poorly functioning manufacturing operation. Many plants literally could not reliably anticipate from one week to the next how much product could be produced, nor at what quality, because Cpk, a measure of product adherence to quality, was typically at 1 or less, compared to a world-class level of greater than 2. Some plants had production variances from their plans of 50% or more, from week to week. Until the company achieved manufacturing excellence, global supply chain objectives would be very difficult to achieve. Clearly, manufacturing excellence is a necessity at Beta, not an option if the company is to achieve its key strategic objectives for supply chain management.

Further, Mr. Neurath had some concern that his message for improved supply chain performance was being misinterpreted by some people in procurement and some at the production plants. For example, he had heard through one of his staff that one of the plants had been advised by the stores manager that someone, apparently under the auspices of achieving supply chain objectives, had stated they were coming to remove half the spare parts in stores, because most of it had not "moved" in over a year. However, he understood that stores inventory levels (discussed in the next chapter) were secondary concerns when it came to supply chain management and, more importantly, that if the parts were not readily available for plant maintenance, it could result in additional downtime, further exacerbating broader supply chain objectives. This was particularly true for those plants that operated in a highly reactive mode. Granted, the best plants operate with a stores level of less than 0.5% of plant replacement value, compared to Beta's typical level of 1–1.5% or more. However, the best plants were typically operated much more reliably, had higher uptimes, lower reactive maintenance levels, and lower maintenance costs. They didn't need the level of spare parts required by most of Beta's plants, and when they did, they could more reliably anticipate those needs, allowing them to more effectively create supplier partnerships, use blanket orders, operate in a consignment mode, etc.

Mr. Neurath understood that given the current level of performance in many Beta plants, one of the worst things to do at this point is to arbitrarily reduce spare parts, putting the plant at risk for its uptime performance and exacerbating its ability to produce and deliver on customer obligations. After some discussion with his key staff, Mr. Neurath concluded that the first order of business was to assure manufacturing excellence, and as part of that to manage feedstock supplies more effectively. Management of stores, as described in the next chapter, will be a part of the overall improvement process, but will have a lower overall priority.

To achieve the goals associated with supply chain management—low-cost producer for each product, on-time deliveries of 99% or better, finished product inventory turns of 20 or better, etc.—Mr. Neurath knew there were several issues that had to be addressed, particularly those associated with manufacturing excellence. He also understood that purchasing had a key role to play, particularly in the area of strategic supplier alliances, and in assuring better specifications for plant reliability and uptime when these alliances were developed. Going with low bid because it was low bid was apparently creating several hardships at the operating level, which he wanted to alleviate. Examples of Beta's efforts to address these two issues in particular are described in the following sections. Lendrum[1] also provides additional information on the development of partnerships and alliances.

A Model for Development of Strategic Alliances—Goose Creek Plant

When discussing strategic alliances, many people immediately revert to "discounts for volume." While this may be part of a strategic alliance, the better alliances usually involve more than just a discount and volume formula for a given product. Indeed, at Beta's Goose Creek plant, a strategy was developed that worked exceptionally well, involving more than volume discounts.

Beta's Goose Creek plant was generally operating at a more advanced level of performance than most other Beta plants, though not world-class. Asset utilization rate was in the 85%+ range; product unit costs were lower than most; advanced operating and maintenance practices (described elsewhere) were being implemented resulting in lower operating and maintenance costs; on-time-in-full rates were at 90% and better in any given month. Overall the plant was reasonably well run. However, as noted, the plant was not world-class. The purchasing manager, an engineer who had also worked in production and in maintenance (a rare combination of experience), had concluded that supporting the global supply chain initiative would require extraordinary effort. One area that concerned him was the actual process for creating these strategic alliances. After considerable thought, he developed and executed the plan of action described below.

If manufacturing excellence was the objective, a key issue for purchasing was how suppliers working in a strategic alliance could help achieve excellence. It then seemed critical to analyze operating results—uptime, product and process quality, equipment life (mean time between equipment failure and total life), process efficiency, and operating and maintenance costs for given sets of equipment. Further, it was also critical to understand key production losses that were resulting from problems with major critical equipment. Having participated in an uptime optimization improvement effort (described in Chapter 2), which includes identification of major losses, the purchasing manager understood that a certain type of pump used in production was causing major losses. These losses were characterized as losses in uptime due to equipment failures, and as out-of-pocket losses due to extraordinary repair costs. He decided to use this as a "test case" to construct a supplier alliance with a major pump supplier to eliminate most, if not all, of these losses.

Working with maintenance and production, he contacted the existing supplier and two other suppliers who had been suggested and set up a meeting with each of them. At this meeting, which also had representatives from production and maintenance, he outlined the current situation with the existing pumps—production losses and maintenance costs attributable to the pumps, their problems as they understood them, etc. He also clearly stated that the goal was to establish a vendor alliance with a single supplier that would eliminate these problems. He made it very clear that continuing to buy spare parts for repairs from the existing vendor and operating in "forever fixing" mode was not an option in the long term, and that having these problems "fixed forever" was a requirement. Privately, he did have some misgivings about the current vendor, because he seemed to be just as happy to sell spare parts for repair, rather than aggressively seek to resolve the problems. Vendors were encouraged to look at current operating and maintenance practices for the pumps and offer any improvement suggestions in the short term. Preliminary goals were put forth for vendor comment regarding:

> Production losses due to pump failures—output, product quality, yields, etc.
> Mean time between pump repairs
> Annual operating cost
> Annual maintenance cost—PM, overhaul, and repair
> Overall pump life
> Initial cost

With this in mind, he asked each supplier to offer a proposal on how Goose Creek could minimize its losses, minimize its unit cost of production, and maximize its uptime. In return, Goose Creek would commit essentially 100% of its business for these pumps to the supplier. Additional opportunities for increases in business in other areas would be contingent upon achieving specific performance criteria in this area, e.g., reduction in losses, improved average pump life, quality technical support, access to results of R&D effort, etc. Further, the Goose Creek plant required that the pump supplier perform a failure modes and effects analysis (FMEA)/reliability centered maintenance (RCM) analysis on its pumps and in conjunction with failure history data, and use that analysis as a basis for its recommendations for spare parts and PM. It was no longer acceptable to recommend spare parts and PM on a take-it-or-leave-it basis—the recommendations had to be backed by solid engineering and statistical analysis. This was to be a true partnership effort.

As an aside, the pump suppliers' review of the operating and maintenance practices resulted several of improvement recommendations in the areas of pump operating procedures (for minimizing cavitation), in pump lubricating practices, in alignment and balancing practices, in overhaul practices, etc. These were incorporated immediately into current operating and maintenance practices for the pumps, and are summarized in the following section.

Pump Reliability Best Practices

At the Goose Creek plant a pump improvement team was established, consisting of specialists from the supplier, two senior operators, the plant engineer, the machine shop supervisor, two senior mechanics, and a condition monitoring specialist. The group met to review best practices for pump operation and repair, and to develop an improvement plan that they would lead in their areas. Over the course of several days, they developed several improvement actions:

- Operator tours were established for each shift to check/log items such as pump suction and discharge pressures, leaks, lubrication levels, unusual noises such as cavitation, etc., and recording the information as required.
- A detailed pump start-up and operation procedure was developed. While it varied for each pump service, it typically included some 20 steps/checks, any one of which if improperly done, could result in pump damage or unsafe start-up. Operator understanding of basic pump operating principles was found in significant need of improvement.
- An in-line spares policy was developed that for each application included consideration of issues such as potential effects on production downtime, effect of buffer stocks, ease of changeover, ease of detecting developing problems, historical pump reliability and fitness for purpose, local environmental conditions, and ease of access.
- When in-line spares were being used, a policy was developed to assure its reliability when needed, e.g., alternate operation, or mechanical and process stream isolation; PM of the back-up spare; pump status card and history, spares availability, etc.
- The pump repair shop was improved by getting work flows and tools better organized, cleaning and tidying the area, better repair standards, establishing a "clean room" for precision work, and a general application of pride and craftsmanship.
- Precision standards were established for shaft precision, balancing, lubrication, seals, isolators, foundations, installation and start-up, a precision alignment checklist, etc.

Additional information can be obtained from The Pump Handbook Series published by *Pumps and Systems Magazine*.

Supplier Selection

After reviewing all proposals and having several discussions, Goose Creek finally selected a supplier and signed a formal contract. It included key metrics for pump performance, i.e., pump life—mean time between repairs and overall life, $ losses from pump failures; production losses and repair costs; and annual maintenance costs, including PM requirements, overhaul, and repair costs. These factored into the RCM/FMEA analysis, which was acceptable to Goose Creek engineers for defining PM and spare parts requirements. The supplier also warranted the pumps to meet certain minimal requirements relative to these measures, so long as the Goose Creek staff performed certain tasks related to the operation and maintenance of the pumps. Of course, they provided the standard warranty regarding the pumps being free of defects. Finally, the pump supplier also agreed to keep certain critical (and expensive) parts available in his facility and to make those available within 24 hours of notice to ship, and made certain other parts available on consignment in the Goose Creek stores.

Included in the contract were data regarding baseline performance of the current operation developed using information that had already been developed and shared with the suppliers. Deadlines were included in the contract for new pump delivery and installation, including a small liquidated damages clause for failure to deliver on time. The pump supplier also included key training and technical assistance for the initial storage, installation, start-up, operation, and maintenance methods.

As part of on-going support and problem resolution, they also included in the contract a process for continuing and regular communication, and for the methodology for failure analysis of any pump failures, e.g., root cause failure analysis and FMEA methodologies. The pump supplier detailed their process for quality assurance in the pump manufacturing effort, and included time for Goose Creek staff to tour their manufacturing plant and review their production methods, and training processes for their technicians.

As noted, all these issues were formalized in a contract between the Goose Creek plant and the pump supplier. The process by which this agreement was reached is summarized as follows:

• Analyze current operating results and losses from ideal as a result of equipment performance, e.g., downtime losses, operating and maintenance costs, product and process quality, equipment life, etc.
• Set operating objectives and cost reduction targets, including operating and maintenance costs, purchase price, including training and technical support, etc.
• Baseline current operation re: key measures for partnership.

- Commit minimum % of business to partner. Set increases in % of business to specific performance criteria, e.g., quality, cost, technical support, targeted improvements, access for results of R&D, etc.
- Set performance standards and dates for achievement, reference baseline data for improvements.
- Agree upon metrics and techniques for their measurement.
- Provide for warranty of performance, e.g., better than any of competitor products; better than average of prior years; free of defects, minimal performance requirements, etc.
- Define technical assistance requirements and commitments, and consequences of not meeting commitments.
- Baseline specifics of processes/products/practices.
- Define schedule improvement in performance, including any lead times, forecasts, etc.
- Define basis for frequent, clear communication, performance reviews, and basis for failure analysis process for product quality faults, etc., including report formats and frequency for communication and reporting.
- Define QA process to be used for products, and include supplier plant tour.
- Define equipment for prototype or pilot run, as necessary.
- Define procedure for resolving any disputes.
- Document and sign a formal agreement.

The results of the alliance were exceptional. Total initial costs for the pumps was actually somewhat higher, considering the training, installation support and continuing technical support, but then so was the initial value. Production losses were essentially eliminated because of pump failures, and maintenance costs were drastically reduced. Mean time between repairs for the pumps more than tripled, and maintenance costs overall were substantially reduced.

Finally, this approach stands in marked contrast to that of Beta's Grundy plant purchasing manager. At this plant, they had received several defective pump shafts, ones in which the pump impeller was not perpendicular to the shaft, visibly so, because it didn't take precision calipers to see the angular offset. The purchasing people accepted the pumps for a 20% credit on the invoice, without checking with the machine shop or maintenance foreman to determine if the pump could be salvaged at all, and if so at what cost. It was not a good trade-off.

Process for Improved Specifications for Equipment Reliability—Mossy Bottom Plant

As previously described, purchasing and the entire procurement process must be an integral part of improved reliability, equipment life, uptime, etc. In the best plants, purchasing is an integral part of the production team, helping to assure maximum reliability in production equipment. Usually, however, ineffective communication and insufficient attention to reliability issues compromise the procurement process, and purchasing. This was the case at Beta's Mossy Bottom plant.

In helping production, maintenance, and engineering assure maximum production capacity, purchasing must consider reliability and life-cycle cost as an integral part of the purchasing process. Reliability and value should be the critical measures for supplier selection. And in fact, the purchasing manager at Mossy Bottom was quick to assert that he does consider life-cycle cost, reliability, and value. Experience has shown, however, that he was often missing key elements, both in his thinking and in his practices, for assuring maximum equipment reliability, and typically had been conditioned to think in terms of lowest delivered cost, as opposed to equipment reliability and lowest life-cycle cost.

The standards for reliability, life-cycle cost, and value, while simple conceptually, can be very difficult as a practical matter. The purchasing manager at Mossy Bottom very often necessarily assumed that the specifications were adequate to assure meeting the plant's needs. Unfortunately, many times the specifications did not specify requirements for maximum reliability, and as we all know, it is often simply not possible to put *everything* into a specification. Further, Mossy Bottom's purchasing department would often substitute alternate vendors who would, at least ostensibly, meet a specification, but in fact have a poor track record.

For example, at a recent reliability improvement team meeting, it was announced that corporate materials management had signed a long-term supplier agreement with a particular pump seal manufacturer. Most of the people at the meeting were very unhappy with the decision, essentially echoing the comment "they'll look good at our expense—those seals require much more frequent replacement, and their technical support is poor." The maintenance department had first-hand knowledge of those suppliers who provide the best quality, highest value, best service for seals, motors, pumps, etc., but were not consulted before the decision was made. On another occasion, purchasing had gone to a different supplier for suction cups that were used in the packaging area for product handling. It turned out that the new suction cups weren't nearly as reliable as the old ones, and created considerable downtime, even though the vendor provided them under the same specification. In this case the savings in the cost of the suction cups was far less than the lost uptime and production losses incurred as a result. The purchasing manager tried to make the right decisions for the business unit, but poor communication combined with autonomous decision making had resulted in poor decisions. Further, they weren't all held to common measures such as maximum uptime, and minimum unit cost of production.

Such problems (or opportunities waiting) should not simply be placed at the feet of purchasing, but more properly should be viewed as driven by the lack of good communication, and the inability to put everything into a purchase specification. In some circumstances, even when everything is in a specification, many suppliers with a history of poor performance will bid to the specification, only to supply unreliable equipment. Equipment histories must be put in place to identify reliable equipment and, combined with a formal communications process between production, maintenance, engineering, and purchasing, including a reliability evaluation process to screen out those suppliers whose equipment falls short in actual use. Such was not initially the case at the Mossy Bottom plant. Writing better specifications, testing supplier equipment (in the factory and at installation where appropriate), documenting problems and equipment histories would also substantially improve reliability in manufacturing equipment. After considerable review and a major effort between production, engineering, maintenance and purchasing, the following processes were put in place at the plant.[1-4] These methods are intended to offer a model for improved specifications rather than represent a comprehensive set of standards, and should be adapted for specific plant processes, needs, etc. Note also that these requirements also apply to contractors, because they are in greater use.

Vibration Standards for Rotating Machinery

For critical equipment, the Mossy Bottom plant required that vibration standards be included in the specification for the equipment, and the supplier would be required to certify that their equipment meets those standards. The vibration standard chosen was General Motors Specification No. V 1.0-1993 for use in setting maximum vibrations standards for particular types of equipment at specific rotational frequencies. The GM specification is applicable to motors, pumps, and fans as well as production equipment such as machine tools. Typically, the specification is applied to equipment larger than about 10 horsepower, unless criticality of the equipment warrants testing at lower horsepower. An additional source of information for specifying acceptable vibration levels is Hewlett Packard Application Note 243-1, *Effective Machinery Measurements Using Dynamic Signal Analyzers*. When applying these standards, the issues following were addressed.

Pride[2] advises that the following procedure should be followed when developing a specification for vibration levels for a given machine:

1. Obtain nameplate data.
2. Define location of measurement points, typically two radial and one axial on either end of the machine train, and two radial on the inboard of the driver and driven machine.
3. Define instrumentation requirements for resolution (number of lines), and sensor types. Hand-held sensors are generally not acceptable.
4. Obtain narrowband vibration spectrum on similar machines, and establish acceptance levels for each narrow band, e.g., GM V1.0-1993. Differences in baseplate stiffness and mass will affect vibration signature. Overall measurements are only for general interest, and not part of the acceptance criteria.
5. Calculate all forcing frequencies i.e., imbalance, misalignment, bearing defect, impeller and/or vane, electrical, gear, belt, etc.
6. Construct an average vibration signature for the similar machines.
7. Compare this average vibration signature to one of the guidelines provided above, e.g., GM Specification V1.0-1993.
8. Note any deviations from the guidelines and determine if the unknown frequencies are system related, e.g., a resonance test may be required to identify those associated with piping supports.
9. Collect vibration data on new components at each of the bearing caps in the radial and axial directions.
10. Compare vibration spectrum with the average spectrum developed in Step 5 and with selected guidelines.
11. Any new piece of equipment should have a vibration spectrum that is no worse than similar equipment that is operating satisfactorily.

With critical machinery, they would also require a factory acceptance test of the equipment, typically including:

1. Driver uncoupled, including vibration and phase data.
2. Driver coupled to machine, including vibration and phase data, fully loaded at normal operating temperature. Also, consider collecting data during start-up and coast-down to look for critical speeds; and for unloaded/cold, during warm-up, unloaded at normal temperature, or for other special cases.

Any failure of the equipment to meet the specification results in rejection.

In some instances a "bump" test could be performed on all piping, foundations, frames, etc. to identify potential resonance-induced problems, and take action as appropriate.

Finally, all tests should be conducted by a vibration analyst who has been certified by the Vibration Institute as a Level I or II Vibration Analyst.

Balancing Specifications

For balancing new and rebuilt rotors, the specification should include (1) the speed(s) for balancing the rotor; (2) vibration acceptance limits; (3) single or multi-plane balancing; (4) trim balance requirements at installation. ISO DR1940 Grades 1.0, 2.5, 6.3, and 16 are routinely used, with ISO Grade 6.3 having been the historical *de facto* standard. More recently best practice, particularly for critical equipment, has come to be ISO Grade 2.5 for most industrial applications, with ISO Grade 6.3 being reserved for non-critical applications. For more precision requirements such as machine tools, ISO Grade 1.0 has become a typical requirement.

Resonance Specifications

In recent years, in an effort to reduce costs, many manufacturers have reduced the mass of much of their equipment, particularly in high-efficiency motors. This reduction in mass can lead to an increase in resonance problems. Therefore, a resonance specification may be appropriate in the purchase specification. The resonance frequency of any component or frame should be at least 30% greater than the *maximum attainable* speed of the machine. Note, however, that it is fairly common to see machinery run at speeds significantly greater than design.

Bearing Installation Specifications

The specification should include a requirement that the supplier publish and use good bearing selection, handling, and installation procedures during manufacture of the required equipment, and should provide the user with the brand and model number of bearings used in rotating machinery. Further, L10 life for bearings should be specified, with a typical industrial requirement being an L10 of 50, meaning that 90% of the bearing purchased should last some 50,000 hours of operation. (Note: That's 6 full years at 90% run time.) Other considerations, such as ABEC number for bearing finish, and bearing fit up, e.g., C3 or C4, should also be included. Requirements for use of an induction heater and oil bath for bearing installation should also be included.

Machinery Alignment

The specification should include a requirement that the supplier publish and use good alignment practices for the supply of machine trains. A standard specification for dynamic check of alignment using a standard vibration specification for validation should be required. Include any belt- and pulley-driven machinery, including tensioning specifications.

Motor Specifications

Beyond the normal specifications, it may also be prudent to require that three-phase motors not have a cross-phase resistance difference of greater than 3%; nor a cross-phase inductance difference of greater than 5%, between any two phases.[2-3] This will minimize one phase running hot, which leads to deterioration in motor life. Motors should be balanced within about 0.05 in./sec. vibration level at normal turning speed. Vibration levels at 120 Hz should be less than about 0.05 in./sec. Levels in excess of this indicate a non-uniform magnetic field, due to voids in the shaft, eccentric shaft, stator faults, imbalance in the stator phases, etc. The feet of the motor (or other machinery) should be co-planar (flat) within nominally 0.005 in. (cast iron) and 0.015 in. (steel). Each motor should have a unique nameplate serial number.

Equipment Identification_____

General—For each machine, the following should be obtained:

Manufacturer _____ ID/Serial No. _____

Drive and opposite end bearings model nos.; all other bearing model nos;
all bearing L10 data
Lubrication requirements—type, frequency, sampling points
Other requirements—jacking bolts, rigid base plates, vibration disks

Motor or Driver

Rated hp _____   Rated voltage_____

Rated amps _____   Efficiency _____

No. of phases _____   Drive and opposite bearing; L10_____

No. of rotor bars _____   No. of stator slots _____

Frame_____   Service factor _____

Rated rpm _____   Type of coupling_____

No. of poles_____   Temperature detectors _____

Electrical classification_____

Driven Equipment

Speed of each stage_____   Model no._____

No. of vanes each stage _____   Input speed_____

No. of blades each stage _____   Constant _____Variable _____

No. of stages _____   Drive and opposite end bearings; L10___

Belt Driven

Diameter of 1st sheave_____   Belt ID_____

Diameter of 2nd sheave _____   Input shaft speed _____

Distance between centers_____

Gear Driven

Input shaft speed_____   Output shaft speed _____

Gear IDs_____   No. of input gear teeth _____

No. of output gear teeth _____   Service factor _____

Figure 5-1. General machine information specification summary sheet.

General Requirements

1. Defects should not be found at bearing-fault frequencies. If they appear at a factory test or at start-up, the fault should be corrected. Similarly, for belt-driven equipment, belt frequency and harmonics of the belt frequency should not appear.
2. Pump suppliers should provide grouting instructions and alignment specifications.
3. When setting up data bases in a CMMS or predictive maintenance system, each piece of equipment and data collection point should have a unique identifier.
4. L10 life for bearings and a requirement for identifying the bearing make and model number for each should be provided by the equipment supplier.
5. Service factors for gear boxes and motors should be specified.
6. Run out measurements should be specified as follows:[2] Maximum bore run out: ± 0.002 in.; Maximum shaft run out: ± 0.002 in.; Maximum face run out: 0.0005 in. Zero axial end play.
7. Jacking bolts should be requested for larger motors, pumps, etc. to facilitate precision alignment.
8. Threaded flange holes should be counter-bored to avoid material being compressed on tightening, resulting in a soft foot effect.
9. Instruction should be given to staff and vendors to assure they do NOT lift motors and pumps by their shaft.
10. As a minimum, the general equipment information sheet shown in Figure 5-1, or similar, should be completed for each major piece of equipment purchased and provided to maintenance and engineering.

This information reflects an example of the process for integrating the procurement function into a world-class reliability program. The key to assuring that purchasing is an integral part of the production team is that they must be advised and conditioned to consider reliability issues, and they must be treated as an integral part of the team, not just someone to call when you want something purchased.

These two areas are considered critical for the future success of Beta and in particular for the Mossy Bottom and Goose Creek plants, and are already the following benefits:

1. Increased communication and teamwork between purchasing, engineering, production, and maintenance—a shift in the culture of the plant.
2. Improved equipment reliability and life.
3. Improved uptime and unit cost of production.
4. A sense of purpose regarding world-class manufacturing.

Beta's Mossy Bottom and Goose Creek plants are currently implementing these practices and have already achieved substantial improvement in these areas. These will be used as models for implementation at other plants within Beta's business units. Purchasing and procurement practices must be made an integral part of plant reliability for assuring manufacturing excellence.

One final tip may be of use in improving supplier performance. At one of Beta's plants, the purchasing manager prominently displayed two placards, one labeled "Top Dog," with a cartoon of a happy puppy; the other labeled "Dog House," with a sad hound hanging low in a dog house. The suppliers who routinely met the plant's requirements for price, quality, delivery, service, etc. were rewarded with their names displayed under the "Top Dog." Of course, the ones who were less than satisfactory in their performance were treated otherwise. None of the suppliers wanted to be in the "Dog House."

Raw Material Cost Improvement

Raw material and feedstock purchases often represent some 50% or more of total manufacturing costs. Much effort is put into reducing direct labor costs, which in many larger manufacturing plants only represent 5–20% of total costs. If we could achieve a 10% reduction in raw material costs, this would amount to a equivalent of 25–100% reduction in direct labor costs. Yet, only recently has Beta begun to look for new methods for minimizing its raw material costs. Certainly, Beta has all along been doing what many others are doing, that is, reducing the number of suppliers in exchange for higher volume and lower pricing; searching world-wide for suppliers that appear to have good value, not just low price; improving manufacturing performance to reduce waste and scrap, etc. However, more recently Beta has decided to try several new initiatives. The first, related to developing strategic alliances for suppliers of critical production equipment, was described earlier.

The second, however, is a more novel approach. As noted, some 50% of Beta's manufacturing costs are for raw materials coming into its factories. Each percentage reduction here has much higher leverage on total manufacturing costs than any other cost component. Granted, consolidating suppliers and constructing alliances should be done. However, what if Beta takes what it has learned, and is learning, and shares that with its key raw material suppliers? What if Beta sets up a procedure wherein part of the procurement qualification process is to compare their suppliers' operations to world-class standards, and to work with their suppliers to make sure these practices and standards are being applied? Beta has recently begun a test effort with a few of its key suppliers. Essentially, the process involves auditing key suppliers against best manufacturing practices, making some estimate of the potential savings possible using better practices, sharing with those suppliers Beta's application of best practice, and then negotiating with suppliers relative to improved raw material costs, sharing in the gains to be achieved. Intense competitive pressures world-wide appear to be lending credibility to this approach.

Finally, while the information in this chapter provides considerable detail about rotating machinery, the intent is not to educate about rotating machinery, but to provide a model that can be expanded to other equipment, and to show how to apply specifics for technical requirements and the development of alliances with suppliers for all plant equipment. For example, specific types of equipment, such as compressors, fans, etc., will obviously require additional detail to assure good specifications; and perhaps more importantly, analogous requirements could be developed for fixed equipment using this model. The use of strategic alliances for equipment suppliers is a key part of the improvement process, but it involves not just cost and volume, it involves improving operating performance. Raw material costs are driven by supply and manufacturing costs. Beta's sharing of best practice with suppliers should improve raw material costs. The information above, like much of Beta's experience, is being shared as part of a process for continuing change and improvement.

References

1. Lendrum, T. *The Strategic Partnering Handbook,* McGraw-Hill Company, Sydney, Australia, 1998.

2. Pride, A. Pride Consulting, Inc., Knoxville, TN.

3. Talbot, C., Mars, M. and M., and DiMezzo,B. "Reliability Improvement Through Vendor Quality Specifications," Owens-Corning, presented at Society for Maintenance and Reliability Professionals 1994 Conference, Barrington, IL.

4. Dunton, T. "Discovering/Providing/Correcting Vertical Pump Misalignment," Update International, presented at Enteract Conference, 1994, sponsored by Entek, Cincinnati, OH.

Stores/Parts Management Practices

6

You never miss the water till the well runs dry.

Rowland Howard

Stores should be run like a store—clean, efficient, everything in its place, not too much or too little, run by a manager with a focus on customer (facility maintenance and operation) needs. Moreover, stores should be viewed as an asset, not a liability or cost. Maintaining a good, high-quality stores operation is in fact the low-cost approach to operating a facility. Yet, Beta International plants typically treated their stores function as if it were a necessary evil, a burdensome cost, a non-value adding function. This was not an enlightened approach. As Beta found, IF properly managed, stores will help assure a high-quality, low-cost operation. If not, stores will continue to be a "non-value adding" and expensive "necessary evil."

What Are Stores?

In most facilities, stores are typically viewed as spare parts. However, a broader and more accurate perspective is that all items not consumed directly or indirectly in production are included under the heading of stores. At Beta, stores are generally classified into five groups:[1]

- Hardware and supplies, e.g., bolts, small tools, belts, pipe, valves, etc.
- Materials, e.g., paint, lubricants, cement, refractory, etc.
- Spare parts, e.g., bearings, gears, circuit boards, specific components, etc.
- Spare equipment, e.g., complete assemblies and machines.
- Special items, e.g., lubricants, catalyst, steel banding, construction surplus, pilot, etc.

The stores function is to provide high-quality spare parts and other material as needed and where needed, primarily supporting the maintenance function. Ideally, stores would always have exactly what was needed, when it was needed, and be able to place it where it was needed at a moment's notice. And it would have no more than what was needed—only that material and spare parts needed immediately, and only for a minimum period in stores. Unfortunately, few of us live in this ideal world, and at many of Beta's plants "stock outs" were a frequent occurrence; reorders were often needed; delivery of spares was sporadic, etc. Beta, like most companies however, found a "solution" to these problems—they carried lots of spare parts in considerably larger quantities than would ordinarily be needed on a daily basis. This resulted in excess inventory, poor cash flow management, and often, sloppy management practices.

There is a better way.

The "Cost" of Stores

Spare parts and stores expenditures at Beta's plants typically ran 25–50% of a given maintenance budget. Further, annual carrying costs (labor, space, insurance, taxes, shrinkage, utilities, etc.), typically ran 30% or so of the value of stores. Perhaps more importantly, if the parts were not available, or were of poor quality because of poor suppliers or poor stores practices, then plant function was lost for extended periods of time. These losses were often larger than the carrying costs. After an indepth review, the cost of stores was recharacterized as losses associated with:[1]

- Working capital "losses"—overstocked, underused material, parts, etc., sitting in stores.
- Carrying cost "losses" for maintaining the stores operation.
- Plant capability "losses" due to lack of timely availability of parts.

- Maintenance inefficiency "losses" due to poor management—wait time, transit time, etc.
- Expediting cost "losses" due to poor planning.
- Shrinkage "losses" due to poor control—waste, theft, deterioration, obsolescence, etc.

At the same time, if we could eliminate or at least minimize these losses, then the "value" of the stores function would be readily apparent. More enlightened managers understand the need to minimize these losses, and therefore put in place practices to assure a so-called world-class operation—minimal losses, maximum support capability. So, how do we set up a good stores operation?

What Stores Are Needed—Kind and Quantity

Beta International had a stores operation at all its plants, some portions centralized, other portions plant specific, but often it was not functioning like a modern store to routinely meet kind, quantity, and availability requirements. Suppose, for example, you went into a local department store in your home town, and found it to be dirty, lacking the items you were seeking, managed by people who didn't seem to care about the store, or you! Would you ever go back? At Beta, however, like most plants, they only had one store, and that's the one everyone had to use. Unfortunately, most of its stores were not being managed like a modern store. To build a good stores operation, Beta had to reevaluate its entire understanding of the customer's needs—of plant maintenance requirements. Therefore, kind, quantity, and availability needs must be driven by a keen understanding of maintenance needs. Further, to facilitate good communication and understanding, maintenance had to put in place a good maintenance management system for equipment identification, work orders, planning and scheduling system, the link to stores, kitting and delivery of parts for given work orders, and a cost accounting link for effective management. So, where did they start?

Bill of Material and Catalog

Beta didn't have a good bill of material for every critical item in its plants, and is now in the process of developing one. This is being done in cooperation with maintenance and using their definition of critical equipment and understanding of spares needs. This updated bill of material will be used in conjunction with other needs to develop a catalog of all stores and spare parts required in each plant. Critical to this process is the identification of simple things like belts, bearings, gaskets, etc. This is a dynamic document and must be updated 2–3 times per year, or as needed, e.g., for a major change in suppliers, for major equipment additions, etc. Further, the catalog includes unique identifier codes, generally numerical, for each catalog item, and provides for a logical grouping of material for use in Pareto analyses, component use frequencies, equipment history analyses, etc. It also includes a standard nomenclature and descriptors for each item. All this (catalog, standard nomenclature, grouping, descriptors) is not as simple as it sounds, and must be developed in cooperation with others whom it may affect, e.g., maintenance, design, suppliers, construction and capital projects. This will assure buy-in, acceptance, common understanding, etc., and will assure greater probability of success in the effort to run a world-class stores organization. Finally, while hard copies are routine, the catalog must also be "on-line" and staff must be trained in using the catalog, both manual and "on-line."

Management Methods

Simple policies and procedures must be developed in cooperation with maintenance and engineering to assure consistency of process and quality of operations. This should include a policy and/or procedure for:[1]

- Development, use, and modification of the catalog system.
- Inventory classification, including process for obsolescence.
- Vendor stocking and consignment programs.
- Economic order practice—quantity, point, level, etc., and dynamic adjustment.
- Consolidation of parts, suppliers.
- Repair/replace policy, including managing reconditioned (vs. new) equipment.
- Alternate sourcing (qualification, detailed drawings availability, etc.).
- Communication to maintenance, engineering, purchasing of key policies.
- An audit process.

Beta is developing policies and procedures in these areas dependent upon current practices and philosophy, the skill level of your staff, resources available, etc.

A quick tip. Many companies have a repair/replace policy for their motors that essentially says that if the cost of the repair/rewind is less than, say 50%, of a new motor, then they will repair. This practice ignores the efficiency loss that often results from a rewind (estimated at up to 3% by some experts for each rewind), which translates to increased power consumption and shorter life for the rewound motor. These costs of increased power consumption, and reduced motor life must be considered and put into a policy for repair/replacement. Beta will be following up on this and develop other examples.

Partnerships with Suppliers

As noted in the previous chapter, suppliers were consolidated and standardized as much as possible. When selecting suppliers, key performance indicators should be used, in conjunction with key performance objectives. Key issues and requirements being used at Beta for supplier relationships are:

- Partnership agreements detailing the basis for the agreement
- Supplier stocking and consignment terms and methods for reducing physical inventory
- Blanket orders wherever possible
- Maintainability and reliability requirements
- Feedback process for resolving problem areas
- Use of electronic communications and order entry wherever possible
- Measurement (and minimization) of emergency or spot orders
- Measurement of stock types

Further, suppliers are routinely asked to provide information regarding spare parts recommendations and frequency of preventive maintenance (PM) requirements. A typical response is a list of spares to be used for annual PM. Rather than simply accept this at face value, which may be related more to next year's sales plan than to good maintenance practices, Beta is now requiring key suppliers to provide the statistical basis for their recommendations, including the basis related to the application of the equipment and its working environment. In certain cases, the supplier is even required to perform an RCM analysis using failure modes and effects, to determine proper PM and spare parts. It's also important to remember that overhaul PMs essentially presume that all your equipment is average, a highly unlikely situation. It may also be that your application is very different from a typical application, and that you do not have consistency in your operation and maintenance practices. Suggestions for developing a strategic partnership with suppliers are provided in Chapter 5.

Standardization

Supplier partnerships will facilitate standardization, but these partnerships must also be combined with seeking opportunities for further standardization. For example, at Beta, methods for standardization will include (1) using materials that fulfill common if not identical requirements, (2) reviewing new equipment and purchases for standardization opportunities, and (3) assuring consistency with corporate supplier opportunities. The standardization process includes input from the maintenance, operations, design and capital projects staff, and purchasing. All appropriate parties must be trained in the standards that have been developed, and a process must be put in place that defines how the standards are changed and/or waived. It is critical that project engineers and purchasing agents work diligently in support of standardization.

The Store

The store itself should be well managed. There are several techniques to assist in managing the store itself:[2]

• Layout
• Procedures
• Work environment and practices
• Technology/methods
• People

Layout

Routine work should be reviewed from a "time/motion" perspective. For example, Beta is currently having its plants review stores, asking:

1. Are material and spare parts conveniently located for minimizing the amount of time required to pick up and deliver to the counter?
2. Is the material received in a way to minimize the time and effort of stocking?

3. Are material and parts conveniently located, especially for frequently needed items?
4. Is the issue counter near the receiving counter?
5. Is management near the hub of the activity—issue and receipt?
6. Is a delivery system in place to provide the parts at the job location?
7. The layout of the stores should be reviewed with minimizing the time required to provide the needed deliveries to maintenance, all things considered.

Procedures

Other issues being reviewed include procedures and processes:

1. Is bar coding in routine use?
2. Is receipt inspection routinely practiced?
3. Are automated reduction and inventory control points highlighted?
4. Are receipts recorded quickly and inspected?
5. Have you considered contracting miscellaneous material purchases, such as shoes, towels, jackets, coveralls, etc?
6. Has the catalog been completed and input into a stores management system, which is linked to the maintenance management system and to accounting?
7. Is bar coding used to minimize clerical requirements?
8. Are carousels in use and controlled by a controller pad linked to the stores management system?
9. Will the carousel bring the material to the counter, and charge the withdrawal to the customer, and mark the withdrawal against quantities for order point determination?
10. Is this process tied to maintenance planning and control?
11. Is material and/or parts kitted by work order, and as required, delivered to the job location?
12. Is a process in place for cycle counting (verifying inventory quantities on a periodic basis)?
13. Is an electronic data entry, and order entry process in place, especially for key suppliers?
14. Is there a process for managing equipment to be repaired or overhauled and restocked, e.g., separate area for "to be repaired and restocked," cost accounting procedure, etc.?

Are the following in place relative to suppliers?

1. Are supplier stocking and consignment terms and methods for reducing physical inventory in place?
2. Are blanket orders used wherever possible?
3. Is there a feedback process for resolving problem areas?
4. Is there a process for measurement (and minimization) of emergency or spot orders?

Work Environment and Practices

As to work environment, Beta asks the following questions to determine if they are using best practices in their stores facility:

1. Are the floors and walls clean and painted (floors with epoxy, non-skid for reducing dust)?
2. Is the stores area clean, comfortable, and well lighted?
3. Is access controlled and/or managed, e.g., limited to users of a swipe card?
4. Is there an air-conditioned, non-static area for PC boards and other electronic equipment?
5. Are you using high density storage for appropriate items?
6. Are bearings and gaskets protected, sealed, and stored to minimize damage or deterioration?
7. Are motors covered to minimize deterioration?
8. Do large, critical motors have heaters to eliminate moisture accumulation in the windings?
9. Are the shafts of rotating machinery rotated regularly to avoid false brinneling?
10. Are shafts to critical rotors stored vertically, and in a nitrogen-sealed, pressurized enclosure?
11. Is carbon steel equipment that may corrode coated with a thin, protective film?

People

Employees represent perhaps the easiest, and simultaneously the most difficult, issue in the stores management function. Most people want to do a good job, given the proper training, tools, systems, procedures, and encouragement. In many stores operations, the stores person has been assigned to the function without much training in store management, other than what might have been garnered through on-the-job training, and the practices that have been handed down over the years. Yet, the cost and value considerations for effectively managing a store dictate much more than a casual and historical approach to stores management.

Having answered the questions regarding stores environment and practices, Beta must now develop an organization with the right people, in the right mix and quantity, and provide the tools, training, and encouragement to assure superior performance. A matrix was created to outline the training its people need to accomplish the tasks identified. Further, measurements are routinely kept of the effectiveness of the stores operations. And, customer satisfaction surveys are performed through the maintenance and operations functions, seeking to develop a strong supportive relationship with maintenance, as well as purchasing, operations, and engineering.

Training

Training is being formulated based upon a series of strategic questions:

1. What are my key objectives (reference key performance indicators)?
2. What are the skills required to achieve those objectives? In what quantities?
3. What are the skills of my people today?
4. What new equipment and/or systems are coming into use in the future?
5. What are my workplace demographics—age, ability, etc.?
6. What are my training requirements in light of my answers?

Beta is using the answers to these questions to develop a strategic training plan that assures the skills are put in place on a priority basis to minimize losses and add value to the organization.

Contracting the Stores Function

While Beta does not share many others' enthusiasm for contracting maintenance (reduces ownership and core competencies, increases loss of equipment and process knowledge, increases risk of downtime, etc.), it may have its place in the stores function. Beta is currently reviewing the characteristics and prospective value of a good stores function, but has yet to conclude that it would be hard pressed to achieve this level of competence in a short period of time without contractors. It may ultimately decide that, all things considered, a good high-quality stores management function could be put in place quickly and effectively using contractors. This is the conclusion in Reference 2, but in that situation there were also additional considerations related to the intransigence of the union and its work rules, etc. Apparently, the union was unwilling to work with management to improve productivity and performance and was replaced by a contractor, who is reported to be doing a very good job. Further, others have found that certain items may be better handled by a "roving trailer" type contractor who handles safety shoes, uniforms, coveralls, etc. Ultimately, all unions must recognize that they are in fact competing for the same jobs as contractors. All things equal, companies will normally stay with their employees. If major differences are demonstrable and/or compelling, then contracting must be considered. Some suggestions on contractors and their best use are provided in Chapter 12.

Finally, though not specifically a contracting issue, in one area a supplier park[3] was created through a cooperative effort of the purchasing managers of several large manufacturing operations. Essentially, the park was built on "spec," and space was leased to several suppliers, e.g., routine bearings, lubricants, hose, piping, o-rings, belts, etc. These suppliers used a common same-day and next-day delivery system, electronic ordering, routine review of use and repair histories (from their records), and an integrated relationship with their suppliers to achieve a superior level of performance and lower inventories than what was otherwise achievable within an individual stores operation at the plants.

Key Performance Indicators

After review of the literature and doing some internal benchmark data collection, the following key performance indicators were developed at Beta. Above all, performance indicators were viewed as an indication of the success of the organizational objectives that were established.[1, 2]

	Best	Typical
Stores value—% of facility replacement value	.25–.50%	1–2%
Service level—stockouts	<1%	2–4%
Inventory turns (see following discussion)	2–3	1
Line items processed per employee per hour	10–12	4–5
Stores value per store employee	$1–1.5M	$0.5–1M
Stores disbursements per store employee	$1.5–2M	$0.5–1M

Further, measures are also being set up for the following:

Use of catalog items in stock—%, quantities
Use of preferred suppliers—%, quantities
Carrying costs—total and % of stores value
Receipt and issue backlog—% and delay days

Beta is currently establishing the processes previously described, and beginning to measure performance; it anticipates substantially improved performance. However, it may be instructive to review a case history on how one of Beta's plants improved its inventory turns and managed its stores operation more effectively. Please note, however, that this plant already had most of the systems previously described in place, so that it could manage its stores operation more effectively.

Minimizing Stock Levels—A Case Study[4]

Beta currently has a major effort on-going to reduce inventory levels, principally finished goods, but also including stores. Certainly they should, because inventory generally represents capital that is not generating a return. Indeed, Beta recognizes that it costs money to store and maintain inventory. It could be compared to stuffing money under a mattress, one which you're renting to store your money in it.

The drive to reduce inventory is often intense at Beta. Some of their plants have attempted to issue decrees, e.g., "A world-class level for inventory turns of spare parts is 2. Therefore, we will be at 2 turns on our spares inventory in two years!" or some other equally arbitrary objective. Middle management has then been left with the goal to reduce inventory, usually with limited guidance from senior management about the strategy of how to achieve this objective, or whether or not this objective can reasonably be accomplished. Nonetheless, most will make a good faith effort to do so. However, most will be caught between the proverbial rock and hard place. If they simply reduce inventory across the board, they could jeopardize their ability to quickly repair failed equipment in a timely manner, due to lack of parts that resulted from reducing inventory, risking unplanned downtime, or incurring extra costs. Further, inventory often will be "reduced" only to find its way into a desk drawer, filing cabinet, storage closet, etc. for future needs. This is especially true in an organization that is highly reactive in its maintenance function, e.g., lots of breakdown maintenance, emergency work orders, run-to-failure, etc. So, what should Beta do?

It was ultimately the decision at Beta that inventory should be driven by reliability and capacity objectives, and a systematic strategy, not necessarily by arbitrary decrees. The first step in establishing a basis for spares inventory management was to segregate inventory into categories that can be managed, such as:

1. Obsolete—to be disposed as economically as possible.
2. Surplus—quantity > economic order point; to be managed in cooperation with suppliers.
3. Project—excess of which is to be returned at the end of the project.
4. High volume/use items—most to be put on blanket order and delivered as needed.
5. Low volume/use critical spares—most to be stored in-house using specific procedures.
6. Low volume/use non-critical spares—most to be ordered when needed.

Other companies may have other categories better suited to their purpose, but this should start the thinking process for improved inventory management, while still assuring maximum equipment reliability.

Integral to this, management should consider:

1. Equipment failure histories
2. Parts use histories
3. Lead times
4. Supplier reliability (responsiveness, quality, service)
5. Stock-out objectives
6. Inventory turns objectives

And finally, all this should be integrated with the following:

1. Strategic objectives as to reliable production capacity.
2. Application of a reliability based strategy for knowing equipment condition.

There are other issues that may come into play at any given manufacturing facility, but these points should illustrate the principles involved.

Beta's Wheelwright Plant

At Beta's Wheelwright plant, the management team had been directed by Beta's senior management to reduce spares inventory, such that turns were 2.0 by year-end. On assessing their current position, they found the following:

Current inventory level:	$10M
Current annual parts expenditure:	$10M

They are presently turning their spares inventory at 1.0 times per year, which essentially means that inventory must be cut in half. This was perceived to be a *major* challenge, particularly in light of their current mode for maintenance, which was highly reactive.

Beta's senior management had further determined that unplanned downtime and maintenance costs were excessive as compared to industry benchmarks. Reactive, run-to-failure maintenance was resulting in substantial incremental costs due to ancillary damage, overtime, the unavailability of spares (in spite of high inventory levels), and most importantly, lost production capacity from the downtime. A team of the staff determined that application of a reliability-based strategy would assure a reduction in downtime and maintenance costs. A major part of this strategy was the application of equipment condition monitoring technologies (vibration, infrared, oil, motor current, etc.) to facilitate knowing equipment condition and therefore:

1. Avoid emergency maintenance and unplanned downtime.
2. Optimize PM's—do PM's only when necessary, because few machines fail at precisely their average life.
3. Optimize stores—plan spares needs based on equipment condition, move closer to JIT.

4. Assist in root cause failure analysis to eliminate failures, extend equipment life.
5. Commission equipment to assure its "like-new" condition at installation, extending its life.
6. Systematically plan overhaul work requirements, based on equipment condition.
7. Foster teamwork among production, engineering, and maintenance.

In doing so, the team felt they could extend equipment life, lowering spares requirements, and planning spares requirements more effectively for both routine and overhaul needs.

On reviewing their inventory they found that the $10M in current inventory could be broken down as follows:

Obsolete	$ 1.0M
Surplus	$ 2.0M
Project	$ 1.0M
High-volume/use	$ 4.0M
Low-volume critical	$ 2.0M
Low-volume non-critical	$ 1.0M

Note the total adds to more than $10M, because of overlapping categories. They ignored this in the short term for ease of demonstrating the principles, but it could be handled through a matrix for multiple categories. Their next steps are described as follows.

Obsolete equipment was identified and brought to the attention of the plant manager. Some $1M, or 10% of the total (and not an uncommon number), was represented by obsolete equipment. It was anticipated that after liquidation income to a salvage operation that an $800K charge would be incurred. The plant manager was initially very reluctant to take such a charge on his statement, but after much negotiation at the vice-president level, it was agreed to amortize the charge over an extended period, as opposed to a one time "hit." An inventory control process was also established to dispose of inventory as it became obsolete, and not to continue to hold it in storage for the next plant manager to handle. The $800K charge on inventory disposal, even though spread over several months, was a painful expense, but one that shouldn't occur again with the new process in place. Inventory level would now be about $9M, and turns were improved to 1.11, representing modest progress.

Next, capital project inventory was reviewed. It was anticipated that half would be consumed by the project before year-end. Another 25% would be returned to the supplier with a 20% return penalty. This was accomplished only after considerable pressure was applied to the supplier. In the future they will have a policy built into major capital projects for returns, and will make this policy a part of the contract with their suppliers. The final 25% was decided to be necessary as critical or important spares for future use, because the equipment for this project was not common to current equipment. The result was a $750K reduction in inventory. However, note that a $50K charge was incurred. Note also that in the future project inventory and the timing of its use/disposal/return must be considered when developing inventory turn goals. Inventory turns were now anticipated at 1.21, allowing more progress. When combined with a commissioning process to test and verify proper installation based on standards for vibration, IR, oil, motor current, and other process parameters, they felt they could substantially improve equipment life and avoid rework. Their experience had been that half of their equipment failures occurred within two weeks of installation. They also applied these same standards to their suppliers.

Next, surplus inventory was reviewed for each of the designated stores categories. Economic order points were reviewed and it was determined that a total of $200K of what was considered to be surplus could be used before year-end. More stringent policies were put into place regarding order points, including consideration of stock-out objectives. More importantly, the Wheelwright plant put in place a comprehensive condition monitoring program that allowed the company to anticipate parts requirements more definitively and to reduce the quantity of its order points. They now planned to provide their suppliers with at least 5 days notice on certain spare parts needs. With good support, good planning, and ease of shipping to the plant, inventory could be reduced even further in the future. For the time being, with this nominal $200K improvement, inventory turns were expected to increase to 1.24, more progress.

Next, a detailed review was performed of critical equipment (equipment whose failure leads to lost production). The equipment was detailed and listed down to the component level, which was kept in inventory. Lead times were reviewed. A 0% stock-out policy was established for this equipment. After a team from production, purchasing, maintenance, and engineering reviewed the listing, lead times, and inventory in stock, the conclusion was reached that "excess" inventory amounted to $500K, but that fortunately most of that would be used during an outage planned later in the year. All things considered, they expected to reduce critical low turning inventory by $300K by year-end. With regard to the longer term, the stores manager for the Wheelwright plant met with other plants concerning their inventory, identified common equipment and spares, and anticipated that an additional $500K in spares will be defined as critical/common, meaning several plants will be able to use this to reduce their slow moving, critical inventory. This inventory, while stored at this plant, was placed under the control of the division general manager. Inventory turns were now at 1.29.

Next, high-volume, high-use rate inventory was reviewed. This inventory typically turned at 2 or more times per year, but the total dollar value of this inventory was not sufficient to substantially increase total inventory turns. Concurrently, the inventory was reviewed against equipment histories, identifying critical equipment overlaps. The inventory was categorized by vendor dollars, and reviewed as to lead times in major categories. Reorder points were reviewed, and in some cases trimmed. Condition monitoring was used as a basis for trending equipment condition, and determining and planning needed spares. Suppliers were contacted and asked to maintain, under blanket order and/or consignment agreement, appropriate quantities of spares for delivery within specified time periods. A stock-out objective not to exceed 5% was determined to be acceptable for most routine spares. All things considered, it was expected that high-use spares could be reduced by $1M by year-end, and probably even more over the next 2–3 years. Inventory turns were now estimated to be at 1.48.

Next, low-volume, non-critical spares were reviewed, again, in light of lead times, equipment history, use history, stock-out objectives, etc. Suppliers were contacted concerning maintaining guaranteed spares under a blanket order and/or consignment agreement, with minimum quantities, etc. All told, it was felt that half of the low-turning, non-critical spares could be eliminated by year-end, with most of the balance eliminated by the end of the following year. With this, inventory turns were now estimated to come in at 1.6, substantially below the decree of 2.0, but substantially above the historical level of 1.0. The company has positioned itself to increase available cash by $3.75M, but about half of this would come through after year-end. A reduction of an additional $1.25M or more (considered well within their grasp) over the next 1–2 years should yield the objective of inventory turns of 2.

They were now ready to present their findings to senior management. After their presentation to management, the objective of two turns on inventory was considered not to be achievable before year-end, but that in light of capacity objectives, a good plan had been established to achieve that objective within 24 months. The plan was approved, with the proviso that the team would report quarterly on its progress, including any updated plans for additional improvement.

Consistent with this, the company now put in place a strategic plan for reducing inventory, which included the approach described, and had the following characteristics:

1. Production targets considered achievable were:

   a. 95% production availability, including 4% planned maintenance and 1% unplanned maintenance downtime.
   b. 92% asset utilization rate, including 2% for process yield losses, 1% for transition losses, and 0% losses for lack of market demand. They could sell all they could make.

2. Inventory targets were set as:

   a. 0% stock-outs for critical spares
   b. 4%—fast turning non-critical
   c. 6%—slow turning non-critical

3. Supplier agreements under blanket order were effected for inventory storage and JIT shipment.
4. Inter-plant sharing of common critical spares was placed under control of the division general manager.
5. The plant set up the systematic application of condition monitoring to:

   a. baseline (commission) newly installed equipment.
   b. trend equipment condition to anticipate and plan spare parts needs.
   c. comprehensively review equipment condition prior to planned overhauls.
   d. engage in root cause failure analysis to eliminate failures.

Summary

By putting these processes in place, the Wheelwright plant was well on its way to improved plant reliability, and concurrently reduced costs and inventory. Good stores management at Beta first required that management recognize the value-adding capability of a good stores function—increased working capital, increased plant capability, reduced carrying costs, reduced shrinkage, and improved maintenance efficiency. The losses associated with poor stores management practices should be intolerable to senior management.

In setting up a quality stores management function, several issues must be addressed:

- Development of a comprehensive catalog for stores requirements.
- Development of policies and procedures which facilitate effective management of stores.
- Establishment of procedures and practices which facilitate maintenance excellence.
- Establishment of supplier partnerships, blanket orders, consignment, etc.
- Establishment of a stores layout which assure efficient operation.
- Comprehensive training of all appropriate staff.
- Consideration of contracting the stores function to accomplish these tasks.
- Comprehensive management of stores and inventory turns by classification.
- Comprehensive performance measurements for assuring a superior stores capability.

Doing all this in a comprehensive, integrated way will assure that Beta has a world-class stores operation at the Wheelwright plant, and over the long term for all of Beta International. Manufacturing excellence requires an excellent stores operation, as well as excellence in maintenance and production. All are an integral part of a financially successful operation.

References

1. Jones, E. K. *Maintenance Best Practices Training,* PE–Inc., Newark, DE, 1971.

2. Hartoonian, G. "Maintenance Stores and Parts Management," *Maintenance Journal,* Vol. 8, No. 1, Mornington, Australia, Jan/Feb, 1995.

3. Schaulberger, S. "What is Supplier Park?," Society for Maintenance and Reliability Professionals, Barrington, IL, Annual Conference, Chicago, IL, October, 1994.

4. Moore, R. "Establishing an Inventory Management Program," *Plant Engineering,* Chicago, IL, USA, March, 1996.

7 Installation Practices

You have the right not to do things wrong.

Winston Ledet, Sr.

Knowing that a job has been done right in a manufacturing plant, consistent with your expectations and standards, is essential for assuring manufacturing excellence. Installation practices that set high standards, and are then verified through a process for validating the quality of the work done, or commissioning, are an essential element of this process. Indeed, we'll see in Chapter 9 that up to 68% of equipment failures occur in the "infant mortality" mode. This strongly implies the need for better design, procurement, and installation practices to avoid many of these failures.

Practices that influence and are related to installation and commissioning were reviewed in previous chapters on Design and Capital Projects Practices, Procurement Practices, and Stores Practices and serve to highlight several opportunities for improvement. Additional information and recommendations, particularly as installation practices relate to contractors are also provided in Chapter 12. Further, this chapter is not intended to substitute for extensive information developed by architect engineers for major construction contracts when constructing and starting up a new plant. Rather it is targeted at particular problems and shortcomings observed at many of Beta's plants related to the smaller capital projects, short shutdowns and turnarounds, and routine maintenance efforts occurring every day. These same principles, however, can be applied and extended to major projects, such as the construction and start up of a new production line or plant.

Beta has been like most manufacturers when installing new capital equipment. They do a reasonably good job with the installation and commissioning of the production *process*. They would generally use considerable care to assure that process pressures, temperatures, flows, critical process chemical or other operating parameters were within specification, and that the production equipment was capable of producing quality product, at least at start-up. In their batch and discrete parts plants, likewise, they always had the supplier do a demonstration run to assure that, for example, machine tools were statistically capable of holding tolerances for a certain number of parts, or that a few batches could be processed and meet specifications. They frequently reminded people that quality (of their products) was a top priority. The care and attention to detail of the process control quality, while still in need of improvement as we'll see in Chapter 8, was significantly better than that given to equipment quality at installation. If the equipment or process ran, did not make any unusual noises or smells, and made quality product, then it must be a good installation and start-up, was the apparent rationale. Beta's plants rarely commissioned the equipment to specific mechanical standards to assure its quality, and its "like-new" condition. This was true of small capital projects, as well as overhauls, shutdowns or turnarounds, and routine maintenance and repairs. Some tips Beta found useful are provided in this chapter. When combined with other sections, this should provide most manufacturers with a model for improvement in this area.

Follow Existing Standards and Procedures

The first suggestion was perhaps the most obvious, and that was to follow existing procedures for installation and start-up. These had been previously developed at great expense, and occasionally following a major failure because of poor procedures or practices. In many situations Beta's plants simply weren't following these established procedures to assure equipment reliability. With new engineers coming in, with the pressure to "get the plant back on line," with the drive to cut costs (at times not withstanding consequences) engineers and supervisors were often ignoring established procedures for best practice. A point to highlight is that they were very good about following safety procedures and practices, and had achieved a better-than-average safety performance. What they didn't follow very well is standard engineering practices. They are now working hard to establish a new culture of doing things right, all the time—a daily struggle—in light of the pressures to improve performance.

Verify and Use Appropriate Manufacturer Recommendations

The second suggestion is also simple, and that is to follow the manufacturer's recommendations. While they may not be 100% correct in their guidelines for every application, it's a good starting point. **Read the manufacturer's instructions and follow them unless there is a compelling reason not to do so.** At many of Beta's plants this was not being done either, or was only being given half-hearted support, principally for the same reasons previously mentioned—not enough time to do the job right, but plenty of time to do it over. Enough said on that point. The use of manufacturer's recommendations can be further enhanced using the strategic alliance process described previously, and which some of Beta's plants are now putting in place.

Installation and Commissioning of Rotating Machinery

One of the bigger areas for improvement is in the area of installation and commissioning of rotating machinery. As many of Beta's plants have found, rotating machinery should generally be installed on a solid foundation, with rigid baseplates, with no looseness, should be precision balanced and aligned, and should be tested for meeting a specific standard of vibration at the time of installation, 1–4 weeks later, and then thereafter consistent with historical experience and/or specialist or manufacturer recommendations. GM Specification V1.0 1993 is an excellent starting point for setting vibration standards for rotating machinery. It provides standards for various types of equipment, but you must decide what, if any, modifications should be used for your application. Following these standards, and

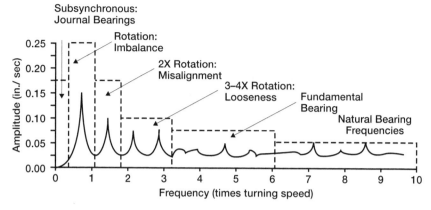

Figure 7-1. *Vibration spectra.*

adapting them as appropriate to other types of equipment, should assure high quality of the installation and long life of the equipment. As always, these should be reviewed and modified as appropriate to suit your particular applications.

For example, Figure 7-1 shows that Beta's standard for commissioning of rotating machinery is being established such that, in general, vibration due to imbalance should be below 0.1 in./sec; due to misalignment should be below 0.05 in./sec.[1] Further, there should be no vibration due to bearing faults at specific ball pass frequencies, there should be no vibration due to looseness, and no significant "other" faults beyond 0.05 in./sec, e.g., electrical vibration faults due to a non-uniformity in the magnetic field of the motor resulting in vibration at 120 Hz (or 100 Hz in most countries).

These standards, when combined with GM Specification V1.0 1993, and adapted for any unique applications specific to Beta's requirements, should serve Beta well for ensuring long-lasting equipment. Unique applications might include reciprocating compressors, shaker tables, etc. These same standards can also be used to set up alarm limits for defining any particular action to be taken for a given level of alarm.

After a critical machine train has been overhauled or repaired, it will be tested at start-up, and corrective action taken as appropriate to assure the equipment meets these standards.

Other requirements being established include (1) a check at start-up of motor current to assure that it is below a certain level; of the running current; and in some cases, a check of the cross-phase impedance to assure a quality motor has been installed. Normally, this should be done at the motor repair facility; (2) verification of proper lubricants being used, consistent with manufacturer recommendations, at proper levels, and with no significant opportunities for contamination of the lubricants before being put into the equipment; and (3) an infrared thermography scan in certain more limited circumstances, e.g., to assure that heat is properly distributed across reactor vessels, to assure motor connections are properly tightened, etc.

Lubrication practices at many of Beta's plants were abysmal. Indeed, in many cases lubricators had been laid off. This is a bit of a mystery, because it's clear that most managers, even very senior ones, understand the need to lubricate their automobiles. In any event Beta's lubricators (where they had them) often used small hand-held pumps to fill reservoirs for certain equipment. The nozzles on these pumps were often left to lay on the ground (dirty); the pumping handle and rod readily accumulated dirt in a "well" where they entered the container. Beta soon found that practices had to assure that clean lubricant was going into the equipment. Otherwise, this dirt that came with the lubricant acted as a "lapping compound," and substantially reduced the life of the equipment. Granted, some of their practices may have been better than open buckets of oil, which was also sometimes used. Beta has also consolidated its lubricants and validated them for application, but through painful experience found that additives in lubricants from different suppliers were not always compatible. Mixing presumably same specification oils, but from different vendors, often resulted in "frothy oil," and destroyed lubricating properties, requiring equipment to be shut down and the lubricant changed, again. The consolidated and standardized lubrication policy should prevent mixing of incompatible lubricants and advise purchasing not to change vendors without approval of maintenance and engineering. More on this issue is provided in the predictive maintenance section of Chapter 9.

Flange and Joint Installation

A standard for the design, specification, and installation of flanges and gaskets had been developed at Beta, but was generally ignored. One of the easier areas for assuring long-term equipment reliability is in the area of eliminating leaks, and in particular in flange and joint installation. Leaks in piping, particularly at flanges and valves are generally inexcusable, and applying their own standards would assure exceptional mechanical integrity of piping and vessel systems. Issues such as flange face configuration and finish, parallelism, torquing, thickness, handling, centerline to centerline offset allowance, gasket types, etc. for various applications were specified. More importantly, mechanics and technicians had to be retrained to follow the standards, like craftsmen who take great pride in their work.

At one Beta plant, a mechanic was observed installing a gasket into a flanged connection. The gasket was lying on a concrete floor (dirty—lots of grit for scratching, adhering to the flange face, etc.). The mechanic was "struggling"—didn't have the part fixed in place for the attachment, and was not using a torque wrench, and was generally attempting to make the installation "free handed." This was not good practice, and Beta has found that if you don't want leaks at flanges and in valves, you must use precision standards and practices, and mechanics and other trade people must be allowed the freedom, and encouraged to do the job with great care and precision, not fast. "Fast" will come with experience. And finally, a similar scenario could be described for cleaning piping and tubing at installation.

Workshop Support

As Beta has found, workshops that support installation efforts and repairs should be more than a laydown, assembly, and fabrication area. They should be very clean, and certainly not dirty and disorganized. They should be operated in a controlled manner, not opened to everyone 24 hours a day, particularly if those who frequent the workshop show little ownership, and low expectations of its contribution. The workshop manager is more than a custodian. His job is to manage a clean, efficient workshop, fully responsible and accountable for its performance, and assuring that all work is performed with great care and precision, and validated for its quality using commissioning methods.

Housekeeping

On many occasions after a turnaround or major overhaul effort, or in some cases even a routine repair, Beta's plants were found to be cluttered—boxes, parts, paper, debris everywhere, scaffolding still up, etc. And, more importantly, there were leaks too, one at the flange of a critical reactor vessel, immediately after a shutdown. This spoke volumes about the care and precision of the installation effort (or lack thereof), and should not be tolerated. It sent a very clear message that standards and expectations were poor, that people running the plant did not care, and therefore no one else should be expected to exercise care and precision. Beta is working hard today to change this culture and attitude, and is having considerable success. If you set high expectations, people will work hard to meet them, in spite of some occasional "grousing." If you set low expectations, people will meet those too, though not working as hard to do so. Setting expectations for precision in the installation effort and validating its quality through commissioning is a must.

Use of the Pre-Destruction Report

At several of Beta's plants, they found the use of a "Pre-Destruction Report" to be exceptionally valuable. At these plants, the maintenance manager or other supervisors were often called upon by production managers to "just fix it!" and considerable pressure was placed on them to "get the plant back on line." This, in turn, often resulted in less than craftsmanship and precision being applied to the maintenance or repair effort. Often, critical work for assuring equipment reliability would not be done in an effort to quickly get the plant back on line.

One ingenious supervisor decided to try to put a stop to this and created the Pre-Destruction Report. When called upon to fix things quickly, as opposed to properly and with craftsmanship and precision, he would ask the demanding supervisor to sign this report. In effect it read:

Pre-Destruction Report

I, (insert name), do hereby authorize premature destruction of the equipment being repaired under Work Order No. (insert number), because I have not allowed adequate time for the perfomance of certain maintenance and/or start-up and commissioning tasks (insert task numbers). I understand that not doing these tasks is likely to reduce the life of this equipment and result in its premature failure. I also understand that it may also increase the overall maintenance costs, and reduce the quality of the product being produced.

_____
Signature

_____
Title

By signing this, the supervisor or manager would be authorizing the performance of bad work, something which few, if any, were willing to do. So long as the maintenance manager was willing to be held responsible for poor work, the production manager was willing to allow it to proceed, and berate future failures with the refrain of "Just fix it!" When he had to authorize it, the tide turned, and greater craftsmanship was allowed, yielding longer equipment life. As Ledet said, "You have the right not to do things wrong."

Summary

Installation and commissioning practices will not correct a poor design. However, it may identify design deficiencies. Therefore, a process must be established to provide feedback to plant personnel regarding potential improvements that have been identified through the commissioning process.

Commissioning should be done as part of a partnership among plant staff. The goal is not to search for the guilty, but rather to learn from our potential shortcomings and put procedures in place that assure continuing excellence. When problems are found, they should be used as a positive learning experience, not a condemnation exercise.

For projects and shutdowns, the commissioning process begins with the design of the project, or the planning of the shutdown. Specific equipment should be identified, procedures and standards defined, and time built into the plan, to verify the quality of the installation effort. In a study by the Electric Power Research Institute in the late 1980s, they found that half of all equipment failures occurred in the first week of start-up, and lasted less than one week. This begs for a better installation and commissioning process,[2] and as Beta has found, particularly for the equipment.

Let's consider Beta's operational and maintenance practices next. As you're reviewing this, consider where these may apply to the installation, start-up, and commissioning process.

References

1. Pride, A. Pride Consulting, internal document, Knoxville, TN, 1997.

2. Smith, A. *Reliability-Centered Maintenance,* McGraw-Hill, New York, NY, 1993.

Operational Practices

If you always do what you always did, you will always be what you always were.

W. *Edwards Deming*

Beta reviewed the operating practices at several of its manufacturing plants, and concluded that poor practices in plant operation, process control, and production planning were often at the root of poor plant reliability and uptime performance, resulting in increased operating and maintenance costs, poor product quality, and poor delivery performance, among other things. Indeed, a preliminary analysis indicated that while maintenance costs were well above world-class, over half of these costs were being driven by poor process control and operational practices. Maintenance had historically been "blamed" for equipment downtime and high maintenance costs, but on closer review, most of the maintenance costs were the result of poor operational practices. The conclusion was reached that Beta had to have much better consistency of process, greater precision in plant control, and much better operator training and expertise to eliminate or minimize the root cause of many problems.

Improving Operating Practices to Reduce Maintenance Costs

At Beta's Wayland plant, an expert had been called in to help reduce maintenance downtime. It seemed that the plant was having numerous equipment failures, resulting in lots of downtime, lost production, and out-of-pocket costs. In the course of the review, an inquiry was made as to key process control parameters, at which time the process engineer brought forth several graphs. In reviewing these graphs, it was determined that the plant should be run with moisture content of the process stream below 30 ppm; that an occasional spike above 30 ppm was acceptable, but even those should last no more than a few hours, and be no more than 60 ppm. This was because excess moisture (>30 ppm) reacted with the process stream, creating acid in the stream which dissolved the carbon steel piping, vessels, and valves.

Further, compounding this effect was the fact that when the acid dissolved the carbon steel, it also released free iron into the process stream, which reacted with other process constituents, creating sludge that fouled the reactor, severely impairing its ability to operate. So, it was very important that moisture levels be controlled very tightly to avoid this problem. Indeed, the design engineers had assumed that the plant could be operated below 30 ppm with ease, and all material specifications were placed accordingly. Apparently, they gave more credit to the process control capability of the plant than warranted, or ignored the potential for upsets in the process stream. Because moisture was an inherent by-product in the production process, it may have served them well to consider better control or alternative materials, or both. Because no system can be perfectly controlled, process transients (both physical and chemical) should always be considered in the design process. However, on reviewing the actual data, which took some time to find because they were not actually used in operating the plant, it appeared that the plant *rarely operated below 60 ppm, which was the maximum at which it should have been operated.* In fact, the plant typically ran above 100 ppm, and more than occasionally spiked the instrument scale above 200 ppm. (See Figure 8-1.) Further, on a more detailed analysis to determine whether these data were correct (in general they were), it was also discovered that:

1. The measurement systems were relatively poor—frequent instrument failure, infrequent calibrations, etc. The instruments were sufficiently accurate to verify that moisture content was way too high, but not sufficiently accurate for precision process control being planned.

2. The control capability was insufficient, both from a process perspective, and from a feedstock perspective. Feedstocks, which came from an upstream plant at an integrated site, typically had moisture content well beyond specification. In addition to this, however, process control capability was limited, partly because of poor instrumentation, and also because of inadequate design and business expectations. Moisture carry-over from a feedback process loop had limited control capability.

3. The plant was being expected to run beyond its design limits to increase yields, which also increased moisture carry-over into the process stream. This effort to make up the difference in production shortfalls proved less than successful and even short-sighted.

4. The laboratory analysis capability for measuring process stream parameters was inadequate. Measurements of the process stream were only taken twice a day, but feedstocks would often change 3–4 times in a given day. And, when they were taken, the laboratory instruments were not capable of providing accurate information on the process condition in a timely manner.

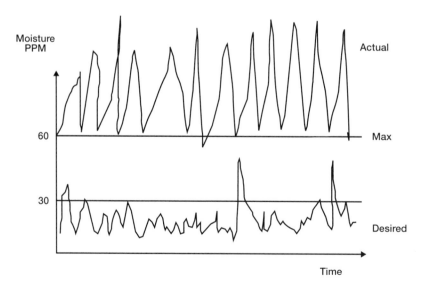

Figure 8-1. Wayland Plant moisture control chart.

After a short operating period, a given reactor (there were several on stream) would have to be shut down and cleaned, or in some cases where the damage was too severe, replaced. Asset utilization rates were running at 50% or less, well below world-class, and maintenance costs were very high—more than 12% of asset replacement value, as compared to an average level of 3–6%, and a world-class level of nominally 2%. Breakdown production losses were running over 20%, compared to an average level of some 5%, and to a world-class level of less than 1–2%.

Was this a maintenance problem? Clearly maintenance costs were excessive, and equipment downtime was large. Was maintenance at the root of the problem? For the most part, it was not. The results of an audit comparing maintenance practices against a world-class standard did indicate that the maintenance department had things it could improve upon. For example, the plant needed better planning and scheduling, better condition monitoring, better training, better equipment history records for Pareto and RCM analysis, better installation and alignment of pumps, etc., but given the constant state of crisis in the organization, they had little time to improve their processes until the root cause of the failures was addressed through better process chemistry control.

Were the operations people at fault? Perhaps, but it turned out that they had no choice but to accept feedstocks of varying quality from upstream plants that were part of an integrated site production process for the entire site where Wayland was located. They had several things they could do to minimize moisture content, and mitigate its effects, but until the question was asked, they did not fully appreciate the implications of current operating practices. They just continued to accept the feedstocks they were given without challenge. To make a long story short, feedstock quality was a serious problem, exacerbated by site operations practices and expectations, exacerbated by poor plant process control, exacerbated by poor maintenance practices, much of which could have been mitigated by better design standards. Everyone had a part to play in this drama, and until they all sat in a room together as a team to recognize that the parts had to be played in cooperation, the solution to improving performance was elusive.

Applying better process control practices, maintenance practices, and working with site management to mitigate feedstock effects, the Wayland plant is now well on its way to substantially improved performance. For example, breakdown losses are now down to 5% or so, a tremendous improvement over the dismal levels of 20%+. They recently also recorded their best production month ever, some 30% better than any previous month in the history of the plant. And yet, they still have much opportunity for improvement. With continued leadership, no doubt Beta's Wayland plant will be among its best performers in the months and years to come.

Consistency of Process Control

Beta's Auxier plant was struggling to meet customer demand at one of its plants. It seemed they could sell everything they could make, but just couldn't make enough. A new plant manager had been hired to help bring the plant to a better level of performance. After spending just a few weeks in the plant, he found, among many things, that each shift within the plant operated the plant using different control points for key process parameters. It seemed that empowerment had been taken to the lowest level possible, and each operator had the power to change control points based on his view of where the process ran best, so long as each kept the process within a control band for key parameters. Good in theory, but bad in practice, without some overall guidance on the process.

The new plant manager gathered his team together, and advised them that the plant had to have consistency of process, but rather than dictate control parameters, he asked that each shift select what it thought were the control points that should be used. Likewise, he and the process engineer selected a set of control points. They concluded the exercise with 4 separate sets of specific control points. Then he advised all the operations staff that for the next four weeks they would run the plant each week strictly using one of each of the set of control points developed during the previous exercise—no deviations during that week from the control points selected without his specific approval. Every shift during a given week had to use the same control points, no exceptions.

At the end of the 4-week test period the plant showed better performance for each week with each of the different set of control points than it had in several months. It also turned out that the points that the plant manager and process engineer had selected ranked 3rd out of 4 in the overall performance. As it turned out, every time a shift supervisor or operator would change the operating conditions without just cause, they would destabilize the system and reduce plant performance. Consistency of process yielded better results in every case, and was much better than the inconsistency between shifts which had previously been in place.

Control Loops

Surveys[1] have indicated that in a typical process manufacturing plant only 20% of control loops perform as desired, and conversely some 80% of control loops can actually increase process variability when operated in automatic mode. Control loops are also reported to account for 90% of the variability in product quality. With this in mind, and given that it is true, is it any wonder that operators are reported to routinely disable process control systems. Control loops and systems must be properly designed, and must be maintained, that is, routinely serviced and calibrated to be effective. Otherwise,

> ". . . operators will leave a controller on closed loop control, if he does not have to worry about the controller getting him into trouble. If he has to worry about what the controller is doing as well as the unit, he will turn the controller off. If operators find they can trust the controller to keep them out of trouble and it does not increase their work load, they will readily accept it."[2]

Further,

> "Process operators are incapable of coping with the multidimensional aspects of (changing operating conditions) when the plant is operated at its constraints," necessitating precision process control.[3]

Beta's experience has been quite consistent with these situations. For example, at Beta's McDowell plant, the process control system engineer was asked how often the operators bypass or disable the control system, to which he replied that they rarely did this. One of the senior operations supervisors was then asked to check the digital control system (DCS) to see how often in the past month the system had been disabled or bypassed. It turned out that in the previous month this had occurred some 300 times, on average every 2–3 hours. Clearly, the control system was not being used as intended, for whatever reason. Further emphasizing the point, one of Beta's statistical process control (SPC) specialists, who has only recently come into higher respect and appreciation, has indicated that if process control systems are not maintained, some 50% lose their effectiveness after 6 months of operation.

Let's consider some fundamental issues related to statistical process control.[4, 5] It is generally agreed that one must:

1. Understand your key process variables, those used to control the process.
2. Plot each key process variable for a routine period and determine the mean and standard deviation. Verify that the data are normally distributed.

Establish the upper control limit (UCL), the mean plus 3 standard deviations, or $\bar{x} + 3\sigma$, and the lower control limit (LCL) is $\bar{x} - 3\sigma$. Six σ is then the natural tolerance. The process is *not* in control if:

1. There are any points outside the control limits.
2. There are 7 consecutive points trending up.
3. There are 7 consecutive points trending down.
4. There are 7 consecutive points above the mean.
5. There are 7 consecutive points below the mean.

We should not confuse upper and lower control limits with upper and lower specification limits (USL and LSL). Control limits are inherent in the system's natural variability. Specification limits represent our expectation for the process or the product, which may or may not be met within the inherent capability of the system. When expectations are not met, then the process may not be *capable* of achieving production requirements.

Control performance capability, or Cpk, is a measure of the ability to deliver quality product through quality processes within a plant. It demonstrates what the process can best achieve and should be the objective of any control improvements. It is defined as the lesser of $(USL - \bar{x})/3\sigma$, or $(\bar{x} - LSL)/3\sigma$. For example, if Cpk is greater than 1.5, you could expect that just over 0.1% of your product would be off specification; whereas if Cpk = 1, then you could expect that over 2% of your product will be off specification. The higher the value of Cpk, the less off-spec product, and vice versa. Many believe that a Cpk of 2 is about optimal. Higher values probably mean that the specification limits are set too high. Lower values mean the process is not in sufficient control. Beta is presently spending considerable effort to assure that processes are in control, and that Cpk of key variables of the production process are measured, not just the end quality of the products. Controlling the process effectively leads to higher quality products.

In summary, basic process control in a process plant requires:

1. Knowledge of key process variables and measurement methods.
2. A process control philosophy.
3. Understanding of control limits for each variable.
4. Measurement capability—accurate, well maintained instrumentation for key variables.
5. Control capability—controller/operational set points and biases.
6. Operation within control limits (and if not, an understanding why not for each event).
7. Understanding of process variable lag/lead times and interrelationships.
8. Logic and sequence interlocks.
9. Alarm points and philosophy.
10. Hazard operations analysis, if necessary.
11. Timely, appropriate, and accurate laboratory/QC analysis.
12. An understanding and rigorous application of SPC principles.

A similar model could be developed for non-process applications.

Finally, specific products should have very definitive "recipes" for running the production process to assure meeting product specifications. For most operators these recipes and the basis for running the plants for each "recipe" should be second nature for them, through training and practice. Assuring quality of production process will assure quality of the product.

Operator Basic Care

Not withstanding application of good basic process control, operator basic care (some might even call it PM, depending on the circumstance) is one of the simplest, most powerful, and yet scarcely used tools, in most manufacturing plants today. If we operated our manufacturing plants with the same care and diligence that we do our cars, at least those of us who care about our cars, plant reliability, uptime and costs would immediately improve, substantially, if not dramatically! Only the most callous of individuals would ignore the basics of maintaining their car—lubrication, fuel, water, routine PM, looking, listening, smelling, feeling, taking care of "funny" noises before they become catastrophic failures, etc. If we could combine basic care with good process control, we would be well on our way to world-class. Yet in most manufacturing plants, and Beta's plants are no exception, the sense of care and ownership is more the exception than the rule. Why is this? The answers are not clear. Part of the answer, no doubt, is the sense of disenfranchisement that cost-cutting and downsizing creates among employees, particularly down in the ranks. For example, one of Beta's mechanics asked in despair "Where's the dignity?", after learning of his friend being abruptly laid off, having served the company some 20+ years. He went on to remark that the shop floor people understood that the company had to be competitive, but the process being used for becoming competitive (downsizing) left most scared and powerless, like waiting for a death sentence. This is not an environment that creates a sense of loyalty and ownership.

Another part lies in the fact that management has not stated its expectations of the shop floor. Beta has encouraged its senior management to state that they expect the operators and mechanics to treat the equipment in the plant with care, like they would their own car. Not stating the obvious leaves it in doubt, or at the very least, does not reinforce the expectation. At one of Beta's plants someone remarked, "This is the place where you make your living. If you don't take care of the place where you make your living, it may not be here to take care of you." They went on to remark that while the employees did not literally own the equipment, they did own their jobs related to the equipment, and should take that ownership as part of their craftsmanship. Sometimes ownership is created by stating that it is expected.

Finally, another part (and there may be more not discussed here), lies in *not* creating an environment which fosters ownership and care.

Establishing Operator Care/Ownership

At Beta's Bosco Plant, the question was raised at to whether or not Bosco operators were doing any basic care or PM of the equipment. The answer was no, not really. The reasons were numerous, and related to union work rules, historical behavior, culture, etc. The general conclusion was reached by management that operators should do some PM, but how to go about this was another question. Many thought the idea was good, most thought that operators, and the union bosses, would not go along with this.

After much thought, it was decided to conduct a reliability workshop with the shop floor—operators, mechanics, union stewards, and plant engineers. The goal of this workshop would be to explore expanding operator basic care and PM, but operators would decide, in cooperation with union stewards, plant engineers, and mechanics, electricians, etc. exactly what would be done. Teams of people from each area of the plant were assembled, and first a half-day reliability workshop was presented, stressing the need to stay competitive, outlining best practices, and stressing their opportunity to have some say in the future of their plant. It was also stressed that in this effort we must:

1. Assure that no safety hazards were created.
2. Provide for adequate training in any new skills required.
3. Resolve and/or negotiate any union work rule issues.
4. Not have a negative impact on existing job requirements.
5. Work as a team for the good of all employees.

Most people, when offered the opportunity to do a good job, will take it enthusiastically. These employees did. After the reliability workshop, the larger group was broken into smaller groups, and examples were provided of what operators were doing at other plants. This was not offered as an example of what was expected of them, but rather to stimulate their thinking about what was possible or reasonable. Examples included:

1. Lubricating of equipment—understanding levels, frequencies, types.
2. Minor adjustments, e.g., checking/tightening belts, conveyors, parts, interlocks, etc.
3. Cleaning of equipment.
4. Minor PM, e.g., changing packing, filters, etc.
5. Minor instrument calibrations.
6. Preparatory work for the following day's maintenance, e.g., draining, loosening, etc.
7. Log sheets for noise, air pressure, temperatures, steam/air/gas leaks, housekeeping, etc.
8. Log sheets for specific process conditions.
9. Above all, look, listen, smell, feel, and think about the plant and its care.
10. Other ideas that the group developed.

After considerable discussion and effort, each team recommended what was reasonable to expect operators to do, without affecting existing job requirements, and including requirements for training, safety, union rules, etc. Each group had a little different view, but in the end all the issues were resolved, and operators were soon involved in greater basic care and PM, and more importantly had created a sense of ownership among everyone.

Eventually what evolved with operations input was actually a maintenance hierarchy:

1. Operator basic care and PM, ownership.
2. Area or focused factory crafts/trades, support functions.
3. Central maintenance support functions.
4. Contract maintenance.

Shift Handover Process

The exchange of information between shifts, especially as it relates to plant and equipment performance, can be crucial to plant success. Beta reviewed its shift handover process and found it to be lacking when compared to best practice.[6] In many circumstances, shift handover was not much more than a wave in the hallway or dressing rooms, or sometimes even in the parking lot. Certainly, there were times when supervisors and staff spent considerable time discussing what had happened on the previous shift and advising of problems or issues. But, this was more by happenstance, and far too dependent on the personalities and moods of the individuals involved.

Therefore, Beta established a shift handover procedure, which defined current plant or process condition, any problems or upsets which had occurred, any unusual events, etc. In fact, Beta assured that the shift supervisors and senior operators actually wrote the procedures for each plant, creating a sense of ownership of the process. The general rules of the shift handover process included:

1. It must be conducted face to face.
2. It must follow specific procedure(s), based on an analysis of needs. Procedures are especially important:

   a. When there's a big difference in experience between shifts.
   b. After a major maintenance or capital project effort.

   c. Following and during the lengthy absence of key personnel.

   d. After a significant transient, particularly if plant/system lag or response time an overlaps shifts.

3. It must allow as much time as necessary for communication, especially when problems have occurred on the prior shift.

4. Both shifts are responsible for communication, teamwork, and joint ownership.

Examples of issues discussed include equipment and process conditions, any maintenance activity and lock-out condition, any significant transients or upsets, any personal issues or absences, any new products, practices, procedures, etc.

Production Planning

One of the more troubling issues at several of Beta's plants was that of production planning. As noted in Chapter 3, production planning was often subject to the whims of marketing, or more accurately sales, and changed from moment to moment at many plants. While integrating their marketing and manufacturing strategies, and having a process for rationalizing product mix would help tremendously, Beta also felt that several actions were also necessary at their plants to assure plant facilitation of the integration process. Among these were:

1. Creation of a written sales and production planning procedure, including forecasting, supply/demand balancing, verification of production forecast against demonstrated plant performance, conformance to production plan and causes for failure to do so, etc.

2. Refinement of a sales/production forecasting system. A simple tool called a "stagger chart"[7] (see Table 8-1) would be used to track actual performance against forecast.

3. Balancing of supply, demand, and inventory levels.

4. Planning of raw material requirements as a result of these reviews.

5. Linking current performance to business financials and trending this performance.

6. Creation of a longer term logistics requirements plan from this procedure.

7. Creation of a process for resolving conflicts in the supply chain.

Table 8-1
"Stagger Chart"

Forecast Made in:	Jan	Feb	Mar	Apr	May	Jun	Jul	Aug	Sep	Oct	Nov	Dec
	Forecasted Incoming Orders for:											
Dec	100	125	135	120								
Jan	**105**	120	140	135	130							
Feb		**95**	130	125	140	130						
Mar			**115**	140	145	140	150					
Apr				**110**	130	120	120	140				
May					**115**	120	135	140	145			
Jun						**105**	115	125	130	130		
Jul							**100**	110	120	125	120	
Aug								**110**	120	130	140	140

Numbers in bold represent ***actual*** *performance against forecast. Note that, at least for this sales group, which is typical at Beta, they are almost always more optimistic than their actual performance, but at least now Beta has a calibration capability which should be fairly accurate for the existing set of products. Beta is also exploring using software programs that incorporate "fuzzy" logic into the forecasting process, and other statistical tools such as those suggested by Shipman,[8] but at present this is only at the developmental stage.*

8. Linking to the supplier information systems for planning purposes.
9. Integrating more fully the production planning and maintenance planning functions.
10. More comprehensive training of production planners in the planning systems, and in integrated logistics and supply chain issues.

Advanced Process Control Methods

Beta's first order of business is to establish the basics of process control as previously described. However, at one of its advanced operations, the Pikeville petrochemical plant, Beta has implemented a program for more advanced process control.[9] Essentially, advanced process control was applied in a multi-variable environment, one which needs integration of key parameters to achieve specific objectives related to quality and uptime. The first step in the effort was to build a dynamic model from data associated with the key variables, e.g., a mathematical representation of the production process, including thermodynamic, equilibrium, and kinetic relationships, as well as key process constraints. The model was developed and run on-line to initially predict system behavior and track driving variables. Coefficients were used to fit the model to the variables that represented the dynamics of the process, and calculate the "trajectories" of the process.

Once satisfied with the dynamic model, an optimizer was imbedded into the model, which included economic considerations related to the process plant, e.g., raw material cost, product being made, process rate, gross margins anticipated, etc. Next, the model was tested in a non-control mode for two weeks, including several changes to the process to assure that the model is properly predicting system behavior. Once satisfied with this, an advance controller was designed to support the plant's economic objectives, fine tuned, and implemented through a commissioning process that verified that the controller could effectively use the dynamic model to optimize economic performance of the plant. Beta has achieved millions in savings using this more advance methodology. That said, the process will not work unless the basics are in place first.

Finally, several of Beta's plants have tried with varying degrees of success to use a more advanced technique called design of experiment (DOE), which helps determine the sensitivities of product outputs to various input parameters, facilitating greater control of those input parameters that offer the greatest opportunity for optimization of outputs. The technique has proven itself in several instances to be very beneficial. However, it does require considerable discipline, as well as the ability to vary and accurately measure key variables that control the production process during a given time period. This discipline and capability are, for the most part, in need of improvement throughout Beta's manufacturing operation. Once the basics are well established, this technique represents an opportunity to take Beta's plants to the next level of performance.

Summary

In Beta's effort to improve manufacturing and to achieve a level of excellence, they found several areas that needed improvement. Their following conclusions are based on those areas where it has been observed that their plants didn't do a very good job. Beta is currently implementing processes to assure that these areas are addressed:

1. Review of instrumentation and control systems, and their maintenance, to assure process measurement and control capability. This will also include an assessment of QC and laboratory analysis methods for validation of process information.
2. Improved production planning methods as previously described, integration with sales and supply chain issues.
3. Advance methods as appropriate to the current practices of a given plant.
4. Back to basics for all plants to assure their operators are properly trained and employing best practices, as described as follows.

Specific improvements for operators, their training and practices, include:

1. Training in process basics and control limits, and using their expertise to assure precision control of both the physical process (pressure, temperature, flow, etc.), and in many cases at Beta, the chemical process. This is particularly true in plants that require precision process chemistry control. A similar statement could be made for Beta's batch and discrete plants, but with different control parameters.
2. Use of control and trend charts to measure and trend all key process indicators, physical, and as necessary, chemical. Trends should be used to anticipate and trend potential problems developing and mitigate them long before they become serious.
3. Training in statistical process control, inherent variability, inherent stability of a given process, and ability to use this knowledge to operate within the basic stable envelope of a given process. Many operators go "chasing their tails" trying to stabilize a process when it is already within its inherently stable limits, often actually creating instabilities that would not otherwise exist.
4. Training in the basics of pump and valve operation. This knowledge must be used to operate a more stable and reliable plant. Far too often, pumps are run in a cavitation mode because operators do not understand the characteristics of a cavitating pump, what causes cavitation, proper "net positive suction head," proper discharge conditions, etc., or how to address problems causing cavitation. Likewise, valve operation is not fully understood or appreciated and must be improved.

5. Training in startup, shutdown, and other transition periods such as moving from one product or process stream to another. This is from a standpoint of assuring that process "recipes" are followed, as well as good process control. Frequently, changeovers and transient periods will result in the most harm to equipment due to process stream carryover, cavitation of pumps, control valve chatter, "hammer" on piping and heat exchangers, running seals dry, etc. Transient control must be given particular attention to avoid equipment damage and ultimately loss of production in both process and batch plants.

6. Training in the basics of condition monitoring and trending. Control charts must be used as a form of condition monitoring, but other techniques and technologies are available that may be made part of the operator's capability. Methods such as vibration, oil, infrared, leak detection, and motor current monitoring will be used to *supplement* an operator's knowledge of process and equipment condition to assure greater precision in process control.

7. Training in and providing basic care and PM of the equipment they operate. In the better plants, operators spend some 30% of their time doing so. Much the same as most people take basic care of their cars, and only go to maintenance when they need to do so, all the while collaborating with maintenance to assure a proper solution is put in place, so should operators do in a manufacturing plant. Experience has shown that operators themselves should determine which PM and basic care they are most capable of doing, considering training, safety, and other operating requirements.

8. Training in and selection of certain visual controls which will facilitate their performance.

9. Routinely walking through the plant, not just for filling in log sheets—they all do that, but for seeking ways in which problems can be anticipated and resolved long before they become serious. Filling in log sheets is only the beginning, not the end. Yet in most plants, too many operators view the job as done when the log sheets are completed. Or, in the case of large process plants, they sit for endless hours looking at mimics and screens. Plant tours should be made an integral part of good plant operation.

10. Keeping instruments and equipment calibrated, and electronic instruments in particular must be kept cool, clean, dry, and powered by "clean" electricity—no voltage or current surges, no spikes, no harmonics, etc. It has been said process control effectiveness deteriorates some 50% after six months of operation without maintenance.

11. Assuring measurement and control capability, as well as laboratory analysis capability must be superior.

12. Finally, and perhaps most importantly, operators must be conditioned to take ownership and pride in their operation. Beta has found that its operators were reluctant to do so with the company focused incessantly on cost-cutting. Beta is now taking the position that a greater degree of success will be achieved if they set a few key goals related to uptime, unit cost of production, and safety, and then provide the freedom, training, and encouragement for the operations, engineering, and maintenance staff to achieve those key objectives. Beta has shifted focus from cost-cutting, per se, to manufacturing excellence, and *expecting* that the costs will come down as a consequence of best practice.

Beta's plants used a self-audit technique to measure its operating performance and rated itself at just over a 50% level. This performance is about average, and fairly typical of most manufacturers. Beta is currently working intensively to improve its performance in these areas.

In summary, Beta's operational practices must be improved to assure precision process control, routine use of control charts for key process parameters, methods for assuring consistency of process, and perhaps most importantly to encourage a sense of ownership and basic care, every day in all its operating plants. Beta must also put in place a measurement system for assuring that all its people understand uptime, OEE, and asset utilization rates as key performance indicators. Beta must measure every hour of lost production and the reason why, and use those measures to drive the improvement process.

Relatively few plants do the basics well. Beta is working hard to make sure it is one of those few who do.

References

1. Aiken, C. and Kinsey, R. "Preventive/Predictive Maintenance: The Secret to World-Class Productivity," conference proceedings, Association for Facilities Engineering, Las Vegas, October 1997.

2. Cutler, C. and Finlayson, S. "Considerations in Applying Large Multivariable Controllers," Instrumentation Society of America, NY, NY, Annual Conference, October 1991.

3. Cutler, C. and Perry, R. "Real Time Optimization with Multivariable Control," *Computers and Chemical Engineering,* Vol. 7, No. 5, pp. 663–667, 1983.

4. McNeese, W. and Klein, R. *Statistical Methods for the Process Industries,* Marcel Dekker Publications, January 1991.

5. Shunta, J. P. *Achieving World-Class Manufacturing through Process Control,* Prentice Hall, Englewood Cliffs, NJ, August 1994.

6. "Effective Shift Handover—A Literature Review," *Health & Safety Executive,* United Kingdom, June 1996.

7. Grove, A. S. *High Output Management,* 2nd ed., Vintage Books, New York, NY, 1995.

8. Petzinger, T. "The Front Lines," *The Wall Street Journal,* October 30, 1998.

9. Williams, S. discussion, Aspen Technology, circa June 1997.

Maintenance
Practices

According to an old story, a lord of ancient China once asked his
physician, a member of a family of healers, which of them was the
most skilled in the art. The physician, whose reputation was such that
his name became synonymous with medical science in China, replied,
"My eldest brother sees the spirit of sickness and removes it before it
takes shape, so his name does not get out of the house. My elder
brother cures sickness when it is still extremely minute, so his name
does not get out of the neighborhood. As for me, I puncture veins, prescribe potions, and massage skin, so from time to time my name gets
out and is heard among the lords."

A Ming dynasty critic writes of this little tale of the physician:
"What is essential for leaders, generals, and ministers in running countries and governing armies is no more than this."[1]

Going from Reactive to Proactive

It could be added that what is essential for plant managers, vice-presidents of manufacturing, and CEOs is no more than this. Most manufacturing plants are operated in a highly reactive mode—routine changes in the production schedule, routine downtime for changeovers and unplanned maintenance, etc., often resulting in a need to ". . . puncture veins, prescribe potions, and massage skin, so from time to time my name gets out and is heard among the lords," rather than being very proactive and assuring that one ". . . sees the spirit of sickness and removes it before it takes shape . . ." As in ancient times, there's more glory today in fixing things after they become a problem than there is in stopping them from happening in the first place. How much we change and yet stay the same. And yet we must change if we are going to compete in a global economy.

This chapter outlines maintenance and reliability best practices. At Beta, like most companies, executives historically viewed maintenance as a repair function, a necessary evil, an unnecessary cost, a fire-fighting function, a group of grease monkeys and knuckle draggers (unspoken attitude), or any combination of these and other unflattering terms.

This was an un-enlightened view, because few had an appreciation for the value a world-class maintenance function could provide to their company. Because of this, a good deal of education was necessary for Beta executives to understand this issue. Hence, the need for a fairly large body of information. We can only hope that you, like

Table 9-1
Comparative Maintenance Practices—1992 and 1997

Maintenance Practices 1992:		Maintenance Practices 1997:		
		Process/	Discrete/	
	All	Continuous	Batch	All
Reactive Maintenance	50%	46%	53%	49%
Preventive Maintenance	25%	27%	29%	27%
Predictive Maintenance	15%	16%	9%	14%
Proactive Maintenance	10%	10%	7%	9%

Note: Some minor rounding error occurs in the 1997 data, and/or some "other" category of maintenance may have been omitted from the categories presented.

many of the Beta executives will take these issues to heart and intensively implement the practices provided below.

From a 1992 study,[2] and more recently in 1997 (detailed in appendix A) the average US manufacturer was reported to have the levels of maintenance practices in their manufacturing plants shown in Table 9-1.

In these studies, participants (70 plants in the 1992 study, and nearly 300 plants in the 1997 study) were asked "What percentage of your maintenance is driven by the following type of behavior?":

1. Reactive maintenance—characterized by practices such as run-to-fail, breakdown, and emergency maintenance. Its common characteristics are that it is unplanned and urgent. A more stringent view of reactive maintenance is work you didn't plan to do on a Monday morning, but had to do before the next Monday morning.
2. Preventive maintenance (time-based)—characterized by practices that are periodic and prescribed. Examples are annual overhauls, quarterly calibrations, monthly lubrication, and weekly inspections.
3. Predictive maintenance (condition-based)—characterized by practices that are based on equipment condition. Examples include changing a bearing long before it fails based on vibration analysis; changing lubricant based on oil analysis showing excess wear particles; replacing steam traps based on ultrasonic analysis; cleaning a heat exchanger based on pressure-drop readings; replacing a cutting tool based on deterioration in product quality, etc.
4. Proactive maintenance (root cause-based)—characterized by practices that focus on eliminating the root cause of the maintenance requirement, or that seek to extend equipment life, mitigating the need for maintenance. These practices use the maintenance knowledge base about what was going wrong with equipment to make changes in the design, operation, or maintenance practices, or some combination, and seek to eliminate the root cause of problems. Specific examples might include root cause failure analysis, improved design, precision alignment and balancing of machinery, equipment installation commissioning, and improved vendor specifications, and better operational practices to eliminate the cause of equipment failures.

What is striking about the two sets of data (1992 and 1997) is their similarity. After years of effort defining benchmarks and best practices, and creating a reliability model for manufacturing plants to follow, the data are essentially the same. As the saying goes, "The more things change, the more they stay the same."

These typical plant maintenance practices were then compared to so-called benchmark plants. These benchmark plants were characterized as those that had achieved extraordinary levels of improvement and/or performance in their operation. For example, a power plant increased plant availability from 50% to 92%; a fibers plant increased uptime by 40%, while cutting maintenance costs in half; a primary metal plant increased capacity by some 30%, while reducing labor levels by 20%; a motor manufacturer increased OEE from 60% to over 80%, reducing unit costs of production commensurately; a paint plant doubled production output, and so on.

The striking characteristics of these benchmark plants, as compared to the typical plant, are shown in Figure 9-1,[2] and are twofold:

1. Reactive maintenance levels differed dramatically. The typical plant incurred some 50% reactive maintenance, while the benchmark plants typically incurred less than 10%.
2. The benchmarks plants had a heavy component of predictive, or condition-based, maintenance practices.

Similar conclusions were reached by Ricketts[3] who states that the best oil refineries were characterized by, among other things, the "religious pursuit of equipment condition assessment," and that the

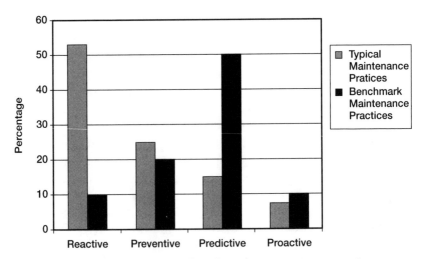

Figure 9-1. Typical vs. benchmark maintenance practices.

worst were characterized by, among other things, "staffing . . . designed to accommodate rapid repair," and failures being "expected because they are the norm." In the same study, he also provides substantial data to support the fact that as reliability increases, maintenance costs decrease, and vice versa.

A more recent study[4] of some 250 small and medium manufacturers in Australia is quite consistent. It reported that companies that adopted a policy of strategic asset management showed increased profits of 25–60%, increased productivity of 25–50%, reduced equipment downtime of up to 98%, and reduced maintenance costs of 30% or more. Table 9-2 provides a summary of additional key results of this review.

Table 9-2
Comparative Results of
Maintenance Practices and Maintenance Costs

Base Case Profile		Effects of Various Practices							
Reactive	58%	<30%	<15%						
Preventive	27%			>50%	>60%				
Predictive	7%					>10%	>25%		
Proactive	8%							>10%	>20%
Maintenance									
Costs	100%	78%	44%	72%	59%	75%	42%	58%	47%
(as a % of PRV)									

In the study, the average of the plant data on maintenance practices is represented as the base case profile. It shows a typical plant having 58% reactive maintenance, 27% preventive, and the balance split approximately equally between predictive and proactive. Maintenance costs were viewed as a measure of success, and were determined as a percent of current plant replacement value (PRV) for each plant, with the average value being normalized to 100%. When comparing the typical plant maintenance practices with other plant maintenance practices, a clear trend is evident. Those plants that experienced lower reactive levels, or reciprocally higher preventive, predictive, and proactive levels, also experienced much lower maintenance costs.

For example, as shown in Table 9-2, when reactive maintenance was less than 15%, maintenance costs were 44% of base case; when predictive maintenance was greater than 25%, maintenance costs were 42% of base case; and when proactive maintenance was greater than 20%, maintenance costs were 47% of base case. Note that while preventive maintenance does improve maintenance costs, it does not do so to the same degree as the other practices. As Beta found at one of its plants discussed in Chapter 12, increasing preventive maintenance was accompanied by an increase in reactive maintenance when maintenance practices did not include predictive and proactive methods.

As one might expect, it was also found that plants with higher rates of proactive or predictive maintenance were also balancing the other practices for improved effect. For example, those plants with more than 25% predictive, also had less than 25% reactive, and were applying the balance of effort to preventive and proactive maintenance, reflecting a balanced, reliability-driven approach to maintenance in their plants. The study also reported that those plants with specific policies for maintenance, including plans and goals for equipment reliability and maintenance performance, also experienced lower maintenance costs than the group as a whole. None of this should be surprising. As Dr. David Ormandy once said "Do all the little things right, and the big things don't happen."

Beta had similarly gone through a review of its manufacturing practices, with particular emphasis on its maintenance practices, and had concluded that in spite of pockets of excellence in some areas, all in all it was among the mediocre in its performance in essentially all areas, including maintenance, or as one of its executives proclaimed, "Beta is thoroughly average."

"Worst Practices"

Reactive maintenance at levels beyond about 20–30% should normally be considered a practice to avoid in most manufacturing plants, or a "worst practice." Reactive maintenance tends to cost more (routinely twice as much as planned maintenance[5]), and leads to longer periods of downtime. In general, this is due to the ancillary damage that often results when machinery runs to failure; the frequent need for overtime; the application of extraordinary resources to "get it back on line," NOW; the frequent need to search for spares; the need for expedited (air freight) delivery of spares, etc. Further, in a reactive mode, the downtime period is often extended for these very same reasons. Moreover, in the rush to return the plant to production, many times no substantive effort is made to verify equipment condition at start-up. The principal criterion is often the fact that it is capable of making product. Hudachek and Dodd[6] report that reactive maintenance practices for general rotating machinery costs some 30% more than preventive maintenance practices, and 100% more than predictive maintenance practices. These results are consistent with that reported for motors.[7] Most Beta plants experience reactive maintenance levels of near 50%, and sometimes more. There should be little wonder why maintenance costs for Beta are well above world-class, and in some cases even worse than average.

Best Practices

Plants that employ best practices, that operate at benchmark levels of performance, have a strong reliability culture; whereas those that are mediocre and worse, have a repair culture. At Beta, this was true—the plants that had the best performance held the view that *maintenance is a reliability function, not a repair function.* Of course, they understood that repairs were often necessary, but these repairs were done with great care, precision, and craftsmanship, and with a view that the equipment must be "fixed forever" as opposed to "forever fixing"; building reliability into the equipment. They also understood that the reciprocal was *not* true, that is, reliability is a maintenance function. Reliability required doing everything right, in design, purchasing, stores, installation, operations, and, of course, maintenance. Unfortunately, most of Beta's plants viewed maintenance as a rapid repair function.

Beta's Repair Culture

In Beta's repair culture, the maintenance department was viewed as someone to call when things broke. They became very good at crisis management and emergency repairs; they often had the better craft labor—after all, the crafts were called upon to perform miracles, but they could never rise to the level of performance achieved in a reliability culture. They often even viewed themselves as second-class employees, because they were viewed and treated as "grease monkeys," repair mechanics, and so on. They often complained of not being able to maintain the equipment properly, only to be admonished when it did break, and then placed under extraordinary pressure to "get it back on line, now." They were rarely allowed the time, or encouraged, to investigate the root cause of a particular problem and eliminate it. Seeking new technologies and methods for improving reliability was frequently not supported—"it's not in the budget" was a familiar refrain. The times when they were allowed to investigate the root cause were a kind of "reactive proactive"—the problem had become so severe that it had reached a crisis stage. They were eager, sometimes desperate, to contribute more than a repair job, but were placed in an environment where it often just was not possible. They were doomed to repeat the bad practices and history of the past, until the company could no longer afford them or stay in business. The good news is that this is now changing at Beta, which has a newfound resolve towards creating and sustaining a reliability culture.

In a reliability culture, reliability is the watchword. No failures is the mantra. Equipment failures are viewed as failures in Beta's processes and systems that allowed the failure to occur in the first place, not failures in the equipment, nor in the employees. In a reliability culture, preventive, predictive, and proactive maintenance practices are blended into an integral strategy. Condition monitoring is pursued, as Ricketts put it, "religiously," and to the maximum extent possible maintenance is performed based on condition. Subsequently, condition diagnostics are used to analyze the root cause of failures, and methods are sought to avoid the failure in the future.

Maintenance Practices

Before we explore specific maintenance practices that assure plant reliability, however, we need to consider equipment failure patterns as shown in Figures 9-2[2,8] and 9-3,[9] which profile the conditional probability of failure as a function of age for plant equipment.

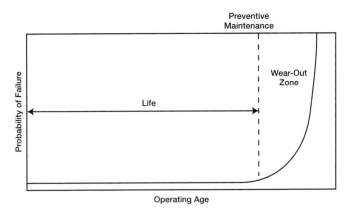

Figure 9-2. Classical failure profile used in preventive maintenance.

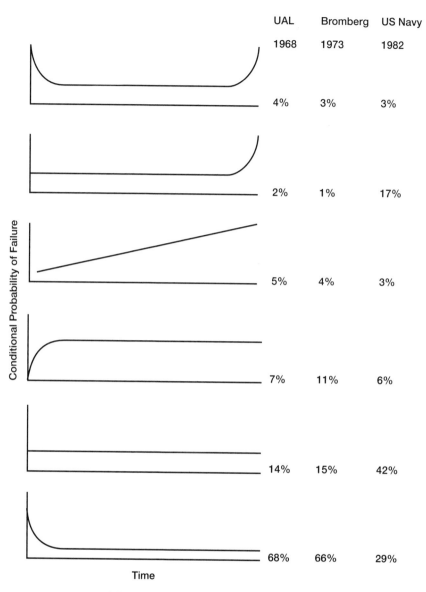

Figure 9-3. Age-related failure curves.

Referring to Figure 9-2, preventive maintenance, or PM (interval based), often takes the form of periodically overhauling, repairing, or otherwise taking equipment apart, replacing certain parts, and re-assembling. It assumes that a given set of equipment will experience a few random, constant failures, but after a time will enter a period where the conditional probability of failure rises sharply (the wear-out zone). Therefore, the invasive PM (overhaul, repair, etc.) should be done just prior to entering the wear-out zone.

There are several problems with using this failure profile as the basis for routine invasive maintenance. First, and perhaps foremost, most equipment does not fit this profile. Referring to Figure 9-3, typically only about 1–2% of equipment fits this profile. While the US Navy reported that some 17% fit this profile, most of that was related to sea water corrosion, which had a definitive wear-related failure mode.

Further, most plants do not have the data or equipment histories that allow determination of the conditional probability of failure; or if they do, the data look something like Figure 9-4,[10] which happens to be for 30 bearings that were run to failure. These bearings were from the same manufacturer's lot, installed with the same procedures, operated under the same loads, and run to failure, and yet experienced very high variability in failure period. Recognize that these data could represent any type of equipment for which histories have been collected, e.g., heat exchangers, electronic boards, etc. In any event, it should be obvious that using data like this is relatively meaningless when trying to determine PM intervals for changing bearings. For example, using mean time between failure (MTBF) assures both over-maintaining, for those that have considerable life remaining beyond

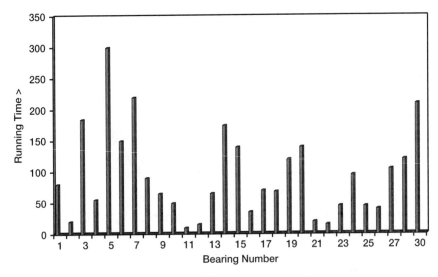

Figure 9-4. Bearing failure component histogram.

their mean time between failure (MTBF), and under-maintaining, for those that fail before the PM interval is ever reached. Only 5–10% of the bearings in Figure 9-4 could be considered as failing at an "average" interval. Hence, the data are not very useful for determining PM interval for bearing changes, for example, in pumps, fans, compressors, etc. However, such data can be very useful for other purposes. For example:

1. The data could be used to facilitate root cause failure analysis and/or to recognize patterns of failure in clusters for a given set of equipment.
2. The data could be used to determine intervals for predictive maintenance such as vibration monitoring. For example, if we replotted the data from lowest to highest, what we would find would be a constant rate of failure at about every 10 units of time. If the decision was made to try to avoid all catastrophic failures, we could monitor the bearings at something like one half or one fourth of the failure rate, and thus assure that we identify pending failures well before they become catastrophic failures, allowing us time to plan the maintenance requirement, and minimize production losses and maintenance costs. Note that this assumes perfection in the vibration analysis effort, something which is problematic. The best vibrations analysis programs are reported to have a 90–95% success rate for fault detection.
3. The data could be used to begin a discussion with the supplier who might ask questions about your design, specification, storage, and installation practices. What did you specify for this application? Do you use proper storage and handling procedures? Do you use an induction heater and/or oil bath for installation? Do you use a clean room for pump overhaul? Do you use proper lubricants and lubricating procedures? Do you do precision alignment and balancing of the equipment? This could be very helpful in eliminating the root cause of the failure.
4. The data could be used to begin a discussion with operations or design to determine if operational or design issues such as cavitation, excess vibration, process conditions, poor shaft design, etc. are creating the poor performance.

And so on. The data serve as a basis for determining whether PM does apply, and if not, as a basis for further investigation and problem resolution to get to the root cause of the failures, and eliminate them.

Along the same line, most people have come to accept intuitively the "bathtub" failure pattern, that is, equipment tends to have some early life failures, some constant rate of failure during its life, and eventually the equipment just wears out. This is shown in Figure 9-3. However, as the data indicate, this only applies to some 3–4% of equipment.

Figure 9-3 shows that depending on the study, "infant mortality" or early life failures represent some 29–68% of failures. This typically means within 60–90 days of startup. This has *profound* implications relative to a given plant's maintenance strategy. PMs make no allowance for these infant mortality failures. Indeed, these failures are more properly eliminated through better design, procurement, installation, commissioning, start-up, and operational practices, *not PM*. Reinforcing this point is the following:

1. The Nordic paper industry, which routinely replaced bearings on a PM basis, found that on actually inspecting the bearings, only 5% could have led to catastrophic failure; 30% had nothing wrong; and 65% had only minor defects due to poor lubrication, alignment, balancing, or installation.[11]
2. The US Navy, which found that some 10–20% of all maintenance work at one of its facilities required some type of rework, suggesting a high probability for introducing defects doing time based PM on equipment.[12]
3. Beta's Maytown plant found that when they increased PM, without applying predictive and proactive methods, reactive maintenance also increased. See Chapter 12.

Figure 9-3 also shows that the next biggest age-related failure pattern is constant, and depending on the study, makes up 14–42% of failures. This also has *profound* implications on your maintenance strategy. If your conditional probability of failure is a constant random series of events, then the best strategy is to assure that you have good condition monitoring in place to detect onset of failure and developing failures long before they become serious, allowing for planning and scheduling of the maintenance requirement. The type of condition monitoring recommended is not just the standard predictive maintenance tools, such as vibration, oil, infrared, etc. technologies. It also includes process condition monitoring, and the integration of the two to assure minimal opportunity for failures. This same high-quality condition monitoring can also be used effectively during installation and start-up to assure the quality of the maintenance and start-up effort, and to minimize infant mortality failures.

When combined, infant mortality and constant rate failure patterns make up some 71–82% of all failures. Developing and applying a maintenance strategy that specifically addresses these failure patterns will have a profoundly positive effect on your maintenance, and operational, performance. Assuring that these failures are eliminated or mitigated is essential to assure world-class maintenance.

Beta's engineers often underestimated or misunderstood the effects just described. Design, procurement, installation, start-up, and operating practices can have an enormous effect on equipment reliability, and consequent uptime and costs. Many of these can be prevented or mitigated by specifying more reliable equipment and requiring the use of non-intrusive testing, i.e., commissioning to specific standards discussed previously. These specifications must be verified by performing post-installation checks at a minimum. For major equipment, the vendor should test the equipment prior to shipment and provide appropriate documentation. The equipment should be retested following installation to ensure the equipment was properly installed and not damaged during shipment. And, as always, better operational practices will minimize equipment failures.

Preventive Maintenance

As data from numerous studies and substantial anecdotal evidence suggest, a program dominated by a PM, or time-based, maintenance strategy is not likely to provide for world-class maintenance, and hence manufacturing performance. Given this is the case, when should preventive maintenance be used?

Best practice for preventive maintenance should allow for time-based maintenance, but only when the time periods are justifiable. For example, appropriate PM might be used:

1. When statistical data demonstrate that equipment fails in a generally repeatable wear-related mode. Note that this "rule" also applies to vendors and their PM and spare parts recommendations—it must be backed by statistical data, not just arbitrary proposals.
2. For routine inspections, including regular condition monitoring.
3. For basic care and minor PM efforts, such as filter changes, lubrication, minor adjustments, cleaning, etc.

4. For instrument calibrations.
5. For meeting regulatory driven requirements.
6. For other purposes based on sound judgment or direction.

Beyond the routine PM outlined, the preventive maintenance function should be used as an analysis, planning, and scheduling function. This will almost always include a comprehensive computerized maintenance management system (CMMS). Using this as a tool, the maintenance function can establish and analyze equipment histories, perform historical cost analyses, and use these cost and equipment histories to perform Pareto analyses to determine where resources should be allocated for maximum reliability. The specific functions for a maintenance planner are:[13]

• Establish work order process and standards

  - unique equipment IDs
  - ease of capturing repair frequency, nature, cause, correction, result of repairs
  - general requirements, including permits

• Issue work orders, plus any instructions, work plans, and sequence of activities
• Establish and analyze equipment histories
• Pareto and cost analysis
• PM selection, scheduling, and optimization
• Maintenance planning and coordination:

  - with maintenance supervisor and trades
  - with stores: parts, tools, special equipment
  - with production, including job status
  - with projects, including contractors required
  - keep current documentation, drawings, procedures, permit process, etc.
  - keep current equipment bill of material
  - publish schedules, periodic reports
  - intensive coordination during shutdowns

• Coordinate closely with reliability engineering

Preventive maintenance requires good maintenance planning, assuring coordination with production, and that spare parts and tools are available, that permits have been issued if necessary, that stores inventories and use histories are routinely reviewed to minimize stores, maximizing the probability of equipment uptime. Beta also found that a lock out/tag out pocket guide[14] for its skilled trades, as well as solid training in procedures, helped reduce the risk of injury during maintenance. In summary, best practice in preventive maintenance includes:

1. Strong statistical base for those PMs done on a time interval.
2. Exceptional planning and scheduling capability.
3. Maintenance planning and production planning being viewed as the same plan.
4. Solid equipment history analysis capability.
5. Strong and flexible cost analysis capability.
6. Comprehensive link to stores and parts use histories.
7. Comprehensive training in the methods and technologies required for success.
8. Comprehensive link between maintenance planning and scheduling, condition monitoring, and proactive methods.

Best practice for use of the CMMS supports those methods and includes:

1. Good work order management.
2. Routine planning and scheduling of work (>90%).
3. Equipment management, including cost/repair histories, bills of material, spares.
4. Pareto analysis of cost and repair histories.
5. Quality purchasing and stores management interface with purchasing.
6. Good document control.
7. Routine use of personnel and resource allocation.

Additional detail on the comprehensive implementation of a computerized maintenance management system is provided in Chapter 11, "Computerized Maintenance Management Systems."

When one of Beta's vice-presidents for manufacturing was presented with a plan for purchasing a computerized maintenance management system, the vice-president asked "What's the return on investment for this system?" To his question the reply was "It doesn't matter," surprising this vice-president. He was then quickly asked, "Does the company have a finance and accounting system to manage its cash and other financial assets?" To this he replied "Of course, it does. The company couldn't be run effectively without it." And then another question to him "What's the return on investment for that system?" Then there was a pause, but no response. And then the statement was made to him "Your division has several hundred million dollars in fixed assets. Do those assets not require a system to assure their proper management?" The system was approved, without any return on investment analysis.

Predictive Maintenance

This is an essential part of a good manufacturing reliability program. Knowing equipment and machinery condition, through the application of vibration, oil, infrared, ultrasonic, motor current, and perhaps most importantly, *process trending technologies,* drives world-class reliability practices, and assures maximum reliability and uptime. It is generally best if all the traditional predictive technologies are in a single department, allowing for synergism and routine, informal communication for teamwork focused on maximizing reliability. For example, knowing that a bearing is going into a failure mode weeks before probable failure allows maintenance to be planned and orderly—tools, parts, and personnel made available to perform the

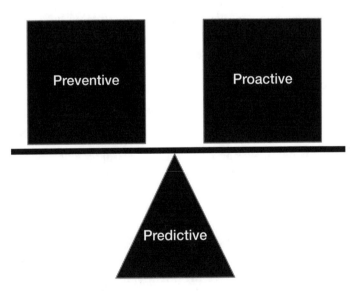

Figure 9-5. Balancing maintenance requirement.

work in a planned shutdown. Moreover, it also allows a more accurate diagnosis of the cause of the failure so that action can be taken to prevent the failure from occurring in the future. Condition monitoring allows overhauls to be planned more effectively, because it is known what repairs will be needed. Overhauls can be done for what is necessary, but *only* what is necessary. Therefore, they take less time—much of the work is done before shutdown; and only what is necessary is done. Condition monitoring allows for checking repairs at start-up to verify the machinery is in like-new condition. Condition monitoring allows better planning for spare parts needs, thus minimizing the need for excess inventory in stores. Indeed, as shown in Figure 9-5,[2] predictive maintenance, when it includes process condition monitoring, can be viewed as the process by which the need for preventive maintenance and proactive maintenance can be balanced.

Best predictive maintenance practices include:

1. "Religious" pursuit of equipment condition assessment, including linking to process condition and control charts.
2. Application of all appropriate and cost-effective technologies.
3. Avoiding catastrophic failures and unplanned downtime by knowing of problems in equipment long before they become an emergency.
4. Diagnosing the root cause of problems and seeking to eliminate the cause.
5. Defining what maintenance jobs need to be done, and when they need to be done—no more, no less.
6. Planning overhaul work more effectively, and doing as much of the work as possible before shutdown.
7. Setting commissioning standards and practices to verify equipment is in like new condition during start-up.
8. Minimizing parts inventory, through knowledge of equipment and machine condition and therefore the effective planning of spare parts needs.
9. Comprehensive communications link to maintenance planning, equipment histories, stores, etc. for more effective teamwork.
10. Comprehensive training in the methods and technologies required for success.
11. An attitude that failures are failures of the processes in place, not the equipment nor the people.
12. Continuously seeking ways to improve reliability and improve equipment performance.

One of Beta's plants illustrates the value and potential conflict in applying predictive maintenance. Beta, like most manufacturers, has several large air compressors at each plant. These compressors are typically on an annual or bi-annual PM, which often includes an overhaul schedule by the vendor. Accordingly, the PM/overhaul plan and schedule routinely include this PM effort. As Beta was approaching the time for this work, several routine tests were performed that were a part of its new predictive maintenance program for doing condition monitoring. Using routine condition monitoring, the maintenance manager found that just 2 weeks before the scheduled overhaul:

1. All vibration levels in all frequency bands and at all fault frequencies were below the lowest alarm level prescribed by GM V1.0 1993, as modified by plant engineering.
2. All oil analysis parameters, e.g., viscosity, viscosity index, additives, water, and wear particle were in the normal range per the vendor's original lubrication specification sheet.
3. Motor current readings indicated that in-rush current and normal operating current were within normal limits on all phases.
4. Cross-phase impedance measurements on the motor indicated inductive and resistive impedance were within 5% and 3% respectively for all phases, Beta's standard for this motor.
5. A recent infrared thermographer's survey indicated that the compressor had no unusual hot spots.
6. Ultrasonic leak detection has, however, found a number of leaks in the compressed air piping system. These leaks have historically been given inadequate attention because of other more pressing work, like overhauling the compressor.

Further, on checking operations logs and confirming them, Beta found that:

1. Discharge pressures, temperatures, and flow rates were all normal.
2. High moisture content is indicated in the instrument air. Apparently this too has been ignored to handle more pressing problems.
3. The next time during which the overhaul can be performed is not for another year.

With all this in mind, does Beta's maintenance manager overhaul the compressor? Would you?

If history is any indicator, the overhaul will be performed. Most of Beta's maintenance managers will not "take the risk." But then, where is the greater risk? Is it in overhauling the compressor, for sure spending the money and risking the introduction of defects. Or, is it in continuing to run the compressor, risking that the technology and monitoring may have missed a developing fault that will result in failure. Those who have confidence in their condition monitoring program will *not* overhaul the compressor, but they will continue to appropriately monitor to detect any onset of failure. Those who have poor monitoring capability, or lack confidence in what they have, will overhaul. There's estimated to be a 10–20% likelihood of introducing defects when this is done. There are risks either way. Who's right? Only time will tell, but what can be said is that the best plants use condition monitoring and inspections religiously to determine the work to be done, and to verify its quality at completion.

Let's consider another way of looking at this issue. Suppose your car dealer recommended that you overhaul your car engine at 100,000 miles. Let's further suppose that you've checked and there's no indication of any problem. For example, the compression is good, gas mileage is good, acceleration is good, and you haven't detected any unusual noises, smells, vibration, etc.? Would you overhaul the engine? Not likely is it? So why persist in doing things in our manufacturing plants that we wouldn't do with our personal machinery? Some food for thought.

Beta's Current Predictive Maintenance Practices

An initial assessment of several of Beta's plants, revealed several issues concerning Beta's practices. Because of regulatory requirements, Beta had very good capability, resources, and practice for nondestructive examination (NDE), or condition monitoring of stationary equipment, principally pressure vessel and piping inspection using various NDE technologies. However, consistent with its generally highly reactive maintenance organization, Beta had only limited capability and/or resources in the area of predictive maintenance (PDM) for equipment condition monitoring. Notwithstanding a few people's clear understanding of rotating machinery and vibration analysis, the resources and expertise needed to fulfill its prospective needs throughout the company, or for that matter at a single large integrated site, was very limited—insufficient resources, technology, training, management processes, etc. Further, the application of other technologies such as infrared thermography, motor current analysis, oil analysis, etc. was also very limited, and in some plants essentially non-existent. Beta was well behind its competitors and well below world-class in machinery condition monitoring practices.

This was surprising, but particularly in light of the demonstrated value of vibration analysis at one site, which had an acknowledged and published 10:1 benefit-to-cost ratio for the current vibration monitoring program. This same program was also vastly underutilized. Beta would be hard pressed to achieve and sustain manufacturing excellence without a comprehensive equipment condition monitoring program that was fully integrated with precision process control and operations input.

In reviewing any number of plants, it was found that maintenance planning and scheduling alone was not sufficient to support world-class maintenance and manufacturing; nor was condition monitoring alone sufficient. Rather, the best plants (highest uptime, lowest unit cost of production) were very proactive about using their CMMS to do equipment histories and Pareto analysis, using maintenance planning and scheduling tempered by process and equipment condition monitoring in a comprehensive way, to focus on defect elimination to achieve superior performance. All the technologies were necessary, none alone were sufficient.

Beta's Predictive Maintenance Deployment Plan

Survey of Existing Capability. Initially, Beta surveyed its existing capability in condition monitoring, both capability and application. At the same time, the survey also included actual application practices, e.g., commissioning of equipment to strict standards, routine condition monitoring and trending, root cause diagnostics of failures, etc. The results of the survey were then used to determine the prospective needs within the operating plants, to correlate those needs to operational performance and production losses, and to work with them to assure their buy-in and support of any needs identified to their specific plants, as well as to develop a broader corporate strategy for the technologies and their implementation.

Creation of Core Capability. Further, the survey was used to develop a corporate level specialist support function, which would provide support in the key predictive and proactive maintenance methods. Other companies had used this practice very effectively to help drive the reliability improvement process. For example, one company had a corporate support function with a senior specialist in each of the technologies, i.e., vibration, oil, infrared thermography, ultrasonic emission, motor current, alignment, balancing, etc. These specialists were recognized as leaders in their specialty, and facilitated the implementation of the technologies throughout the company. Their actual functions included, for example: surveying a given plant to assure that the technology applies, assessing the prospective benefit, working with the plant to set up a program—equipment, database, commissioning, trending, integration with other technologies and with process monitoring, continuing quality control and upgrade, problem solving and diagnostics, and last, but not least, training in the technology to assure excellence in its use. The specialist did not necessarily *do* the program, except perhaps in a start-up mode, but rather facilitated getting it done, and may from time to time help identify and use contractors for certain support functions. In other words, these specialists facilitated the review and implementation of given technologies which are considered to provide maximum benefit to a given manufacturing plant. Beta is using this model for the predictive maintenance implementation process.

Proactive Maintenance

At the best plants proactive maintenance is the ultimate step in reliability. At plants that have a strong proactive program, they have gone beyond routine preventive maintenance, and beyond predicting when failures will occur. They aggressively seek the root cause of problems, actively communicating with other departments to understand and eliminate failures, and employing various methods for extending equipment life. Predictive maintenance is an integral part of their function, because the predictive technologies provide the diagnostic capability to understand machinery behavior and condition. Proactive maintenance is more a state of mind than a specific methodology. The following are specific concepts and techniques being used at Beta's plants.

In a proactive culture the staff have realized, for example, that alignment and balancing of rotating machinery can dramatically extend machinery life and reduce failure rates. They have also learned that doing the job exceptionally well in the plant is not sufficient, and that improved reliability must also come from their suppliers. Therefore, they have supplier standards that require reliability tests and validation, and they keep equipment histories of good supplier's equipment performance. They constantly seek to improve the way they design, buy, store, install, and operate their plants so they avoid the need for maintenance. For example, their motor specifications would probably require that most motors: 1) be balanced to less than 0.10 in./sec vibration at one times turning speed; 2) have no more than 5% difference in cross-phase impedance at load 3) have co-planar feet not to exceed 0.003 in. Proactive maintenance practices (but not just "maintenance") that have yielded extraordinary gain at some of Beta's better plants include:

1. Root cause failure analysis.
2. Precision alignment and balancing.
3. Supplier standards for reliability.
4. Training of purchasing staff in reliability standards.
5. Installation commissioning standards to verify proper installation.
6. Comprehensive training in the methods and technologies required for success.
7. Good material selection for fixed equipment and good process control thereafter.
8. Keeping instruments cool, clean, dry, calibrated, and powered by precision power.
9. Design practices that incorporate the knowledge base of operations and maintenance to eliminate failure modes.
10. Continuous communication with production, engineering, and purchasing to maximize reliability.

Let's consider some of these issues, and what Beta's review of its plants, as well as research at other plants found.

Precision Alignment. Beta's research on precision alignment of rotating machinery found that after implementing a precision alignment program, Boggs reported an increased plant availability by 12%, an increased bearing life by a factor of 8, and reduced maintenance costs of 7%, all from precision alignment.[15] Further, McCoy reported precision alignment reduced electrical energy consumption by up to 11%.[16] Intuitively, this energy savings makes sense—misaligned machinery tends to vibrate at higher rates than aligned machinery. Imagine the energy it takes to "shake" a 200-horsepower motor and pump. As a practical matter, this would mean that in most Beta plants the energy savings alone would more than pay for implementation of a precision alignment program, and as a bonus they would get much longer machinery life, and uptime.

Figure 9-6,[17] which is the middle graph of a series of graphs for this type bearing, shows that for every minute of misalignment (⅟₆₀ of one degree) the life of that type bearing is reduced by about 20%. As a practical matter, this means that precision alignment, laser or even reverse dial indicator done with care, will substantially improve equipment life. Beta's maintenance department can *not* achieve that kind of precision with "a straight edge and flashlight." It also implies that as a practical matter over a 12-in. distance, you want to hold 0.001-in. tolerance to assure long life. It further requires a good stiff base plate, a solid foundation, minimal shims (made of stainless steel), no rust or other debris to create soft foot, and no "pipe spring" to negate the precision work being done. Some of Beta's plants require that piping flanges be fit up "centerline to centerline" within

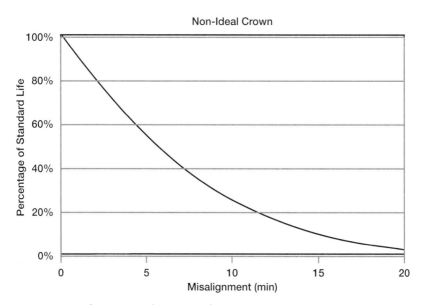

Figure 9-6. Life vs. misalignment for a 309 cylindrical roller bearing: radial load = 3,530 lb (C/4)(15,800 N).

0.040 in. Precision and craftsmanship are essential for world-class maintenance and reliability.

Further, *flex couplings do not eliminate the need for precision alignment.* Consider the following scenario. Let's take an 8-ft-long *perfectly round, perfectly straight* shaft. Let's place a flexible coupling in the middle of this perfect shaft. Next, let's bend the shaft at the coupling (misalignment) to a 30 thousandths total indicated runout (TIR), typical as a result of poor alignment practices. Next, let's place this bent shaft in a machine train (pump and motor). Then, spin the shaft at 1,800 rpm (run the pump). Does this sound like good practice to you? Would you knowingly place a bent shaft in your automobile? In your machinery now? Why would you put one into your critical equipment? Precision alignment is critical to long equipment life.

Illustrating the benefit of precision alignment is the experience of Beta's Wayland plant, where pump repairs were cut in half after they implemented a precision alignment program. See Figure 9-7.

Precision Balancing. Figure 9-8[18] represents prospective increases (or decreases) in equipment life (in this case a pump) for use of a given International Standards Organization (ISO) grade for balancing. In this particular case differences of about 1.5 ounce-inches of imbalance on a 175-pound shaft rotating at 3,600 rpm result in years' increase, or decrease, in the life of the equipment. This is a dramatic change for such a small difference.

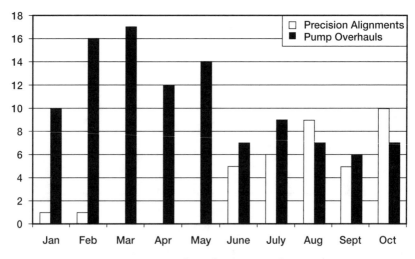

Figure 9-7. Benefits of precision alignment.

In this same effort, Spann reported that his company had been ordering pumps balanced to ISO Grade 6.3, but had never checked to see what was actually being received. On checking, he found that the balance standard being received was substantially poorer than what was specified. On further investigation, he also found that ISO Grade 2.5 would best serve many purposes for his plant, all things considered. He also found that multi-plane balancing of pump impellers was essential when the impeller length was greater than 6 times the pump diameter. Over 3 years, the plant improved output by some 50,000 tons, in large measure due to improved balancing standards, and reduced vibration tolerances for rotating machinery. As a bonus, their maintenance costs also were also reduced by some $2M per year.

Oil Analysis as a Proactive Tool. Check new oil, as well as unused oil for contamination prior to use. Fitch[19] and Mayo[20] reported that new oil is not necessarily clean oil, having been contaminated from internal and external sources, such that its ISO grade quality for purity was well below what was acceptable for the application. Further, oil analysis can detect developing problems related to moisture contamination, wear particle, etc. long before the problem shows up as a

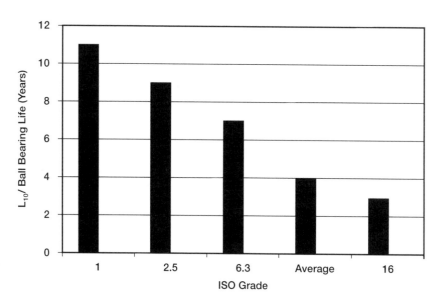

Figure 9-8. Benefits of precision balance.

vibration problem. In addition, minimizing excess temperature will maximize lubricant life. Studies have also shown that for mineral oil with oxidants, for every 25°C increase in temperature above 80°C, lubricant life is reduced by a factor of 10. Similar data could be developed for other lubricants, but as a practical matter, this means that lube oil coolers should be maintained to assure proper cooling; bearings should not be over-lubricated such that they generate excess heat in the grease; and equipment that has been re-rated and is now being run hotter, longer, harder, etc., should have its lubrication requirements reviewed and upgraded as necessary to meet the new operating conditions. Indeed, lubricants should be checked and modified if necessary as a part of re-rating equipment.

Power Quality. This is becoming an increasingly important issue. Larkins[21] reported that the use of new power saving devices and methods such as power factor correction, improved lighting ballast, energy efficient motors, variable-speed AC drives, etc., are all introducing the opportunity for high-frequency harmonics. He further reported that the quality of the power being received from the electric utility can also be of poor quality with surges, sags, etc. It was recommended that a precision recorder be used from time to time to monitor a given plant's power quality looking for harmonics, voltage sags, interruptions, and other disruptions. Using this information, the plant can then address the problem with the power company, within its own design processes using better performance specifications for suppliers, and with suppliers of electrical equipment themselves. Solutions include better specifications, putting the burden on suppliers to guarantee no high-frequency harmonics, isolating variable-speed drives, and derating isolation transformers.

Valve Diagnostics. Recent advances in control valve and transmitter diagnostics have shown that considerable savings are available with these advances.[22] For example, some 230 control valves were scheduled for overhaul, but had added the diagnostics. Of these, 37.1% only needed adjustment, 27.2% were repaired on line, 4.5% required nothing, and only 31.2% had to be pulled and overhauled. For transmitters, 63% only required routine checks or had no problems.

Root Cause Failure Analysis. This is arguably the most powerful tool for proactive maintenance, and for that matter proactive operation and design. Numerous courses are taught by universities, companies, and consultants, so we will only do a brief overview of the methodology here. One consultant has characterized it as the "5 whys," or asking yourself why at least 5 times, and normally you can get to the root cause of a given problem. Note, however, that for each of the levels after the first why, there is the potential for many responses, so the process may grow geometrically. As a practical matter, however, the solution often converges fairly quickly. According to Pride,[23] Nelms,[24] and Gano,[25] the basic steps can be characterized as follows:

1. What happened? Describe the effect.
2. Why did it happen? Describe at least two potential causes.
3. Repeat the process until the root cause is found (typically at least 5 times).

Some useful hints for the process are:

1. Causes may not present themselves in order of occurrence, so don't expect it.
2. The sequence of causes will likely branch, so chart the cause/effect. Wishbone charting is also useful.
3. Each event may have many causes, but eliminating the root cause will prevent the event.
4. It may be useful to work backward from the event.
5. Document acceptances and rejections of root causes.
6. Correlate primary effect to causes.

Most root causes can be boiled down to three areas—people, equipment, and procedures. Improve the people through training and leadership, the equipment through better design, operation and maintenance practices, and the procedures, and good things will happen. If you don't, bad things will happen. Failures are a consequence of poor processes, not poor people or equipment. Proactive methods will assure excellent processes and defect elimination.

Focused Factories and Maintenance Practices: Centralized vs. Decentralized Maintenance

Some, in their zeal for focused factories, have suggested that centralized maintenance has crippled our factories' ability to perform as well as they once did; that computerized maintenance management systems (CMMS) are a burden and there's simply no need for work orders; that machines should be completely rebuilt during maintenance, replacing all parts subject to deterioration, regardless of condition; that having redundant equipment provides the best automatic backup during maintenance; and that the vast majority of factory successes center on equipment modifications and physical improvements in factory floor and office layout.[26] However, Beta's experience does not support these strategies. Many methods related to focused factories are exceptionally good, and have helped Beta make substantial improvements, especially at its batch and discrete plants, where focused factories seem to work best. Beta has improved asset and equipment utilization on its almost universally underutilized assets, and by paying greater attention to every detail of operations and maintenance, Beta has made substantial improvement. However, as Harmon[26] states, producing high value requires quantum improvements in equipment reliability at minimal preventive maintenance costs. In Beta's experience this quantum improvement in equipment reliability at minimum cost is only possible through using the methods previously described, and is highly unlikely, if not impossible, employing the strategies Harmon suggested.

Let's consider the experience at one of Beta's plants that was using the focused factory concept: Beta's Allen Central plant, a discrete parts manufacturing operation, had recently converted to small focused factories for each major product line, had decentralized maintenance, had begun employing TPM practices, Kaizen, or continuous improvement methods, etc., and had shown considerable overall improvement. However, at least as practiced at Allen Central, and because historically maintenance had been a rapid repair function anyway, this only "put the fire fighters closer to the fire." Granted, this should allow them to reduce the duration of the fires, but did little to eliminate the cause of the fires.

Production had been rapidly ramped up to meet dramatically growing demand, and rather than improve overall equipment effectiveness, or OEE (too slow a process), Allen Central did indeed elect to buy more equipment for automatic backup, increasing capacity, and coincidentally, capital, operating, and maintenance costs. Neither work orders nor the computerized maintenance management systems were used to any great extent. We could go on, but in effect, the plant was using the maintenance strategy suggested by the focused factory concept. The results—reactive maintenance was over 70% of the total, maintenance costs were running at nearly 6% of plant replacement value, or nearly 3 times a nominal world-class level. OEE, when we measured it, was typically about 50% at the bottleneck process, some 10% below average, and 35% below world-class, much of which was due to equipment breakdowns.

After a benchmarking review and considerable effort, Beta has since begun employing OEE as a key performance indicator; has begun to employ its maintenance management system to good effect, particularly for inspections and routine PM; has begun to engage operators in minor PM and basic care; has established a condition monitoring program for critical production equipment; and has re-centralized some of its maintenance function. Additional detail for the process used is provided in Chapter 13, "Total Productive Maintenance (TPM) and Reliability Centered Maintenance (RCM) Methods."

After much discussion and review, Beta concluded that simply putting the fire fighters closer to the fire would not achieve the desired results. Initially, a maintenance hierarchy was established, with the following priorities for maintenance:

1. Operator minor PM and basic care, e.g., tighten, lubricate, adjust, clean.
2. Area, or focused factory maintenance teams.
3. Central maintenance support.
4. Contractor maintenance support.

Each affected group was trained in the relevant maintenance technologies and methods, and in equipment repair for the equipment in his factory. Central maintenance was assigned the following responsibility to develop standards and practices for maintenance, and to facilitate and support their deployment:

1. Installation and commissioning procedures.
2. Precision alignment procedures, training, and fixtures for machine tools.
3. CMMS application support—set-up, support, training, equipment histories, Pareto analysis, etc. (the shop floor still did the work orders and scheduling)
4. Predictive maintenance, including working with the shop floor and operations to assure actions were taken on problem machines.
5. Machine repair shop operation.
6. Major stores requirements; minor stores needs were still situated at the factory floor.
7. A manufacturing equipment reliability engineer.

In general, central maintenance is now responsible for facilitating the success of the focused factories, and provided services that were not cost-effective if done within each of the factories. The manager of central maintenance became much more proactive about understanding the needs and requirements of each factory, meeting regularly with each of the factory maintenance managers and production managers to develop a better understanding of needs. Central maintenance became a value-adding contributor, not a cost to be avoided.

Within central maintenance were senior skilled trades, who had picked up the informal title of leadmen (all were in fact men, but it wasn't clear what would happen to informal titles when a female came into the group). These individuals had the responsibility for understanding best practice in their trade, e.g., mechanical, electrical, instrumentation, etc., and for making sure these best practices were being applied at the factory floor level by the maintenance team, including training as needed. These leadmen filled in during times of peak demand or labor shortages within a given factory, and had 2–3 people reporting to them who also filled in. They also helped manage the maintenance requirements for the second and third shifts, using their staff to smooth out work load requirements. Finally, one of the senior leadmen managed the machinery repair shop. Much of this work had been contracted out, but still at this large Beta factory, a small repair shop was in routine use to support factory floor needs.

Beta's Allen Central plant concluded that a hybrid of centralized and decentralized maintenance was best at this plant, and more importantly, contrary to conventional wisdom from focused factory enthusiasts that applying a reliability strategy that combines preventive, predictive, and proactive methods, in cooperation with production would provide for the quantum improvement in equipment reliability at minimum maintenance cost.

The Need for Integrating Preventive, Predictive, and Proactive Practices

At the best plants, preventive and predictive technologies are used as *tools, not solutions,* to help create a proactive culture, and are combined with operational, design, procurement, installation, and stores practices to assure the success of the plant. The need to view preventive and predictive technologies as tools to become proactive is best illustrated by Ledet,[27] while working at a large chemical manufacturing company:

"In the middle 1980s, this chemical manufacturer began an effort to improve its maintenance practices, and employed several methods. After several years, they decided to "measure" whether or not these efforts were successful. They surveyed their plants, with the results below:

"1. One group of plants that came to light had evolved a strong maintenance planning and work order management culture. Few jobs were done without a work order; everything had to be planned and/or scheduled. At these plants, where PM and maintenance planning and scheduling were highly valued, a slim +0.5 to 0.8% improvement in uptime was realized on the whole. It turned out that people were so busy doing work orders and planning, that they didn't have time to do the good reactive maintenance that they had previously done to put the plant back on line quickly, and hence achieved little improvement in uptime.

"2. A second group of plants employed all the latest predictive technologies, almost to the exclusion of other methods. In their zeal to use these predictive technologies, they also neglected to put in place a proper maintenance planning and scheduling function, or to get buy-in from the operations staff. At these plants a −2.4% improvement in uptime was realized—they *lost* uptime. Apparently, the data on equipment condition were being collected, but not being used by operations or maintenance to change any practices or processes. Resources had been re-allocated, but resulted in a negative effect.

"3. A third group linked preventive maintenance, and in particular maintenance planning and scheduling, to predictive maintenance or condition monitoring. At these plants the condition of the equipment was used to adjust the PM or maintenance activity such that better use of resource was achieved. At these plants, an average of +5% higher uptime was achieved.

"4. Finally, there was a small group of plants that used all the technologies, but with a very different perspective. They viewed the CMMS, maintenance planning and scheduling, and predictive technologies as *tools* that allowed them to be proactive, *not solutions* in themselves. At these plants the CMMS was used to collect equipment histories, and this information was used to do Pareto analyses and prioritize eliminating the major defects first. Maintenance planning and scheduling was balanced against equipment condition. Predictive maintenance was used for more than just trending the condition of equipment and avoiding catastrophic failures. It also included equipment commissioning, and root cause diagnostics. A proactive culture was created that was facilitated by various tools to eliminate defects and get to the root cause of problems. This group achieved on average a +15% improvement in uptime."

With such data, it's clear that the technologies and methods must be integrated to assure optimal performance. Further, Ledet also confirmed Beta's general experience and found that plants tend to move from one domain of behavior to another, as depicted in Figure 9-9.[27] As depicted, the lowest domain is the "regressive domain," essentially allowing a plant or business to deteriorate to the point of being nonfunctional. Once the decision has been made (or perhaps re-made) to stay in business, people become very motivated to keep the company or plant in business, responding to urgent needs and moving into the "reactive domain," keeping the operation running, often at significantly greater maintenance costs. After some time, however, it will be natural to want to improve and get out of the reactive or fire-fighting mode, at which point the better plants will begin to move into a mode wherein maintenance requirements can be anticipated, planned,

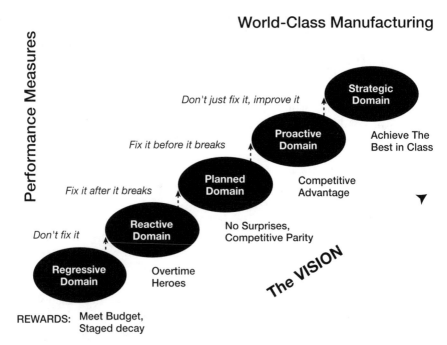

Figure 9-9. The five maintenance domains. (Source: W. Ledet. The Manufacturing Game, Kingwood, TX)

and scheduled—the "planned domain." Those with the best leadership and greatest sense of team work will eventually move from the "planned domain" to the "proactive domain," wherein defect elimination is viewed as the key to success. Eliminating the root cause of defects yields superior performance. Finally, a very few plants will move into the "strategic domain," wherein defect elimination is second nature and ingrained in the culture of the organization, and where learning, positive differentiation, supply-chain integration and business alignment are integral to the daily operation. As a given plant moves from one domain to the next, it does not "forget" the learning of the previous domain, but incorporates that learning and those practices into its performance in the next domain.

Life Extension Program

Within its maintenance and engineering effort, Beta has also been developing an asset evaluation program that looks at current asset condition, anticipated life, current and planned operating requirements, such as asset utilization rate, conservatism in design, anticipated capacity increases above design, etc. Also being considered in this evaluation are current and anticipated maintenance requirements—routine, overhaul, replacement. These considerations have been used to develop the matrix shown in Table 9-3 for estimating maintenance and capital needs for major categories of equipment. This is combined with an estimate of the timing of the requirements, and has a relatively large margin of error, e.g., ±40%. Refinements are made as

Table 9-3
Estimate of Maintenance Costs and Life Extension Requirements

Equipment Category	Normal Maintenance*	Overhaul/ Refurbishment*	Replacement*
Civil			
Control			
Electrical			
Rotating Machinery			
Piping			
Vessels			
Specials			

* Estimates to be completed on a plant-by-plant basis.

the timing and criticality of the equipment replacement or repair comes closer. These estimates also exclude capital expansion and de-bottlenecking projects. Note that condition assessment is performed using predictive and NDE technologies, as well as production perfor-mance, and is critical to the ability of the team to understand current condition and implement the life extension program.

Maintenance Practices and Safety Performance

For several years now, Beta has engaged in an intensive program to improve safety performance, and has had considerable success. Improving procedures, training, and perhaps more importantly awareness and attitude, have contributed to dramatic improvement in safety performance. However, in recent years, this improvement trend appears to have stalled. Figure 9-10 shows that one of its division's safety performance in lost-time accidents had improved five-fold between 1988 to 1994. However, observing the period 1993 to 1997, indicates that the injury rate may have in fact stabilized at a loss-time accident rate that is now oscillating between 0.4 and 0.5. This is of considerable concern to Beta's management. The current view is that the improvements to date resulted from improved awareness, train-ing, procedures, etc., but that if further improvements are to be achieved, then the current "system" must somehow change. Beta's

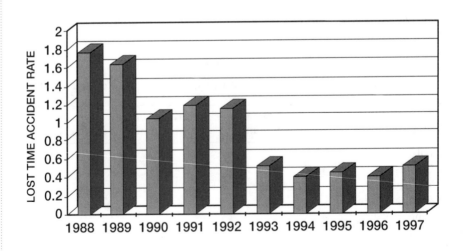

Figure 9-10. Safety rate/200K hours.

reactive maintenance level is typically at about 50%, with substantial need to improve maintenance practices. The view is that this level of reactive maintenance is likely to expose people to greater risk of injury, and more often. And while the empirical data are limited, this view will add additional impetus to Beta's drive to world-class manufacturing (and maintenance) performance, because safety is a key driver at the executive level.

Summary

Most maintenance requirements, and costs, are "preventable," but as has been demonstrated, not by using the traditional preventive maintenance methods. For example, a study of some 15,000 work orders[28] found that 69% of the maintenance costs were preventable by using better design and engineering, better construction, better operations practices, better maintenance practices, and of course, better management practices. Indeed, better design and operations practices were found to make 50% of the maintenance costs preventable. This is consistent to a study done by the Department of Trade and Industry in the United Kingdom, which also found that over 50% of maintenance costs were a result of poor design and operational practices.

What Beta has found is consistent with what Schuyler found:[29]

"When maintenance costs are reduced with no change in maintenance strategy, mechanical availability is reduced (e.g., moving from A to B using "fixed interval" maintenance strategy). Under the same conditions, when mechanical availability is increased, maintenance costs increase. As shown [in Figure 9-11], the only way to simultaneously reduce maintenance costs and increase mechanical availability is to move toward more proactive maintenance strategies."

Schuyler also points out as maintenance costs increase for a given strategy, there may be a point of diminishing, or even negative, returns. That is, there may be a point at which incremental investment under a given strategy will result in lower availability. He also states that data from analyzing many of his company's plants substantiate Figure 9-11.[30]

Beta understands that the comprehensive application of preventive, predictive, and proactive maintenance practices in an integrated philosophy, integrated with operations, engineering, purchasing, and stores practices, is essential to its success. Application of best practices

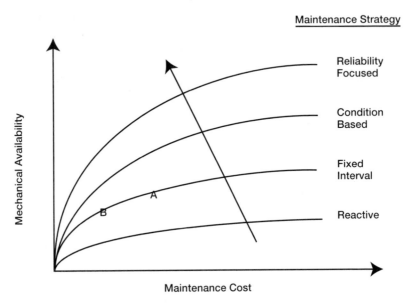

Figure 9-11. Equipment availability as a function of maintenance costs under various maintenance strategies.

is the key to the success of each of their manufacturing plants, particularly as it relates to effective application of supply chain and lean manufacturing principles. Beta has found that by learning what the best plants were achieving and how all Beta's plants compared (benchmarking), by emulating how those best plants were achieving superior results (best practices), and by adding a measure of common sense and management skill, Beta's plants could substantially improve on its current level of performance, and perhaps in the long term, even exceed the current benchmarks. Beta is using the knowledge of the maintenance function to assure that it designs, buys, stores, operates, and maintains its plants for maximum reliability and uptime. Uptime and overall equipment effectiveness are improving dramatically, resulting in increased production, better asset utilization, higher profit, and eventually world-class performance at its plants.

References

1. Tzu, Sun. *The Art of War,* Random House, NY, NY, July 1989.

2. Moore, R., Pardue, E., Pride, A., Wilson, J. Reliability-Based Maintenance—A Vision for Improving Industrial Productivity, Computational Systems Inc., Industry Report, Knoxville, TN, 1992.

3. Ricketts, R. "Organizational Strategies for Managing Reliability," National Petroleum Refiners Association, Maintenance Conference, New Orleans, LA, May, 1994.

4. De Jong, E. "Maintenance Practices in Small and Medium Sized Manufacturing Enterprises," The National Centre for Advanced Materials Technology, Monash University, Melbourne, Victoria, Australia, 1997.

5. Idhammar, C. "Preventive Maintenance, Planning, Scheduling and Control," University of Dayton, Center for Competitive Change, Dayton, OH, 1997.

6. Hudachek, R. and Dodd, V. "Progress and Payout of a Machinery Surveillance and Diagnostic Program," *Mechanical Engineering,* vol. 99, no. 1, 1977.

7. "Maintenance Management, Comparative Cost of Maintenance Strategies," *Modern Power Systems,* July, 1994.

8. Nowlan, F. "Reliability-Centered Maintenance," United Airlines, NTIS Document No. AD/AO66-579, Washington, DC, December, 1978.

9. Pride, A. and Wilson, J. "Reliability as a Corporate Strategy," American Institute of Plant Engineers (now Association of Facilities Engineers), Cincinnati, OH, Annual Conference, May, 1997.

10. Eschmann, P. et. al., *Ball and Roller Bearings: Theory, Design & Application,* John Wiley & Sons, 1985.

11. "Early Detection of Bearing Failures Affects Reliability and Availability at Nordic Paper Plants," *Reliability,* Knoxville, TN, May/June, 1994.

12. Discussion with Alan Pride, Pride Consulting, Inc., Knoxville, TN, 1994.

13. Day, J. "Maintenance Vision for the 21st Century," *Reliability* directory issue, Knoxville, TN, 1996.

14. *Lock Out Tag Out Pocket Guide,* Genium Publishing, Schenectady, NY, 1993.

15. Boggs, R. "Rotating Misalignment—The Disease, But Not the Symptom," Technical Association of Pulp and Paper Industry, Annual Conference, Atlanta, GA, 1990.

16. McCoy, R. "Energy Savings from Precision Alignment," internal memorandum, Computational Systems, Inc., Knoxville, TN, 1992.

17. "Life vs. Misalignment for A 309 Cylindrical Bearing," *SKF Engineering Data Handbook*, Stockholm, Sweden, 1986.

18. Spann, M. "Balancing Parts—Waking to Reality," Society for Maintenance and Reliability Professionals, Winter Newsletter, Barrington, IL, 1994.

19. Fitch, R. "Designing An In-house Oil Analysis Program," ENTEK Corporation User Conference, Cincinnati, OH, September, 1994.

20. Mayo, J. and Troyer, D. "Extending Hydraulic Component Life at Alumax of South Carolina," *Reliability*, January, 1995.

21. Larkins, G. "Energy Efficiency, Power Quality, and Power Systems Commissioning," American Institute of Plant Engineers (now Association of Facilities Engineers), Fall Conference, Cincinnati, OH, 1995.

22. MARCON Conference Proceedings, Maintenance and Reliability Center, University of Tennessee, Knoxville, TN, May, 1997.

23. Pride, A. "Root Cause Failures Analysis Presentation to PT Badak, Bontang Indonesia," Pride Consulting, Inc., Knoxville, TN, March, 1996.

24. Nelms, R. "Root-Cause Failure Analysis" Seminar, University of Dayton, Center for Competitive Change, Dayton, OH, 1997.

25. Gano, D. "Getting to the Root of the Problem," Apollo Associates, Richland, WA, June, 1997.

26. Harmon, R. *Reinventing the Factory II*, The Free Press, New York, NY, 1992.

27. Ledet, W. "The Manufacturing Game," Annual TQM Conference, November, 1994.

28. Oliverson, R. "Preventable Maintenance Costs More Than Suspected," *Maintenance Technology*, September, 1997.

29. Schuyler, R. "A Systems Approach to Improving Process Plant Performance," MARCON Conference Proceedings, Maintenance and Reliability Center, University of Tennessee, Knoxville, TN, May, 1997.

30. Author's conversation with R. Schuyler, E. I. DuPont, Wilmington, DE, January 14, 1998.

Optimizing the Preventive Maintenance Process

There are no solutions, only consequences.

—*Gilbert G. Jones*

Performing preventive maintenance (PM) on an interval basis has long been recognized as a means for improving maintenance effectiveness, and as a means for improving equipment reliability. Hudachek and Dodd[1] reported that maintenance costs for rotating machinery using *preventive* maintenance were over 30% less than those costs incurred from a reactive maintenance approach. In recent years predictive maintenance using condition monitoring equipment has become more and more important to a good PM program, allowing better maintenance planning by considering equipment condition prior to actually performing maintenance work. Not surprisingly, Hudachek and Dodd also state that maintenance costs for rotating machinery using a *predictive* maintenance approach are nearly half that of reactive maintenance. Numerous other studies depicted in previous chapters, as well as many anecdotes, have provided overwhelming evidence of the benefits of viewing maintenance as a reliability function, as opposed to a repair function,[2] and yet most manufacturing plants continue to operate and maintain manufacturing equipment and processes in a predominantly reactive mode. While this is discouraging, there does appear to be a general shift in the acceptance of reliability principles, and considerable effort to improve maintenance practices, and therefore equipment reliability in manufacturing plants. This is certainly true at Beta. This need for improved reliability has also received increased emphasis at many plants with the advent of OSHA 1910, Section 119j, which requires a mechanical integrity program at plants that deal with hazardous materials to prevent the release of those materials.

Unfortunately, since 1992, when one of the first efforts was made to characterize maintenance practices and behavior for some 70 manufacturers,[3] not much has changed. That is to say, most manufacturers, including many at Beta International, continue to report operating with a typical level of reactive maintenance of near 50%.[4] As someone once said "The more we change the more we stay the same."

In any event, more and more companies, including Beta's manufacturing divisions, are purchasing and implementing computerized maintenance management systems (CMMS) for better management of their manufacturing assets, and to assure better maintenance practices and equipment reliability, including integration of predictive and proactive methods. This section offers a model developed for Beta for optimizing the PM process as managed by a CMMS, and for incorporating predictive and proactive methods. It presumes that you have a functional CMMS. For plants that haven't reached that level of implementation, then a few suggestions are offered on "getting started," including putting in place appropriate equipment histories, even if no equipment history database is available.

First Things First

Optimizing the PM process presumes that you have PM's to optimize. Therefore, you should have completed your CMMS database, including:

1. All critical equipment (stops or slows production, or creates a safety hazard if not functioning properly).
2. All appropriate PMs and related procedures, overhaul or turnaround procedures.
3. A complete equipment database, including a bill of material for spares for your critical equipment.
4. A process for *managing* work orders, including planning and scheduling, Pareto/cost analysis, equipment specific histories, etc.

If not, or if not fully developed, you can still get started using the following process described below, which is similar to that outlined in Chapter 12.

Creating Equipment Histories from "Scratch"

If you don't have equipment histories, a good "jump start" can be created by sitting some of your best mechanics, electricians, operators, etc. (a cross-functional team) in a room, tracing a production block diagram on a white board, and then walking them through the production process. At each step in the process ask—What's been happening here with our equipment that has resulted in failures? How often? How long? How much downtime? How much cost? Keep good notes and keep asking enough questions to allow you to determine what equipment fails, why it fails, how long it is down, and how much it costs to get it back on line (approximations are OK for this brainstorming session). Also note that many times the problems will be related to issues other than maintenance—raw material quality, finished product quality, process problems, etc. But this is good information too, and will facilitate the team-building process. Using this information, define that PM effort for each set of equipment that will alleviate or eliminate the failures being experienced, or at least detect the onset of failure early in the failure process (condition monitoring). Alternatively, define the operating, engineering, procurement, etc., practice that will eliminate or mitigate the failure.

Somewhere in this process, you should also be performing a couple of mental analyses:

1. Pareto analysis—what major issues are causing the most downtime? The most increased costs? The greatest safety hazards?
2. Where are my production bottlenecks, and how have they shifted from where they were perceived to be as a result of equipment and/or process problems?

This process will allow you to better prioritize your resources to improve production capacity and reduce operating and maintenance costs; not to mention getting your production and maintenance people to begin working as part of a team with a common objective—maximum equipment reliability at a minimum cost—a kind of superordinate goal that helps transcend minor, and sometimes petty, differences.

Once you get all that done and have all your PM's defined, as well as planned and scheduled maintenance built into our system, then you can begin the process for optimizing PM's. If you're just beginning, the process will still be very helpful.

The Model (Figure 10-1)[4]

Step 1—Set Up Your Database

Categorize your PM's. The following are suggested, but you may have others that are more applicable in your plant. The key is to be systematic and disciplined about the optimization process. For starting the process, they might be:

1. Regulatory driven or required
2. Calibration and instrument PM requirements
3. Inspection, test and surveillance (including condition monitoring)
4. Manufacturer defined
5. Staff defined
6. Shutdown, turnaround, or outage related PMs
7. Other PMs

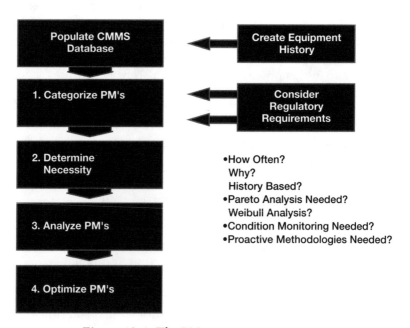

Figure 10-1. The PM optimization process.

Step 2—Determine Their Necessity

Critically analyze each PM in each category. Does the PM support improved equipment reliability, and therefore:

1. Improved production capacity
2. Reduced life cycle cost
3. Better safety performance
4. Better risk management
5. Other company objectives

If it doesn't support these objectives, it may be unnecessary, but let's look at some other issues before we reach that conclusion.

Step 3—Analyze Your PM's

Given that the PM is probably necessary, ask yourself:

1. How often do I need to do this PM? Why?
2. Is the PM interval statistically well founded from equipment histories?
3. Could I use Pareto analysis to prioritize my PM needs or Weibull statistical analyses to help optimize my PM intervals and practices?
4. Could the need for PM be mitigated or optimized using condition monitoring to delay (or hasten) the PM? Some examples include vibration, oil, infrared, ultrasonic, motor electrical analysis; process parameter and operator knowledge.
5. Could proactive methodologies provide longer, more reliable, equipment life, thereby increasing PM intervals, e.g.:
   - Better specifications
   - Better installation procedures
   - Improved joint making
   - Precision alignment and balancing of rotating machinery
   - Commissioning tests and procedures for validation of quality work
   - Better training
   - Root cause failure analysis
6. Would operators be better suited to do certain PM and basic care work, increasing maintenance availability for more complex efforts?

Step 4—Optimization

Using this analysis, begin the process of optimizing your PM activities, step by step. This process will not be easy, nor is it likely to ever be "finished," but rather should be viewed as a continuing process for improvement.

Some Examples

Let's take a few examples and walk through the process.

Instrument Calibration. Define the calibration requirements and intervals for each instrument. At the PM interval, track the "drift" from calibration. Using this information, determine statistically if it is possible to increase the interval, or necessary to reduce the interval, and retain proper instrument measurement requirements. Adjust PM intervals as appropriate, and/or seek new and improved methods or instruments. For example, at several of Beta's plants they have found that once they started tracking calibrations, it appeared that many were "overdone," and some "underdone." For example, if an instrument calibration was checked weekly, and yet in over a year only once required recalibration or adjustment, then this likely means that the calibration and inspection is being overdone. But, a word of caution, if this instrument is monitoring the reactor of a nuclear plant, then it may not be overdone. Failure consequence should also be considered. Similarly, if the instrument requires weekly calibration, it may not be suitable for its intended service and be considered for replacement.

Inspection, Test, and Surveillance. Define the basis for each inspection. Analyze histories of equipment. Note: Use the "developed" histories from the brainstorming if equipment histories aren't available. From the histories, determine a more optimal PM interval. Ideally you might use Weibull analysis, which allows definitive guidelines. For example, if the data are available, you might decide that you want a 97% confidence level that vibration analyses performed on a certain basis will assure preventing a major failure in your equipment. (Note also this presumes that you have best practices in place for acquiring your data.) From this analysis you could set up optimal vibration analysis intervals. For example, at several of Beta's plants, they have also found that after about a year of comprehensive vibration monitoring, doing vibration inspections monthly was probably more often than necessary for many machines. Most of the time, vibration levels did not change very much month to month. But, these plants also included operators taking better care, and being more aware of any abrupt changes in the equipment, at which point they would alert the vibration analyst to check or increase the frequency of data collection. Similar analogies could be offered for other inspection PM.

Manufacturer (and Staff) Defined. Determine when it was defined, and whether there have been any substantive modifications to the equipment that might impact PM practices and intervals. Update as appropriate for those modifications. Challenge the manufacturer as to the statistical basis for his recommended PM intervals, any failure modes and effects or RCM analysis, and the assumptions underlying his recommendations. Review your equipment histories and determine if they support the manufacturer recommendations. Apply predictive and proactive methods to increase, or optimize current intervals and practices.

PMs During Scheduled Outages or Turnarounds. Review equipment histories to understand indications of potential needs. Review equipment condition information, not just the predictive technologies, but also operator knowledge and other plant staff knowledge. Actively seek their input. Establish a proactive process for performing the PM itself. Do only what is necessary, considering the risk of waiting until the next outage (planned or unplanned).

Case Histories

Beta's Abner Mountain plant was a very large facility, which had 5 key steps in the production process. One of these steps was a precipitation process that contained ten separate vessels. A natural consequence of the production process was scaling of the vessels used in the precipitation process. Because of this, each vessel required descaling, which was currently being performed every 30 days. The question was posed concerning the 30-day descaling schedule—Why every 30 days? It seems that the descaling took 3 days, and they had 10 vessels, so the total time to clean all the vessels was one month. It was a matter of convenience. Unfortunately, the vessels were unaware of the convenience issue, because they didn't operate according to the Gregorian calendar in use in the civilized world, but rather according to process conditions. On further discussion, it was found that the scale build-up could be correlated to the process. With that awareness in hand, the Abner Mountain plant began to measure scale build-up and correlate it to process condition, increasing the interval for descaling by over 10% and providing a commensurate increase in uptime, improving operating income by $3M per year.

A point of interest here—Why do we schedule activities on a daily, weekly, monthly, quarterly, annual basis? Because that's how we live our lives. Yet as noted, the equipment in any plant does not operate with any link to the Gregorian calendar by which we live. Scheduling PM activities on a 30-day basis could just as well be scheduled on a 34.72-day basis. The point is that as a practical matter we must live on a daily, weekly, etc. basis, but our equipment doesn't follow this regimen, and we must use better condition monitoring, equipment histories, understanding of process condition, proactive methods to optimize our efforts, not simply follow the calendar on an arbitrary basis, etc.

Another point of interest—Why does plant equipment seem to fail when we're not there? If we only work 40 hours a week, and there are 168 hours in a week, then there are 128 out of 168 hours that we're not there, resulting in a 76.2% probability that we won't be in the plant when the failure occurs, but will be called in for an emergency. Another good reason for condition monitoring technology to help make sure we know about a pending failure well in advance so we can get the equipment corrected during normal hours.

Beta's Estill plant had 84 extrusion machines, that received a PM on a weekly basis, which took some 4 hours to perform. Again, this weekly PM did seem to help them improve uptime, but was not related to equipment histories and was not backed by equipment condition monitoring. It was arbitrarily based on the resources available and their ability to maintain the equipment on that schedule. The suggestion was made to increase the interval from every 7 to every 8 days. If no significant increase in downtime occurred after a suitable time period, then increase the period to 9 days, and so on. The recommendation was also made to put in place some condition monitoring technologies, including operator observations and control charts; to develop quick change over techniques; to proactively seek more reliable processes and equipment, such as precision balancing, alignment, and installation of the equipment, so that over the long term, the process could be truly optimized. Beta's Estill plant has achieved substantial reduction in equipment downtime, and continues to implement these methods.

Other examples could be cited, but this should be adequate to illustrate the process.

Mechanical Integrity

As noted in the introduction and discussed in additional detail in Reference 5, the advent of OSHA regulations on process safety management per 29 CFR 1910, Section 119j, Mechanical Integrity, has provided increased emphasis on mechanical integrity of equipment which contains hazardous material. Indeed, it is easy to infer from Section 119j that run-to-failure is not an acceptable mode for maintenance practices, because run-to-failure carries a substantial increase in the risk of release of hazardous materials. The principle motivation for having good reliability in mechanical equipment should be to provide maximum capacity at a minimum cost. However, in many companies the reactive culture is so inherent in the behavior of people that simple economic motivators for a reliability strategy may not be sufficient, particularly when the benefit is often long term, and the pressure to "get the machine back on line" is intense.

However, these regulations may represent an opportunity. If you do have hazardous materials on site, you can use that fact, combined with OSHA Mechanical Integrity requirements, to assure good PM practices, and provide a regulatory "driver" for optimizing the PM process.

Section 119j requires a mechanical integrity program, which includes requirements for written procedures defining all test and inspection requirements, frequencies, record keeping, alerting to overdue inspections, training, quality assurance standards for installation, replacement parts, vendor/supplier qualifications, etc. Making comprehensive use of a computerized maintenance management system, applying a comprehensive reliability strategy, optimizing the PM process using the methodology previously described, will help assure mechanical integrity in a given plant's equipment. *Mechanical integrity is a natural consequence of applying good reliability and maintenance practices.* Maintenance managers should apply that rationale to their advantage.

Summary

The model provided above for optimizing the PM process should be straightforward to apply, but like most worthwhile efforts will take considerable time. It involves systematic use of:

1. A CMMS to manage the maintenance and reliability process, including comprehensive development of histories for analysis of your equipment PM requirements.
2. Condition monitoring technology and operator information to validate the need for PM, validate the quality of the work done, and detect early onset of failure.
3. Proactive methodologies to eliminate the root cause of failures, minimize or mitigate the need for PM, and eliminate defects in equipment and production methods.

In this manner you can position your plant to procure, store, install, operate, and maintain reliable equipment, assuring optimal PM practices, and mechanical integrity.

References

1. Hudachek, R. J. and Dodd, V. R. "Progress and Payout of a Machinery Surveillance and Diagnostic Program," *Mechanical Engineering,* vol. 99, no. 1, 1977.
2. Carey, K. "Systematic Maintenance Strategies." Institute of Industrial Engineer's 11th International Maintenance Conference, Nashville, TN, October, 1994.
3. Moore, R., Pardue, F., Pride, A. and Wilson, J. "The Reliability-Based Maintenance Strategy: A Vision For Improving Industrial Productivity." CSI Industry Report, Knoxville, TN, 1993.
4. Moore, R. Optimizing the PM Process, *Maintenance Technology,* Barrington, IL, January, 1996.
5. Moore, R. "Reliability and Process Safety Management," *Facilities,* vol. 22, no. 5, Cincinatti, OH, Sept./Oct., 1995.

Implementing a Computerized Maintenance Management System

Profound knowledge comes from the outside, and by invitation. A system cannot know itself.

—*W. Edwards Deming*

Most executives wouldn't dream of running their company without an effective computerized accounting and financial management system, and yet many routinely run their production equipment without an effective computerized asset management system for the maintenance and reliability (and cost) of their equipment, often valued in the 100's of millions. This chapter describes how one of Beta's Divisions accomplished that task.

Beta, like most medium-to-large manufacturing organizations, has put in place a computerized maintenance management system (CMMS) at most of its plants, with informal surveys indicating that over 90% of its plants have some form of a CMMS in place. However, a closer review of those plants and questions about the specific use of their systems revealed that most—

1. Are not using the CMMS for all appropriate equipment in their plant. For most plants some 25–75% of equipment is not in the database, and therefore not maintained using the CMMS.

2. Are using the CMMS primarily for issuing work orders and scheduling work, but often not using it for comprehensive planning, or for development of equipment repair and cost histories, or for performing Pareto analyses to help prioritize resources, etc.
3. May be poorly trained in the systematic use by all the appropriate staff of all the capabilities of a good CMMS.
4. Don't fully apply many of the other tools available, e.g., stores and purchasing interface, resource allocation, document retrieval, etc.

Many times, someone was told to go buy a system and use it—a kind of magic elixir for the ills of the maintenance department.

This type of behavior reflects a symptomatic response to maintenance issues vs. a systematic approach, fairly typical with most manufacturers. The logic seems to be "If we just do...., then everything will get better." You fill in the blank with the flavor of the month. It's much like treating a cough with cough drops so the cough goes away, rather than understanding that the patient has pneumonia and requires long-term rehabilitation.

Few companies at the beginning of a CMMS implementation effort recognize that a CMMS is no more than a very sophisticated software shell, which is empty at the beginning—user's must fill the shell with data, and then train most of their staff to assure its effective use. Beta was no exception. Another way of thinking about this would be buying a word processing program and expecting that books would be more readily developed. Certainly they could be, but the word processing software is just a tool to facilitate the creative process.

In fact, the way many of Beta's maintenance departments were using their CMMS, they could achieve the same result with a word processing package, which usually has a calendar to schedule and issue work orders. This is not recommended, but serves to highlight the effectiveness of many CMMS's in use. Something is wrong with this, considering the millions that are being spent for CMMS programs. The fault lies not in the vendors, so much as in the expectations and implementation process of the users. Users must understand that a CMMS is only a shell, which must be filled with data, and then used in a comprehensive way for effective maintenance management. A CMMS won't solve equipment reliability problems any more than an accounting system will solve cash flow problems. Both are systems that must be filled with data, data which are subsequently analyzed and used to good effect.

A good CMMS is most effective when used for:

1. Work order management—scope, effort, trades, procedures, permits, schedule, etc. (more than just issuing work orders).
2. Scheduling of essentially all work, and planning major efforts parts', tools, procedures, skills (not just scheduling).
3. Equipment management, especially cost and repair histories; and bills of material for each piece of equipment, and their related spare parts.
4. Use of equipment histories for Pareto analyses, prioritization and allocation of resources, and identification of key equipment needing root cause failure analysis.
5. Purchasing and stores management for spares, "kitting," planning, and reliability improvement.
6. Document control and ready access to manuals, schematics, procedures.
7. Resource allocation for effective reliability, production, and cost management.

Moreover, preventive maintenance in the classical sense of fixed interval tasks is typically non-optimal—How many of your machines are truly "average"? How often are you over- or undermaintaining using a mean time between failure approach? As we've seen, the data, when available, typically suggest that less than 10% of most equipment life is near the average life for that class of equipment.

As noted previously, preventive maintenance is best:

1. When used in conjunction with a strong statistical basis, e.g., low standard deviations from average for a strong wear-related failure mode; and when condition assessment is used to validate the need for the PM.
2. When condition assessment is not practical or cost effective.
3. For routine inspections and minor PM's, but even then could be optimized.
4. For instrument calibrations, but even then could be optimized by tracking calibration histories.
5. For some manufacturer PM's—that is, those the manufacturer can back up with definitive statistical data.
6. For some staff-defined PM's—likewise, those backed up with definitive statistical data.

7. For regulatory driven requirements, e.g., OSHA 1910, 119j., code requirements, etc., but even then could be optimized with histories and effective condition monitoring.

One last point before proceeding with Beta's case history—a CMMS is no more than a tool, and tools don't provide discipline—processes do! A disciplined maintenance process must be put in place for the tool to be effective, not vice versa.

Case History

With this in mind, this section provides a case history of how Beta International's specialty products division (SPD) with limited previous experience in computerized maintenance management systems effectively implemented its CMMS to help assure lower maintenance costs, higher staff productivity, and improved equipment reliability.

SPD was faced with an extraordinary set of problems—reduced revenues, increased costs, lower capital and operating budgets; and a maintenance department with:

• Expensive breakdowns
• Little planning and scheduling
• Excessive forms, paperwork, and bureaucracy
• Limited equipment histories
• Superficial replacement/repair criteria
• Minimal equipment failure analysis
• Ineffective resource allocation criteria
• Limited control of maintenance costs
• Limited measures of performance or effectiveness

Or, as the saying goes, "Other than that, they were pretty good."

Clearly, something had to be done to improve this situation, and it was viewed by the company as a major "opportunity" for improvement. A part of the solution to this opportunity was to develop a more effective maintenance function, one which provided greater control, improved reliability of the equipment, and greater teamwork between maintenance and operations.

The first decision made was to put in place a computerized maintenance management system—a fairly typical step. However, to assure the effectiveness of this decision, SPD put together a strategic plan that defined:

1. A process for CMMS selection.
2. Potential impediments and their resolution.
3. A process for implementation.
4. A method for measurement of results.
5. A continuous improvement process that would assure successful implementation beyond initial successes, and not just be viewed another "magic bullet."

Preliminary Authorization and Selection

Initially, management gave tentative authorization to select and purchase a CMMS. Prior to making this decision, the selection committee made several site visits to review various vendor products in a real working environment. Their conclusion from this review was that they didn't know how to effectively select a system. This led to hiring a consulting specialist for their selection team to facilitate the specification of the CMMS that would meet their needs. After considerable effort defining their needs and processes, they finalized a specification and put forth a request for proposal (RFP) to several vendors.

After reviewing the proposals, they narrowed their selection process down to a few vendors who performed office demos of their products. From there they narrowed the list even further by performing site visits, *without* the vendor, to validate vendor representations, to see the systems in action, to use the systems in a working environment, and to assure themselves that the system they might choose was effectively employed by others, and would meet their requirements.

Selection Criteria

The selection process and criteria went beyond the site visits and vendor demos. Specifically, the selection criteria included:

Value:

1. Conformance to the RFP (including a client server system architecture)
2. Features and functions (including using the system at a working site)
3. User friendly (or hostile) characteristics (using the system at a working site)
4. Vendor support systems (including calling as a customer and evaluating the support)

5. Vendor training (including attending a training class before purchase)
6. User satisfaction with the system/results (vendor's five, plus a random selection)
7. Vendor customer base (total number of customers served)
8. Vendor financial strength

Cost:

1. Initial cost
2. Continuing costs—training, upgrades, phone support, etc.

Primary decision criteria: Value took priority over cost, so long as cost was within a reasonable range. Low bid was not the criteria. Finally, they found that the actual implementation cost was approximately four times the initial software cost. *Managers take note:* The implementation process is considerably more expensive than the initial cost and should be considered in the decision making process.

Impediments and Solutions

There were several impediments to the project from the beginning, each of which was addressed effectively:

1. Culture of the organization:

    a. "If it ain't broke . . ."; or its brother—"We've always done it this way."
    b. Prospective job change requirements with the union.
    c. "You can't plan maintenance."

2. Management support and resources—staff and capital

Clearly, from the discussion, "it" was broken, and with the loss of revenue and climbing costs, something had to be done. Other efforts were ongoing to improve market share, develop new technology, improve operations, etc. And, this effort was part of an overall effort for improved maintenance practices, which necessarily included predictive and proactive practices.

The union was approached with the concept of using a CMMS for solving their inherent system problems, to make their jobs easier, to reduce the time spent at the parts counter, to have equipment isolated when they arrived, to have the tools available, etc. Reduced revenues, climbing costs, and "broken" processes were all basic drivers for change in the organization. Reluctantly, but with assurances that the process was not targeting head count reduction, they proceeded with implementing a CMMS. Any head count reduction requirements would be managed using attrition, reduced contract labor, lower overtime, and reduced contracting of small capital projects. Performance measures were finally concluded to be the only effective way to measure the success of the implementation process, but only after considerable discussion and negotiation. One fear the union had was that the system, once implemented, would be used to "bid out" all the work to contractors, because it was now all defined in the CMMS. Union leaders were assured that this was not the case, and required routine re-assuring of this. This effort required a continued fostering of trust between union leadership and management.

As noted, "it" was broken. Management was convinced that something had to be done, and authorized the initial study to determine what, how, when, who, where, how much, potential benefit, etc. Following this study, they authorized proceeding with the principal project to specify, purchase, and install the system on a pilot plant, which would in turn be used as the model for the remaining six plants, a total of seven plants having the CMMS installed.

More importantly, however, they recognized that simply installing a system would not be effective without a systematic plan for implementation and continuous improvement, and achieving acceptance by the union and shop floor of the CMMS implementation process. Union support would be needed, because they were responsible for much of the data entry, work orders, repair codes, closing of jobs, etc. To that end, they set up the following:

- Implementation at a pilot plant
- User group, consisting of a representative from each plant
- Newsletter—announcing purpose, successes, failures, actions
- "Continuous" periodic training to update learning
- Routine meetings to address gossip, rumors, perceptions, problems
- Staged approach for easing the effects of change
- Implementation committee for facilitating implementation

Pilot Plant Implementation

One of the first steps was to select a pilot plant for implementation. After much consideration, and developing the confidence that the implementation would be successful, they selected a mid-sized plant that had processes similar to its largest plant. This plant was more manageable and would permit proving the process and technology prior to full implementation. At the same time, they had one representative from each of the other plants join the implementation committee from the beginning to assure other plant needs were met, and that when they began the implementation process, they would have a first-hand understanding of all the major issues that had arisen at the pilot plant. The representative in fact would be responsible for implementation at their plant.

They set initial expectations and goals as to the timing of the implementation, the training required, the potential cost reduction available, and initial schedules for achieving these goals. Start-up activities included:

1. A complete inventory of equipment
2. Definition of initial PMs and procedures
3. Solicitation of departmental support from management and skilled trades
4. Routine informational meetings

Routine informational meetings were very important to explain the objectives and implementation process, to address any rumors, gossip, or misperceptions, to explain the training that would be done, and so on. Rumors and gossip could take on a life of their own, and needed to be addressed quickly and definitively. The consulting specialist continued to facilitate the implementation process and to serve as an outside sounding board and objective mediator on issues of concern.

Committees were created to discuss major issues, to back informational meetings with written word about plans and processes, to discuss successes, and "failures"—including the course of action related to any "failure," and to generally inform all employees of the system.

Procedures

PM procedures were developed using:

• Equipment manuals
• Interviews with appropriate staff
• Discussions with vendors
• Better definition of work requirements
• Better application of predictive technologies
• Better definition of staffing and material/parts needs

Purchasing software was linked to the CMMS, and included stores management. Material planning and an automated pick list and kitting were made a part of the work order process.

Equipment Database. The criteria used to determine whether or not a particular piece of equipment was to be put into the CMMS database were:

1. Is a history of the equipment needed?
2. Is a PM required for the equipment?
3. Will an operator be able to readily identify the equipment?

Based on these criteria, some 20,000+ pieces of equipment were put into the database for all plants. At the largest (and oldest) plant, some 8,000+ items were put into the database over a two-year period using approximately 8–10,000 labor hours.

Use of the System. Skilled trades routinely did their own time reporting, entered work requests directly, entered closing remarks, and closed jobs out. Backlog was reviewed routinely and used to manage trade work assignments, grouping jobs, planning resources, etc. Management routinely used the system to review equipment histories, and to generally manage maintenance activities. Performance measures included backlog, completed work orders, overtime, aged backlog, work order status, work schedule status, actual/planned hours, PM effectiveness, maintenance cost by area, average cost per work order, contractor costs, etc.

Other Issues. In retrospect, the selection of a client server system architecture was essential to the successful implementation of the system, allowing for sharing of data system-wide. However, the ability to integrate various software packages effectively was more difficult than originally anticipated. This will be reviewed in some detail as part of any future systems implementation process.

Results

The results were remarkable. When combined with other efforts, such as predictive and proactive methods, and improved operational practices, they achieved:

1. Acceptance and use of the system by the skilled trades, by management, and by engineering.
2. Better prioritization of work, scheduling, planning, backlog management and resource allocation.
3. Improved equipment histories for better repair/replace decisions, root cause failure analysis, accounting of costs by process and by machine type.
4. Improved accountability at all levels where they were measuring performance.
5. Improved stores management and lower inventory levels, and improved equipment reliability.
6. Much more effective maintenance—better procedures, reduced paperwork, reduced reactive maintenance through preventive maintenance, and elimination of standing work orders (which had been a black hole for money).

The pilot plant became the plant with the lowest unit cost of production among the seven plants:

1. Labor hours per job were reduced by 25%.
2. Job completion times were reduced by 20%.
3. Contract labor was reduced by 60%.
4. Work order volume was actually up 35%, with the elimination of standing work orders

Total Cost Savings Amounted to Well Over $6,000,000.
Clearly, effective implementation and use of a computerized maintenance management system can provide extraordinary benefits to a company. To achieve these benefits, however, a systematic process must be implemented to assure proper system selection, implementation, and use. This process also must be combined with predictive and proactive methods, and must fully integrate the engineering, operations, purchasing functions.

Reference

1. Moore, R. "Implementing a Computerized Maintenance Management System," *Reliability*, Knoxville, TN, Directory Issue, 1996.

Effective Use of Contractors in a Manufacturing Plant

The best laid schemes o'mice and men gang aft agley.

—*Robert Burns*

At one of Beta's major plants, consolidating maintenance contractors, and simultaneously going through a downsizing at a large manufacturing plant did not achieve the results expected. Indeed, through no fault of the contractor per se, the results were significantly worse than the prior year's performance, were no better than the prior two years, and at last report, the plant was still struggling to meet expectations.[1,2]

The Reliability Improvement Program

Three years ago Beta's Maytown plant began a focused effort to improve manufacturing performance. Particular attention was given to improved plant reliability and its potential impact on improved uptime and lower maintenance costs. Revenues of several $100M's were generated, and included a respectable profit on sales. Hence, the company was not faced with a financial crisis, and was simply taking prudent action to assure its long-term financial health.

Over the next several months, certain performance measures were put in place and specific actions taken to improve maintenance performance. These included, among many efforts, measuring uptime and the causes of lost uptime, as well as implementation of certain maintenance improvement tools such as: (1) maintenance planning and scheduling and routine PM activities; (2) specific predictive maintenance technologies; (3) more proactive efforts, such as root cause failure analysis, precision alignment and balancing of critical equipment; (4) operator PM efforts to improve equipment basic care and to relieve maintenance of several routine tasks; (5) assignment of a manufacturing reliability engineer to facilitate the implementation of these practices in a comprehensive manner. In effect, this Beta plant used the reliability strategy described herein as part of a broad improvement process.

These efforts showed substantial improvement over the following year, and as shown in Figures 12-1 through 12-5. Note: (1) Some data were not available for certain months early in the process due to delays in implementing the measurement system, and/or overlaps in different data collection systems; and (2) Some data may have a one month or so lag time between the event and recording the information, and hence may be slightly non-synchronous.

Uptime, Figure 12-1. Maintaining high uptime had become increasingly difficult, with uptimes typically 70% or higher, but rarely better than 80%. Following the implementation of the reliability program, uptimes improved steadily to a peak of 88%, averaging 82% from December through August of the following year.

Maintenance Costs, Figure 12-2. Reviewing the 3-month rolling average chart for maintenance costs, from October till August of the following year, maintenance costs trended steadily downward after implementing reliability practices, going from $980K per month to $480K per month.

Maintenance Efforts by Type, Figure 12-3. Reactive maintenance dropped from about 70% in mid year to about 30% in August the following year. The reduction in reactive maintenance, which typically costs twice that of planned maintenance, was a result of implementing specific preventive (time-based) maintenance, predictive (condition-based) maintenance, and proactive (root-cause-based) maintenance practices in an integrated, comprehensive way. In particular predictive, or condition-based, was used to confirm the need for scheduled efforts, to trend the condition of equipment, to diagnose the root cause of certain repeated problems, and in general to balance the need for preventive and proactive maintenance, making it more optimal.

Maintenance Purchases/Stores Issues, Figure 12-4. Purchasing/stores was estimated to be trending downward between July and August of the following year, consistent with the trend in overall maintenance costs.

Safety Performance, Figure 12-5. Considerable progress had been made in safety performance, and the company had achieved an OSHA recordable injury rate of ~ 3 per 200K labor hours through August. A peak of rate of 9 in June was attributed to a shutdown and extraordinarily high level of maintenance.

Consolidating Maintenance Contractors

In parallel with the reliability program, the company's purchasing department in the second quarter of year 1 made a determination that considerable money could be saved by consolidating contractors on site, reducing the administrative and management effort associated with those contractors. It was felt that this was particularly true for maintenance and related contractors, such as minor capital and construction projects. The decision was made in June and the consolidation process began in September.

Simultaneously, at the corporate level, considerable benchmarking had been performed with the conclusion, among other things, that maintenance costs were too high, and that productivity (units of product per employee) was too low. After considerable debate among

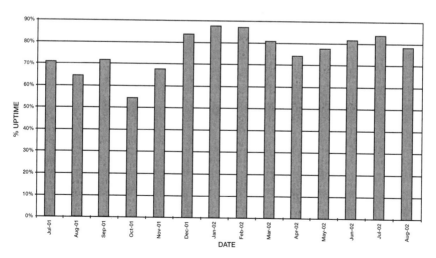

Figure 12-1. Uptime.

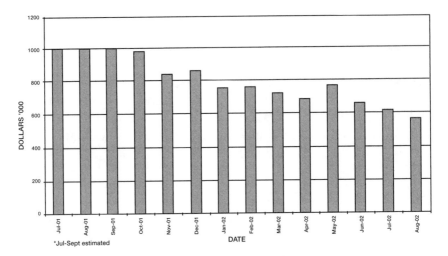

Figure 12-2. Maintenance cost.

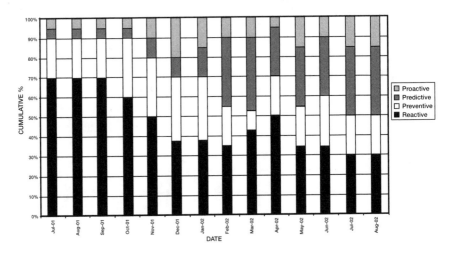

Figure 12-3. Maintenance effort by type.

management, and apparently unable to wait long enough to realize the full benefit of the reliability improvement process that was already established, the decision was made to cut the number of employees, with maintenance employees reduced by about half.

Following these decisions, performance did not improve. Indeed, performance initially deteriorated, and is now only back to about

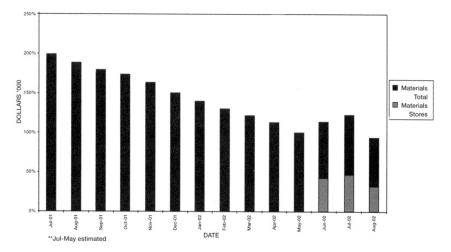

Figure 12-4. Maintenance purchases/stores issues.

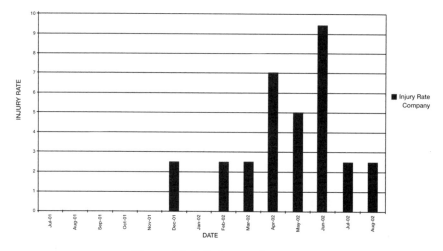

Figure 12-5. Safety performance.

where it was some two years ago. Figures 12-6 through 12-11 provide details of "before and after" performance.

Uptime, Figure 12-6. Uptime dropped immediately to about 65%, and then rose gradually to near 86%, dropping thereafter to an average of about 75% for the period September to June. However, it

text continued on page 236

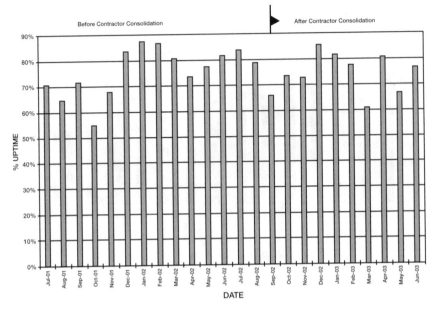

Figure 12-6. Uptime.

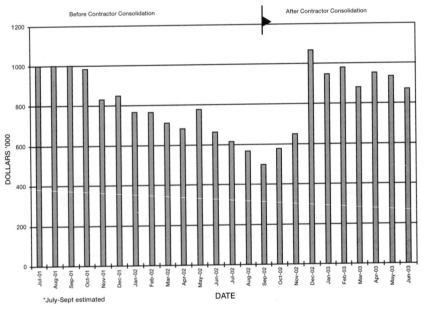

Figure 12-7. Maintenance cost.

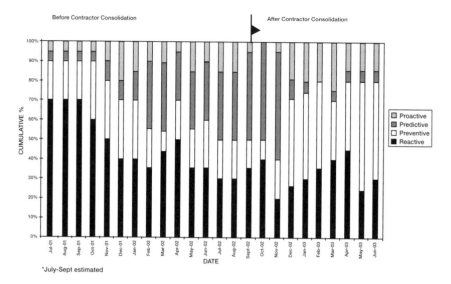

Figure 12-8. Maintenance effort by type.

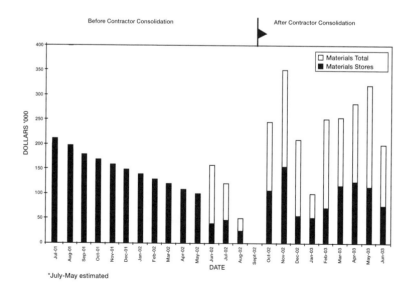

Figure 12-9. Maintenance purchases/stores issues.

should be highlighted that the immediate drop in uptime in September was related to two specific equipment failure events (a large motor and a heat exchanger), and those specific events should not be attributed to the consolidation effort, or to the downsizing effort. As luck would have it, however, the timing of these failures was very inopportune. And, nonetheless, the plant had great difficulty recovering to levels of performance prior to the downsizing and contractor consolidation. Overall, uptime dropped from about 82% to 75% following these actions.

Maintenance Costs, Figure 12-7. In the first quarter of maintenance contractor consolidation, maintenance costs soared to over $1,080K by December, over twice August and September's levels, and even significantly above costs a year prior when the reliability improvement program began. As of June, '03, maintenance costs were still at $880K per month, at a comparable level to where we were in October, '01, nearly two years prior. In effect, after nearly two years for effort, maintenance costs had not improved, and in fact had increased substantially from about a year prior.

Maintenance Levels by Type, Figure 12-8. Likewise, the level of reactive maintenance had trended downward until August, '02, even continuing downward into November to some 20%. However, as the contractor increased their staffing levels and work efforts, predictive maintenance was essentially eliminated, giving way to time-based, or preventive, maintenance, because the contractor was apparently not familiar with condition based maintenance methods for trending, diagnosing, commissioning, etc., for improved maintenance performance. Coincidentally, *reactive levels also began to rise* peaking in May, '03 at over 40%, and comparable to where we had been in early '02, *in spite of substantially increased PM efforts.* Indeed, some studies indicate a 10–20% probability of introducing defects into equipment using a preventive, or time based maintenance approach, as opposed to condition based. This occurs when equipment that is *not* in need of overhaul or repair is in fact overhauled on a time-based approach, and defects are introduced in the process. Hence, sharply reducing the predictive efforts in favor of preventive (time-based) maintenance appears to have had the effect of increasing reactive maintenance and maintenance costs.

Materials Expenditures, Figure 12-9. Stores issues and purchase orders for maintenance parts rose substantially from '02 levels, or

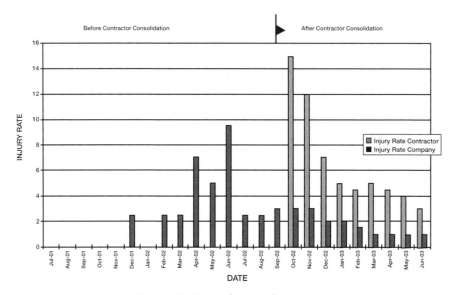

Figure 12-10. Safety performance.

about double what they had been to some $300K per month. Further, purchase order expenses now represent about $150K of the total, or about half. This is considered to reflect contractors not understanding the stores system; or preferring use of purchase orders; or stores not having the material required; or some combination.

Safety Performance, Figure 12-10. Contractor injury rate initially soared to five times that of employees, but has since improved to three times worse than that for employees.

Scheduled Maintenance, Figure 12-11. Maintenance that was scheduled was initially less than 20%, but rose substantially to a peak of near 75%, thereafter deteriorating to near 65%.

All in all, performance has been substantially below expectations by almost any measure—worse than a year ago before the consolidated contractor came on board, and no better than two years ago, when reliability concepts were first introduced to the company.

What Happened?

There were many factors at work, many of which were beyond the control of the contractor. The basis for bringing in the new contractor

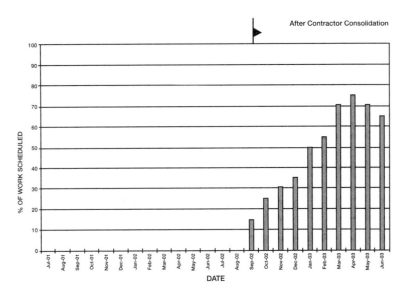

Figure 12-11. Scheduled maintenance.

was driven by a need to consolidate contractors to save money, and perhaps to a lesser extent a perception among some that labor costs for contractors were cheaper than in-house labor. In fact, costs actually increased dramatically following consolidation of contractors. The factors associated with this are discussed below. No particular order of importance or magnitude of importance should be attached to the order of presentation. Rather, it should be viewed as the confluence of a set of these circumstances which lead to less than adequate performance, and should be seriously considered when evaluating the use of contractors in the future.

Contractor Experience. The contractor's staff had limited experience with the plant or equipment that they were maintaining. As a result, a substantial learning curve was necessary for becoming familiar with plant equipment, policies, procedures, practices, location, etc. Further, the contractors had limited experience with use of condition monitoring (predictive maintenance) to help optimize time-based maintenance—not too soon, or too late. As a result, they relied primarily on a preventive, or time-based, approach to maintenance, which is typically not optimal in and of itself. This is evidenced by the increase in reactive maintenance levels, which occurred concurrent with (and in spite of) a substantial increase in time-based maintenance. Condition monitoring should be routinely applied to verify that the maintenance task is necessary, to delay doing some tasks, and to validate the quality of the work performed during start-up and commissioning. Finally, many of the contractor staff were taken from the construction ranks, where different work processes and methods are practiced, resulting in a more difficult transition into an operating plant.

Displaced Contractors. Many existing contractors, who were in effect being eliminated, remained on the job for about three months after bringing in the new contractor who would be consolidating contract maintenance. Their motivation in assisting the new contractor was limited. Not surprisingly, existing contractor charges increased substantially during this "transition period" prior to their departure. A transition period may be prudent, but better management may have helped mitigate these costs.

Shutdown Impact. Just prior to the advent of the new consolidated contractor, a major shutdown of the entire plant had occurred, which included major maintenance efforts, as well as bringing on line a major new production process. The start-up was difficult and time consuming, leaving few resources to manage the integration of the new consolidated maintenance contractor. All this was concurrent with a major downsizing, and the attendant morale problems inherent in such a change. Confusion was substantial, and morale/productivity were low.

Transition Process. The process for introducing and integrating the contractor with the plant's work management process, methods, practices, etc., was poor. There was inadequate understanding of the work order process used at the plant, of the planning and scheduling process, of the CMMS currently in use, etc. There was insufficient management interface, because of the shutdown and start-up efforts, to allow for adequate communication and management of the integration effort.

Major Equipment Failures. Two major equipment failures occurred just as the consolidation, and downsizing processes were beginning, resulting in a large drop in uptime. The timing of the failures was at best inopportune, likely resulting in delays and additional costs during the transition process. Indeed, as noted, the plant struggled to fully recover to previous uptime levels.

Loss of Key Management Staff. Concurrent with the arrival of the contractor, two key managers at the plant transferred, exacerbating the overall management process and contractor integration.

Loss of Skilled Staff. Many of the employees lost in the downsizing were skilled in maintaining the plant equipment, but began to leave just about the same time as the contractor consolidation began. Morale was quite low, and the enthusiasm for working with and "training" the new contractors was limited.

Current Situation

As the old saying goes, "You can't go back." The plant has gone through the effort of bringing in, training, and integrating a consolidated contractor, whose people are now at last familiar with the equipment, work process, policies, etc. to perform in a reasonably effective manner. However, costs are still substantially above what they should be for world-class performance; are above what they were a year ago when the contractor arrived; and are above what the contractor targeted for achievement at the time of their arrival.

Given this, the Maytown plant will (and should) continue to use the contractor to support world-class performance. However, in the short term more regular and intensive meetings will occur with the contractor to establish and continuously improve on the relationship, and to create clearer expectations. At this point, making the contractor an integral part of the operation is a necessity, not an option; and establishing expectations and performance measures targeted at world-class performance is also a necessity, not an option. These performance measures will be "value added" type measures described later. The guiding principle behind these measures is that *the contractor must deliver an effect, not simply supply a service for a fee.* Effects desired include improved equipment life, higher availability and uptime, lower maintenance costs per unit of contractor supply (e.g., normalized to account for issues such as total assets under their care, or total product produced), excellent safety performance, etc. In other words, the contractor will be held to the same high standards as the balance of the organization, and become a genuine partner in the plant's success. For example, measures of effect (and success) will include:

- Uptime (increasing)
- Production losses (units, $) resulting from equipment downtime (decreasing)
- Maintenance cost as a percent of unit cost of product (decreasing)
- Maintenance cost as a percent of asset replacement value (decreasing)
- Mean time between repairs, e.g., average equipment life (increasing)
- Overtime hours percentage (decreasing)
- Rework effort, nonconformance reports, warranty claims (decreasing)
- Safety record, injury rate (decreasing)
- Housekeeping (improving)
- Permit failures, work rule violations (decreasing)
- Grievances (decreasing)
- Turnover (decreasing)

The contractor will also be required to provide certification of skill type and level for each person provided, as well as assure that personnel are properly trained in safety practices and policies.

A fresh look will be taken of the plant's operation, and firm leadership will be exercised, particularly regarding expectations of contractor performance. Maintenance excellence is not an option, it is a requirement. To achieve this (which is not just doing a lot of PM), a balanced maintenance program will be reestablished including greater application of predictive and proactive methods. Greater teamwork between maintenance and operations will also be established, and teamwork will be required between both functions with a view to work collectively to eliminate losses from ideal. Too much is at stake for the success of the business. Therefore, the plant, in cooperation with the contractor, will assure that:

1. A strong predictive, or condition-based, maintenance program, including operator input of equipment and process condition, is reestablished.
2. Existing PM tactics are reviewed with the intent to optimize them. Maintenance planning and scheduling will be tempered with good condition monitoring and the quality of the maintenance effort will be validated with a commissioning process.
3. Operations personnel will become much more involved in the operational reliability and the things they can do to improve performance, including operator PM as appropriate. Operational excellence is also a requirement, not an option.

Lessons Learned

Beta's lessons learned are substantial, and may be summarized as follows:

1. Maintenance is a core competency, and may be difficult to consolidate in contractors.
2. When bringing in a contractor, a specific integration process must be established that includes training and indoctrination of the contractor in, and holding the contractor accountable for:

   • General company policies and procedures.
   • Company work practices, use of its CMMS, planning and scheduling, etc.
   • Continuation of and/or use of certain technologies and methods, e.g., predictive maintenance tools, alignment and balancing, etc.
   • Certification of skills determined by the company to be required for the contract.
   • Company safety performance.
   • Use of company procedures for material and parts procurement.

This process should include a specific individual on site who is held accountable for assuring a smooth integration of the contractor into the work processes, e.g., a project manager.

3. Success-based performance measures and expectations must be established at the front end that define the *effect* that the contractor will deliver.
4. Consolidation of contractors is a substantial change in the organization, and should generally *not* be done concurrently with other major changes, e.g., immediately following a major shutdown and during a start-up period; transfer of key management personnel (for other than disciplinary reasons).
5. Displacing existing contractors also needs a process for integration of and/or elimination of the need for those contractors who are being displaced. It is not sufficient to allow them to define the integration process. This task should also be the responsibility of the project manager for the the contractor consolidation process.
6. If contractors are consolidated during a downsizing, recognize that the employees who are leaving are not likely to be enthused about transferring their knowledge. Morale will likely decline, and this is a "cost" that must be considered.

Even in the best of circumstances, major changes to any "system" will always result in transitory effects—the system will generally get worse before it gets better. This too is a cost that should be considered in the decision-making process. This case study provides an order of magnitude estimate of the cost effects that could occur, and will help avoid those costs. Perhaps the best policy would be to avoid the costs in the first place. *Simply replacing one set of warm bodies with another will not necessarily deliver the effect desired. The processes that result in improved performance must be put in place.* Beta has learned from this exercise, and as a result has developed a policy statement regarding the best use of contractors.

Best Use of Contractors

In many organizations today, the heavy focus on cost cutting has lead to an increased emphasis the use of contractors, or in some cases, contractor consolidation, as a potential solution for reducing overall costs. Moreover, in recent years maintenance in particular has been the subject of increased attention for using maintenance contractors for the replacement of maintenance employees. While that was not the intention in this case, replacing employees with contractors has occurred at several Beta plants worldwide.

As you might expect, the use of contractors in many of Beta's manufacturing plants and facilities has been a sore point with the skilled trades, and particularly in a strong union environment . While some of this may be normal tension between the "shop floor" and contractors, particularly during a time of downsizing, the intensity appears to be growing as more contractors come into use. Further, many skilled trades working in Beta's chemical plants or other hazardous areas express concerns similar to those related to the Value Jet crash, which according to the *Wall Street Journal*[3] ". . . raised troubling questions about the safety implications of such penny-pinching practices as contracting out maintenance, hiring less-experienced workers, and focusing less intensely on training." This clearly begs the question—Are contractors appropriate for a given manufacturing organization?

The answer is clearly yes, for in almost all organizations contractors play a critical, if not essential, role. However, given the experience cited, caution is urged for all organizations and how they assure effective use of contractors. Lower head count and/or lower charge rates from contractors (consolidated or otherwise) may not be the only issue to consider. The real question about the use of contractors is how do they support corporate goals related to manufacturing excellence, such as uptime, unit cost of production, safety performance, maintenance cost as a % of plant replacement value, etc. What is the risk in using (or not using) contractors relative to these goals? What specific roles are best suited for contractors? What processes are used to integrate contractors into an overall business strategy? Does a simple cost-cutting strategy work?

As outlined in Chapter 1, a simple cost-cutting strategy has a low probability of providing the manufacturing improvements desired. Further, the better companies have concluded that equipment reliability and uptime should take priority over cost cutting, and that maintenance contribution to uptime is worth ten times the potential for cost reduction. *But,* the expectation is still clear—lower costs will result from applying best practice.

Moreover, Schuyler[4] reports that reducing maintenance costs, with no change in maintenance strategy, results in a reduction in mechanical availability (and presumably a reduction in plant uptime and/or increase in plant costs), and states that ". . . the only way to simultaneously reduce maintenance costs and increase mechanical availability is to move toward more proactive maintenance strategies." See Figure 9-11 for an illustration of this concept.

Replacing the maintenance function (or any function for that matter) with contractors may not be the proper strategic decision. For example, would you replace your operations function with contractors? Your engineering function? Your accounting function? Are they "core"? Why would Beta not view the years (perhaps decades) of experience developed by its maintenance function as part of a core competency, much the same as they do the other functions? At Beta, as well as many other manufacturing organizations, maintenance is indeed coming to be viewed as a core competency for manufacturing excellence, which is as it should be. Given this, what is the proper use of contractors? Good contractors have a place in most organizations, and the following policy is Beta's model for when contractors should be considered and/or used:

1. For doing the low skill jobs such as landscaping, custodial duties, etc., which are not part of the company's core competency.
2. For doing the high skill jobs, e.g., turbine generator balancing, infrared thermography, machine tool installation and qualification, etc., where the skill is not routinely used, and cannot be

justified on a routine cost basis (and the individuals with these skills often leave to make more money working for contractors).

3. For supporting major overhauls and turnarounds, when keeping the level of staff required to support annual or biannual efforts is not economically justified.

4. For emergency situations, when the workload overwhelms the existing capability.

5. For other situations where the use of contractors is clearly the best interest of the business.

Contractor Selection

When selecting contractors, Beta will also use the following model for selecting and managing contractors, including keeping records of contractor performance in key areas:

• Define the scope of work in light of the specific type of contract to be implemented, e.g., lump sum-fixed price, time and material, cost plus incentive fee, etc.

• Define the experience or expertise required, including any licenses or skill certifications.

• Determine the contractor's track record with the organization, as well as other skills required:

Administration
Project management
QA
Safety
Planning and scheduling
Cost control
Timely completion
Subcontractor relationships
Internal Conflicts
Housekeeping, especially at job completion
Engineering and reliability improvement skills
Quality of their work—equipment life, unit cost, etc.

• Define working relationships

Functional level
Flexibility
Personnel compatibility (at multiple levels)
Cultural compatibility

- Internal and external union agreements compatibility

  Track record on harmony or disharmony, e.g., grievances, strikes, etc.
  Process for handling conflicts

- Pre-award

  Capability
  Availability

- Terms and Conditions

  Design in ownership for results, warranty of quality
  Payment terms

- Scope of work

  Basic requirements
  Effect desired—value added
  Boundaries

- Financial issues

  Contractors reputation regarding contract disputes, add-ons
  Contractor's financial strength
  Basis for resolving financial disputes

- Safety, Health, and Environment Issues

  Historical performance record
  Current policies and practices
  Current safety training

- Compatibility with company administrative systems

  Time sheets
  Work orders
  Accounts payable
  Reporting systems

- Accreditation

  Systems in use for company
  Systems in use for individual employees

- Attitudes

  Supportive of company business goals—value added
  Measurements systems in place for this

• Ownership of intellectual property

   Drawings
   Process technologies
   Patents

Further, contractors will be held to the same high standards as employees for: (1) safety performance (in my experience, contractor safety performance is typically much poorer than employee safety performance); (2) installation and commissioning in verifying the quality of their work; and (3) housekeeping at the conclusion of a job. Beta recognizes that contractors have a potential inherent conflict, particularly in maintenance. One of the goals with any business is to grow the business ("grow or die"), and it is reasonable to conclude that a given contractor's goal is to grow their company's business by increasing revenue. As a result, there could be considerable temptation to increase the maintenance effort, rather than focus on long-term equipment reliability for reducing the maintenance effort (and revenues) over the long haul. At the very least, their enthusiasm for reducing the long-term maintenance level of effort could be diminished by their desire to grow the business. This is not to say there is anything dishonest or wrong with this inherent desire. Indeed, in many organizations the maintenance department often puts forth a large backlog as proof of the need to retain a given number of employees, sometimes without a careful analysis of why such a large backlog exists, and of how to eliminate the need for the maintenance that makes up the backlog. It is just human nature to want to protect one's job and/or to grow a business, and caution should be exercised regarding this issue when hiring contractors.

Moreover, Beta believes that a contractor may be less likely to have the same level of loyalty to the company as its employees, particularly if Beta's management exercises clear leadership and creates an environment supportive of mutual loyalty—company to employee and employee to company. Such a condition requires mutual trust and respect, something in need of improvement at Beta, where cost cutting had become a way of life. While mutual loyalty may seem like an outdated concept in today's world of downsizing and the apparent lack of mutual loyalty in many companies, it is now and will always be a concept that merits consideration and fostering. Properly done, a good operations and maintenance organization can offer greater loyalty to the company, and can outperform a contractor in core competencies over the long term. Measuring uptime or OEE, and defining the causes of losses from ideal performance in a team environment with maintenance and operations working with a common sense of purpose and toward common goals is more likely to be successful, especially when both operations and maintenance are viewed as core competencies.

Concurrently however, employees within Beta must recognize that they are indeed competing with contractors, and therefore must constantly seek to add greater value, e.g., greater equipment reliability, higher uptime, lower unit cost of production, better safety, etc., than might be done by a contractor. Let's consider the situation at a non-Beta plant. The plant was not particularly well run, but not necessarily because of current plant management. Over several years, and under considerable political pressure from senior management to avoid a strike and keep the plant running at all costs, the plant came to have 14 unions operating within it. As you might expect, each union had its rules, its contract, its "piece of turf" that it wanted to protect. Job actions were threatened, grievances were filed, and overall the plant just was not operated very efficiently. Its unit cost of production was quite high compared to comparable companies in the U.S. At the same time, the plant was faced with reduced revenues, and increased costs. Clearly in this circumstance, contracting the maintenance and operations functions becomes an option, even at the peril of the strife that will likely ensue at the plant. Changes will occur at this plant. It's only a matter of time.

Finally, it is recognized that this experience does not cover all circumstances wherein contracting any given function may be appropriate, such as at a new plant that is essentially a "green field," or when costs are truly extraordinary, or in a situation of intransigence with several different unions at one site, etc. For example, at one of Beta's plants, the machine repair shop was contracted out after management concluded that bringing their own staff to a world-class level of performance would take some 3 years or more, because the staff lacked adequate experience in machinery repair. Contracting the function was expected to reduce the time by 18 to 24 months, bringing substantial incremental benefit. Applied judiciously and integrated with existing maintenance employees, contractors can make an exceptional addition to any manufacturing team, but must be held to the same high standards as the balance of the organization, one which is driven to achieve world class performance.

Summary

Beta has learned an enormous amount through this experience, and has developed a solid understanding for more effectively employing contractors. Contractors play a key role within most all organizations, but consolidation of contractors requires a specific set of objectives and processes. Further, caution is urged relative to the temptation to replace core competencies such as maintenance (or operations, or any other function) with contractors, and the models and policies developed from Beta's experience are offered as bases for developing policies and practices for the use of contractors. Contractors must be conditioned to deliver an effect, not simply supply warm bodies for a fee. Finally, most maintenance departments, and employees for that matter, must recognize that they are competing with contractors and therefore must add more value to the operation than a contractor otherwise would, in increased performance or reduced unit cost. To do so assures greater probability of continued employment. To not do so creates greater risk of loss of employment to a contractor.

References

1. Moore, R. "Switch in Contract Maintenance Proves Costly," *Maintenance Technology*, vol. II, no. 2, February, 1998.

2. Moore, R. "Using Maintenance Contractors Effectively, *Maintenance Technology*, vol. II, no. 3, March, 1998.

3. *The Wall Street Journal,* June 20, 1996, New York, NY.

4. Schuyler, III, R. L. "A Systems Approach to Improving Process Plant Performance," Maintenance and Reliability Conference, University of Tennessee, Maintenance and Reliability Center, Knoxville, TN, May, 1997.

Total Productive and Reliability-Centered Maintenance

Put all machinery in the best possible condition, keep it that way, and insist on absolute cleanliness everywhere in order that a man may learn to respect his tools, his surroundings, and himself.

—Henry Ford,
Today and Tomorrow

A recent experience at one of Beta's large discrete parts manufacturing plants shows how combining Total Productive Maintenance,[1] or TPM, and Reliability-Centered Maintenance,[2,3,4] or RCM increased teamwork between the maintenance and production functions, improved equipment reliability and uptime, and lowered operating costs. Among the tools applied at Beta's Allen Central plant are TPM, with a particular focus on operator care and minor PM, or as some people would say, TLC—"Tender Loving Care" in the form of actions such as Tightening, Lubricating, and Cleaning. Other tools are also being introduced and applied in an integrated way, including continuous improvement teams, improved cell design, pull systems, process mapping, etc., but the focus of this case history is how TPM was integrated with RCM.[5]

The application of TPM at this plant, and other plants, has focused most of its attention on operator PM and basic care, operator "condition monitoring," etc. These practices are essential for assuring manufacturing excellence, but used alone are not likely to be sufficient. In this case, the focus on TPM did not adequately consider other, perhaps equally valid or even more advanced, methodologies, such as reliability-centered maintenance, predictive maintenance, root cause analysis, maintenance planning, etc. This view was confirmed by the maintenance manager for the business, who felt that while TPM was an effective tool for assuring basic care for the equipment, for detecting the onset of failures, and often for preventing failures in the first place, it frequently overlooked other maintenance tools and requirements. This, in turn, often resulted in equipment breakdowns, and in frequent reactive maintenance, not to mention the largest loss—reduced production capacity. As a result, we embarked upon an effort to combine the best of TPM and RCM to provide the most effective processes for both maintenance and production. In the process we expected to be able to provide manufacturing excellence—maximum uptime, minimum unit cost of production, maximum equipment reliability. Each methodology is discussed individually and then the process for combining them is provided.

Total Productive Maintenance Principles—TPM

Total productive maintenance, or TPM as it is commonly called, is a strategy for improving productivity through improved maintenance and related practices. It has come to be recognized as an excellent tool for improving productivity, capacity, and teamwork within a manufacturing company. However, the Japanese cultural environment in which the TPM strategy was developed may be different from the culture in other manufacturing plants world-wide, particularly in US plants, and as such may require additional consideration.

TPM was developed in Japan by Seiichi Nakajima.[1] With its Japanese origins, the strategy places a high value on teamwork, consensus building, and continuous improvement; and tends to be more structured in its cultural style—everyone understands their role and generally acts according to an understood protocol. Teamwork is a highly prized virtue; whereas individualism may be frowned upon. This basic underlying genesis of the Japanese TPM strategy is a significant issue to be understood when applying TPM to a given manufacturing plant. This may be especially true in a US manufacturing plant, because US culture tends to value individualism more, and to value people who are good at crisis management, who rise to the occasion to take on seeming insurmountable challenges, and prevail. We tend to reward those who respond quickly to crises and solve them. We tend to ignore those who simply "do a good job." They are not particularly visible—no squeaking, and therefore no grease. This "hero worship" and individualism may be an inherent part of our culture, reinforcing the behavior associated with the high levels of reactive maintenance at most plants, possibly making the implementation of TPM more problematic.

This is not to say that TPM faces overly serious impediments, or is an ineffective tool in non-Japanese manufacturing plants. On the contrary, when an organization's leadership has made it clear that the success of the organization is more important than the individual, while still recognizing individual contribution, a team oriented corporate culture develops that transcends the tendency for the individualistic culture, and success is more likely. Many plants world-wide have used TPM effectively, and most plants have tremendous need for improved communication and teamwork that could be facilitated using the TPM methodology. Most would be better off with fewer heroes, and more reliable production capacity. Considerable progress have been made through programs and strategies like TPM, but it is still evident that in many plants there still exist strong barriers to communication and teamwork.

How often have you heard from operations people, "If only maintenance would fix the equipment right, then we could make more product!" and from maintenance people, "If operations wouldn't run the equipment into the ground, and would give the time to do the job right, we could make more product!" or from engineering people, "If they'd just operate and maintain the equipment properly, the equipment is designed properly (he thinks) to make more product!" and so on. The truth lies in "the middle," with "the middle" being a condition of teamwork, combined with individual contribution and responsibility, and effective communication. This chapter provides a case history of one of Beta's plants for effecting this "middle," particularly as it relates to combining two strategies, TPM and RCM, which sometimes appear to be in conflict when applied at the same plant.

Total productive maintenance implies that all maintenance activities must be productive, and that they should yield gains in productivity. Reliability-centered maintenance implies that the maintenance function must be focused on assuring reliability in equipment and systems. As we'll see, RCM also calls for an analysis for determining maintenance needs. Properly combined, the two work well together.

The basic pillars of TPM and some thoughts on their relationship to an RCM strategy are:

- **TPM calls for restoring equipment to a like-new condition.** Operators and production staff can contribute substantially to this process. At the same time, according to RCM studies, up to 68% of equipment failures can occur in the infant mortality mode—at installation and start-up, or shortly thereafter. Good TPM practices will help minimize this through restoration of equipment to like new condition and operator basic care. However, it is often the case that more advanced practices may need to be applied, e.g., a stringent commissioning of the equipment, as well as the process, using condition-monitoring tools and standards for methods such as vibration, oil, infrared, analysis instruments and software, to verify this like-new condition. It may also be especially important to understand failure modes and effects to take steps in both operations and production to mitigate or eliminate those failure modes. Many will say that TPM calls for application of predictive maintenance, or condition monitoring. However, this tends to be quite limited and usually only involves operator "condition monitoring," e.g., look, touch, feel, etc., certainly good practice, but at times insufficient. Further, condition monitoring as practiced under TPM may not have a strong foundation, such as a failure modes analysis, which drives the specific technology being applied. For example, reasoning such as "it's a bearing and we do vibration analysis on bearings" without defining whether the failure modes require spectral, overall, shock pulse, etc. techniques, may not provide an adequate analysis method for the machinery in question.
- **TPM calls for operator involvement in maintaining equipment.** This is a must in a modern manufacturing plant. However, the operator often needs to be able to call upon specialists in more advanced technologies, when a problem starts developing in the equipment. These specialists can use RCM principles such as failure modes and effects analysis, as well as condition-monitoring tools, such as vibration analysis, to identify and prioritize problems, and get to their root cause.
- **TPM calls for improving maintenance efficiency and effectiveness.** This is also a hallmark of RCM. Many plants make extensive use of preventive maintenance or so-called PM's. However, while inspection and minor PM's are appropriate, intrusive PM's for equipment overhaul may not be, unless validated by equipment condition

review, because according to RCM studies little equipment is truly average. RCM helps determine which PM is most effective, which should be done by operators, which should be done by maintenance, and which deserve attention from design and procurement. PM's become more effective because they are based on sound analysis, using appropriate methods.

- **TPM calls for training people to improve their job skills.** RCM helps identify the failure modes that are driven by poorly qualified staff, and hence identify the areas for additional training. In some cases it may actually eliminate the failure mode entirely, thus potentially eliminating the need for training in that area. RCM is highly supportive of TPM, because training needs can be more effectively and specifically identified and performed.

- **TPM calls for equipment management and maintenance prevention.** This is inherent in RCM principles by identifying failure modes and avoiding them. Equipment is thus more effectively managed through standards for reliability at purchase (or overhaul), during storage, installation, during operation and maintenance, and in a continuous cycle that feeds the design process for reliability improvement. Maintenance is prevented by doing things that increase equipment life and maximize maintenance intervals; by avoiding unnecessary PM's through condition knowledge; and by constantly being proactive in seeking to improve reliability.

- **TPM calls for the effective use of preventive and predictive maintenance technology.** RCM methods will help identify when and how to most effectively use preventive and predictive maintenance through a failure modes analysis to determine the most appropriate method to detect onset of failure, e.g., using operators as "condition monitors," or using a more traditional approach in predictive tools.

One final thought: In many plants TPM has come to be thought of as operator PM, and measuring OEE and losses from ideal. Certainly that's part of it. However, as noted, TPM is about much more, and particularly maintenance prevention. As we've seen from RCM studies in Chapter 9, one study showed that up to 68% of the conditional probability of equipment failure is in the infant mortality mode or early life. Properly practiced, TPM can assure prevention *of* maintenance, instead of preventive maintenance.

Reliability-Centered Maintenance
Principles—RCM

The primary objective of RCM is to preserve system function, as opposed to equipment function. This implies that if the system function can continue even after failure of a piece of equipment, then preserving this equipment may not be necessary, or run-to-failure may be acceptable. The methodology itself can be summarized as follows:[2,3,4]

1. Identify your systems, their boundaries, and their functions.
2. Identify the failure modes that can result in any loss of system function.
3. Prioritize the functional needs using a criticality analysis.
4. Select the applicable PM tasks, or other actions, that preserve system function.

In doing the analysis, equipment histories are needed, and teamwork is also necessary to gather the appropriate information for applying the above steps. However, not having equipment histories in a database should not negate the ability to do an RCM analysis. As demonstrated in the following, equipment histories can be found in the minds of the operators and technicians. Moreover, operators can help detect the onset of failure, and take action to avoid these failures. Similar to TPM, RCM describes maintenance in four categories: preventive, predictive, failure finding, and run-to-failure. At times the difference between these can be elusive.

RCM analysis as traditionally practiced can require lots of paperwork—it's very systematic and can be document intensive. It has been shown to be very successful in several industries, but particularly in airlines and nuclear industries, which have an inherent requirement for high reliability, and a very low tolerance for the risk of functional failure. This intolerance for risk of functional failure has also lead to redundant equipment and systems to assure system function, a principle that, when applied to industrial manufacturing, could put considerable pressure on manufacturing capital and operating budgets.

When applying RCM methods, the system selection criteria typically include a Pareto analysis of those systems that have a large impact on capacity, high maintenance costs, frequent failures and/or corrective maintenance, safety, and the environment. Within a system, components, failure modes, failure causes, and failure effects are systematically defined at the local, system, and plant levels. In turn, this information is used to establish PM requirements. Typical failure mode descriptors might be words such as worn, bent, dirty, binding, burned, cut, corroded, cracked, delaminated, jammed, melted, pitted, punctured, loose, twisted, etc.

RCM is a good, disciplined methodology in that it documents processes, focuses effort on function, facilitates PM optimization (don't do what you don't need to do to prevent failures—you may introduce more than you eliminate), facilitates teamwork, and facilitates equipment histories and the use of a computerized maintenance management system.

There are, however, some potential RCM pitfalls. For example, it implies that if backup equipment exists, then run-to-failure is acceptable, because it has no effect on system function. However, this could be risky in that run-to-failure may result in ancillary damage; or the backup, if not cared for, may not operate, or operate long; or it may reinforce a historical culture of run-to-fail, and reactive maintenance, which typically costs much more.

Moreover, its traditional or historical focus has tended to primarily be on PM activities, versus a more proactive, integrated approach, which includes the effects of product mix, production practices, procurement practices, installation practices, commissioning practices, stores practices, etc. The more advanced application by most current

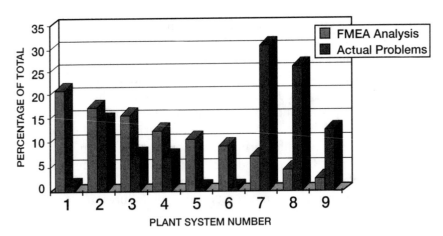

Figure 13-1. Comparison of FMEA analysis to actual plant problems.

practitioners does include these effects, and caution should be exercised to assure that these issues are included.

Another caution is related to the experience of Beta's Wayland plant. RCM uses a failure-modes-and-effects analysis method to analyze potential failures. Using this information then, for example, PM's are put in place to avoid or mitigate the failure mode. At Beta's Wayland plant they did a fairly thorough FMEA, or Failure Modes and Effects Analysis. The results of this analysis, which was done not long before the plant began operation, provided a rank order of the criticality of the systems in place at Wayland. However, after several years of operation, the actual problems, as measured by system downtime, differed substantially from the original analysis. See Figure 13-1.

The reasons for these differences are not clear. It could be that once the analysis was completed, people tended to spend a great deal of energy making sure that Plant System No. 1 was superbly operated and maintained, perhaps ignoring Systems No. 7, 8, and 9, to their great detriment. It could be that the analysis lacked complete data regarding equipment operation and maintenance practices. It could be other factors were involved. In any event, Figure 13-1 highlights the fact that a FMEA, which tends to be "forward thinking about what the problems could be," may not necessarily agree with what problems are actually experienced. However, it does represent a good learning and systems thinking process and should be used in that light. Most RCM type analysis done at Beta has relied heavily on actual historical operating experience.

The primary objective of RCM is to preserve system function. It calls for a systematic process for definition of system boundaries and functions, for the analysis of failure modes that result in loss of function, and for putting in place those tasks that preserve system function. It can be an excellent part of an overall maintenance and manufacturing strategy.

Case Study

At Beta's Allen Central plant, the first step was to bring together a cross functional team of people to review a critical production line with the goal of identifying the failures resulting in a loss of function. Because Beta was having difficulty meeting production demand, and could sell all it was making, loss of production capacity was a huge functional failure. This team included production supervisors, operators, maintenance supervisors, engineers, mechanics, technicians, electricians, etc.—people who knew the production process and the equipment. As necessary, support staff such as purchasing and stores people were brought in to help in defining and eliminating failures.

From the outset, however, a *functional failure* in the system (the production line) was defined as *anything* that resulted in *loss of production output,* or resulted in incurring *extraordinary costs.* That is to say, we did not restrict ourselves to a functional failures of equipment, but rather focused on the production line as a system experiencing functional failures, e.g., no production. We also looked at the frequency of these functional failures and their effects, principally their financial effect as measured by the value of lost uptime or extra costs.

Using the uptime improvement model described in Chapter 2, we initially focused on the first production step, say Step A, but once we finished with identifying all the major functional failures (loss of production, and or extraordinary costs) in Step A, we looked downstream and asked questions: Are failures in Step B causing any failures in Step A? Are failures in utilities causing any failures in Step A? Are any failures in purchasing or personnel causing failures in Step A? And so on. We walked through each step in the production line looking for areas where actions (or failures to act) were resulting in production losses or major costs (functional failures). We also made sure that all the support functions were encouraged to communicate with the team regarding how the team could help the support functions more effectively perform their job through better communication.

A point worth mentioning is that this is likely to be an imprecise process, bordering on controlled chaos, and given the inability to accurately measure the losses, we're often only "guesstimating" at their value. However, these estimates will be made by those who should be in a position to know best, and they can be validated later. Perhaps more importantly, an additional benefit is that we have our staff working as a team to understand each other's issues, and using this information to focus on common goals—improving process and equipment reliability, reducing costs, improving uptime, and in the final analysis improving the company's financial performance.

For example, we found that:

1. Raw material quality was a contributor to functional failures, e.g., lost uptime, lost quality, poor process yields, etc. Operations and maintenance have little control to correct this problem, but, they can advise others of the need to correct it.

2. Gearbox failures were a contributor to mechanical failures. There's generally little that an operator can do to detect a gear box failure with the typical operator PM, if the gear box was poorly installed or specified.

3. Operator inexperience and lack of training was also concluded as a significant contributor to production losses. The problems resulting from their inexperience was often logged as maintenance downtime. For example, on one machine it was initially felt that electrical problems were the major source of maintenance problems. However, on review, it turned out that electricians (under a work order) were coming to the machines to train inexperienced operators in machine functions and operation.

4. Production planning was driven by a sales force lacking concern as to its impact on production, and the inherent "functional failures" that occur when equipment is required to make frequent changeovers. While their decisions may be right strategically, it almost always requires a more comprehensive review, and better integration of the marketing and manufacturing strategies, as discussed in Chapter 3.

5. Spare parts were frequently not available, or of poor suitability or quality. Purchasing was driven to keep inventory low, without sufficient consideration as to the impact of a lack of spares on production. Better specifications and understanding of maintenance needs were required, and low bid should not be the only criteria.

6. Inherent design features (or lack thereof) made maintenance a difficult and time consuming effort, e.g., insufficient pull and lay-down space, etc. Lowest installed cost was the principal criterion for capital projects, versus a more proactive lowest life-cycle cost.

7. Poor power quality was resulting in potential electronic problems, and was believed to be causing reduced electrical equipment life. Power quality hadn't been considered by the engineers as a factor in equipment and process reliability.

8. Lubrication requirements had been delegated to the operators without adequate training, procedures, and supervision.

9. Mechanics were in need of training on critical equipment and/or precision mechanical skills. A few needed a review course on the equipment itself, and in bearing handling and installation.

10. Lay-down and pull space for maintenance was not adequate in some cases, resulting in additional downtime and maintenance

costs. This was due to the focused factory and lean manufacturing efforts that had reduced floor space substantially for all manufacturing cells, without giving due consideration to maintenance requirements.

11. And last, and perhaps most importantly from an equipment reliability standpoint, precision alignment of the machine tools was sorely lacking and if implemented should dramatically improve machinery reliability, and hence reduce system failures.

Beyond these general findings about functional failures in the system, we also found that three separate sets of production equipment were key to improving the overall system (production line) function. Functional failures in this equipment were resulting in the bottlenecking of the production line. It varied from day to day as to which equipment in the production process was the "bottleneck," depending on what equipment was down. Therefore, all three steps in the production process and equipment were put through a further RCM analysis to develop the next level of detail.

At this next level, a method was established for assessing the criticality of the equipment by creating a scoring system associated with problem severity, frequency, and detectability. This is shown in Table 13-1.

Table 13-1
Criticality Ranking

Rating	Severity Who	Severity Repair Time	Estimated Frequency	Problem Detectability
1	Operator	n/a	Quarterly	Operator, little inspection required
2	Maintenance	<1 shift	Monthly	Operator, w/considerable inspection
3	Maintenance	>1 shift	Weekly	Operator normally unable to detect

The score for a given problem was the multiple of the three factors, Severity × Frequency × Detectability. If a given problem was given a score of more than 4 by the group, then it was considered to require additional attention. Scores of less than 4 were those that operators could routinely handle, and/or were of lesser consequence. For example, suppose a functional failure was detectable by the operator, e.g., broken drill bit. Further, suppose it was occurring daily, and could be repaired in one shift. Then it would received a score of 1×2×3, or a fairly serious problem. Very few problems occurred weekly, and required more than one shift to correct, and were not detectable by an operator. Finally, this scoring system could obviously be further refined to provide greater definition on a given system or set of problems. You are encouraged to develop your own models and to use models already existing in your organizations for product or process FMEA's.

One finding of this review process was that a considerable amount of equipment really needed a complete overhaul. That is, it needed to be restored to "like new" condition (a TPM principle), but it was found using RCM methods as we looked at the failure modes and effects associated with the system that defeated function. This equipment subsequently went through a "resurrection" phase wherein a team of people—operators, electrician, electronic technicians, mechanics, and engineers—thoroughly examined the equipment and determined the key requirements for an overhaul, including the key steps for verifying that the overhaul had been successful. Less intensive, but equally valuable, (and summarizing) the following model was found to be effective:

Component/		———————Failure———————					Rating
Process	Function	Mode	Effect	Cause	Prevention	Detection	Action
							S×F×D

This model was then used to analyze the equipment and assign a criticality rating that dictated the priority of action required for resolution of the problems being experienced. See Tables 13-2 and 13-3 for specific examples of results of this analysis.

Some Additional Benefits

Further, as we went through this analysis, we began to determine where to best apply certain technologies. For example, precision alignment of the machine tools turned out to be of critical importance throughout the plant, because in the view of the staff, much of the production losses were a result of failures caused by poor alignment. Further, it was also determined that if poor alignment were causing extraordinary downtime and costs, in the short term we could use vibration analysis (a so-called predictive technology) to confirm proper alignment and to anticipate problems and be prepared to respond to them in a planned, organized way. In the long term, the engineers had to look for more constructive solutions by improving the basic

Table 13-2
Example of Three-Hole Drill Analysis*

Function:	Drill three holes in a part, each having a given diameter, depth and cycle time	
Functional failures:	Poor cycle time	Broken drill
Effect:	Reduced production rates	Stopped production
Rating	1	3
Frequency:	Weekly	Daily
Cause:	Dull drill bits	Misalignment (after RCA Analysis) Tool and fixture design
Rating	3	3+
Detection:	Increased cycle times	Machine stops
Rating	1	1
Prevention:	Better drill bit material	Alignment of tools Improved installation and operation

In this example, the severity code of the broken drill bit is 9+. When added to other issues such as quantity of downtime, bottlenecking, etc., this became a critical problem throughout the plant, and was addressed as rapidly as possible, using root cause failure analysis and putting in place practices to eliminate the problem.

Table 13-3
Example of TPM/RCM Results*

	Detection	Prevention	Action
Bearing failures	Noisy Vib. Analysis	Improved installation, specs, operation	Maintenance training, care, tools, commissioning
Quill damaged	Visual Noisy	Operator cleaning, lubrication Improved design	Improved installation Operator PM
Part concentricity	Quality control Visual	Operator inspection Improved design	Routine inspection Frequent replacement
Leaky hydraulics	Visual Pressure gauge	Operator tightening Better design	Operator tightening Improved installation

Notice that a combination of operations and maintenance, as well as design and purchasing actions were often required to truly address the problems. TPM and RCM principles were routinely applied, but often extended beyond this to get better application of existing methods, such as root cause analysis, and better tools, such as alignment fixtures and tools.

design (a more proactive approach), and to incorporate into the purchasing standards requirements for better alignment fixtures and capability. Further, we considered how best to prioritize our production and maintenance planning efforts, anticipating where resources were best applied. What also came from the analysis was that we were doing preventive maintenance to little effect—either overdoing it on some equipment and achieving little uptime improvement, or underdoing it on other equipment and experiencing unplanned equipment downtime. In this manner we began to optimize our PM practices. We could go on, but the point is that if you don't understand where the major opportunities are, then it is much more difficult to apply the appropriate technologies and methods to improve your performance in a rational way. Using a TPM/RCM approach we found these opportunities more quickly. Finally, as a consequence, the new "model" for behavior among the staff is now changing to "fixed forever" as opposed to "forever fixing."

We also found that it was critical to our success to begin to develop better equipment histories, to plan and schedule maintenance, to be far more proactive in eliminating defects from the operation, regardless whether they were rooted in process, equipment, or people issues. This was all done with a view of not seeking to place blame, but seeking to eliminate defects. All problems were viewed as opportunities for improvement, not searches for the guilty. Using this approach, it was much easier to develop a sense of teamwork for problem resolution.

Summary

The first step in combining TPM and RCM is to perform a streamlined RCM analysis of a given production line. The RCM analysis would define a functional failure as anything that causes loss of production capacity, or results in extraordinary costs. It is focused on failure modes, frequencies, and effects, and is extended to identify those failure modes that would be readily detected and prevented by proper operator action. It also details those failure modes and effects that require more advanced methodology and techniques such as predictive maintenance, better specifications, better repair and overhaul practices, better installation procedures, etc. so as to avoid the defects from being introduced in the first place. The next step is to apply TPM principles related to restoring equipment to like new condition, having operators provide basic care (TLC) in tightening, lubricating and cleaning, and applying more effectively preventive and predictive techniques. Operators represent the best in basic care and condition monitoring, but very often they need the support of more sophisticated problem detection and problem-solving techniques. These are facilitated by integration of TPM and RCM methods.

Results

Process. The results thus far have been very good and are getting better. The cross-functional teams have identified areas wherein operators through their actions can avoid, minimize, or detect developing failures early, so that maintenance requirements are minimized, and equipment and process reliability are improved. Moreover, more effective application of maintenance resources is now being applied to assure that they are involved in those areas that truly require strong mechanical, electrical, etc. expertise in getting to the more serious and difficult issues. The process is in fact similar to how we maintain our automobiles, that is we as operators do routine monitoring, observation, and detect developing problems long before they become serious. As we detect problems developing, we make changes in the way we operate, and/or we have a discussion with a mechanic. As necessary, we bring our car into the mechanic, describing the symptoms for a more in-depth diagnosis and resolution of the problem. Similarly, we as operators of our automobiles can preclude failures and extend equipment life by applying basic care such as routine filter and oil changes, which don't require much mechanical expertise, leaving the mechanic to do the more serious and complex jobs, such as replacing the rings, seals, transmission, etc.

Equipment. The machines to which the methodology has been applied have been very much more available. For example, before this method was applied to one production area it was common that 6 out of 16 machines would be unavailable for production, with only one of those typically being down for planned maintenance. After the process was applied 15 of 16 machines are now routinely available, with one machine still typically down for planned maintenance. This represents an increase of 50% in equipment availability. In another area maintenance was routinely called in for unplanned downtime. After application of this method production personnel were trained in routine operational practices that essentially eliminated the need for maintenance to "come to the rescue," eliminating many unnecessary work orders, improving equipment availability, and reducing costs. The methodology continues to be applied in the plant with continuing improvement.

In closing, it must be said that methodologies such as TPM, RCM, TQM, RCFA, etc. all work when consistently applied. However, as a practical matter, each methodology appears to have its focus or strength. For example, TPM tends to focus on OEE/loss accounting, maintenance prevention, and operator care. RCM focuses on failure modes and effects, and assuring system function. Both are good methodologies. Both work. However, in this instance, we've found that combining the two actually led to a better process and to improvements in teamwork and cooperation at the production level, leading to improved performance and output, and lower operating costs.

References

1. Nakajima, S. *Total Productive Maintenance,* Productivity Press, Portland, OR, 1993.

2. Nowlan, F. S. "Reliability-Centered Maintenance," United Airlines, NTIS Document No. AD/A066 579, December, 1978.

3. Smith, A. M. *Reliability-Centered Maintenance,* McGraw Hill, New York, NY, 1993.

4. Mourbray, J. *Reliability-Centered Maintenance,* Butterworth-Heinemann Ltd, Oxford, England, 1991.

5. Moore, R. and Rath, R. "Combining TPM and RCM," *Maintenance Technology,* vol. II, no. 6, June, 1998.

14 Implementation of Reliability Processes

Enumerate a few basic principles and then permit great amounts
of autonomy. People support what they create.

Margaret J. Wheatley

If we are to successfully implement best practices for assuring a
highly reliable manufacturing process, then we must achieve buy-in
and ownership of the process from top to bottom within a given
organization. At the senior level, executives must "enumerate a few
basic principles and then permit great amounts of autonomy," and, as
Wheatley[1] also states, ". . . minimizing the description of tasks, and
focusing on the facilitation of processes for following those basic
principles." Through this new found autonomy, people will support
what they create, because their participation in the creation process
assures their commitment. It is also essential that we understand
where we are and where we want to be (through benchmarking), creating a kind of cognitive dissonance. And, understanding the gaps, we
must develop our improvement plant, execute it with a team of committed people, and measure our performance along the way. These
are fairly simple, yet powerful concepts, which are far more difficult
in practice. Yet we have little choice in reality.

Where to start? Beta executives have measured their plants performance as compared to benchmark plants, and identified areas for

improvement. (I hope you've been doing something similar to this as you've read this book.) This effort must be recognized as only the *beginning*, not the end, and must *not* be followed by decision making that involves an arbitrary ax. Any dummy can wield an ax. It takes a real leader to define the basic principles and then facilitate other's success. Once these benchmarks are established, best practices must be understood that support achieving benchmark performance. This is key to the success of the implementation effort. Most people in most organizations understand what best practice is. However, common sense just isn't common practice, and most are not "allowed" to actually do best practice. I hope this book will lend credibility to what is already generally known by those who are actually required to do the work in the plants.

In particular, Beta manufacturing executives have asked:

1. What is my asset utilization rate? As compared to benchmark?
2. What are the causes of losses from ideal rate?
3. What are we doing to eliminate these causes?
4. What is our unit cost of production? (Less so than total costs)
5. What is my personal responsibility for facilitating improvement?

Note that this requires a comprehensive measure of asset utilization and losses from ideal utilization. Figure 1-5 provides a model for this measurement.

With a model such as this, Beta is now beginning to systematically measure its losses, and use those measurements to take steps to mitigate or eliminate those losses. If we measure it, we'll manage it. Indeed, these measurements should drive the creation of our reliability improvement plan, which outlines our losses and our steps for resolution. A typical Beta reliability improvement plan could be outlined as follows:

• Executive summary
    Value of the improvements
    Key steps to assure achievement
    Investment required ($ and people)

• Operation's rating relative to benchmark measures

• Analysis of strengths and weaknesses

• The plan
    Improvement opportunities
    Next steps, prioritized by importance, including milestones

Technologies to be applied
Team members, roles
Resources required (people, cost, tools)
Specific performance measures
Expected results

• Basis for periodic reviews and updates

The following section describes a sample reliability improvement plan, reflecting the Whamadyne experience.

Beta has found that the implementation process typically requires 2-4 years to accomplish, and the first year is normally the most difficult. New processes are being implemented, new roles are being established, chaos may be common. However, if the few key principles and goals have been established, this effort will actually tend to be self-organizing. *Establishing common goals using a common strategy will result in organizational alignment toward those goals.* People can, in times of great need, discern what is important and act quickly upon it, particularly if the leadership has made those needs clear. Figure 14-1, depicts what may happen to maintenance costs during this one-to-two-year period:[2]

It is common that maintenance costs will actually rise during the first year or so. This is because of any number of needs. For example, it is likely that (1) some equipment needs to be restored to proper

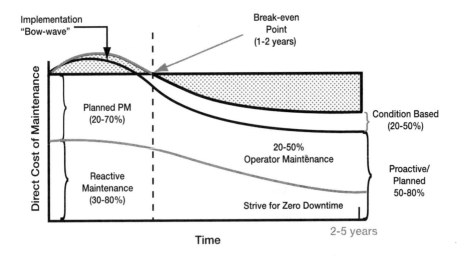

Figure 14-1. Effect on maintenance costs.

operational condition, (2) training in various tools and methods is being deployed, (3) new systems are being implemented, and/or (4) contractors may be required in some cases to help with the implementation process. Considerable effort is required during this period, and a rise in maintenance costs of some 5–20% is not uncommon. Only a few companies are known to have actually gotten most of this accomplished within the one year business cycle and did not incur incrementally higher maintenance costs (the "bow wave" effect). However, this is considered the exception, and most executives would be at risk in "hanging their hat on that nail." However, some relatively good news is also available, and that is, as shown in Figure 14-2, as these practices are implemented, the total opportunity cost of plant operation (the sum of maintenance costs and production losses) is reduced.

Ormandy[3] experienced similar results, but, total costs were defined as the sum of maintenance costs plus production losses that had been occurring. As the practices were implemented maintenance costs increased initially by some 15%, but with time were reduced by 20%. More importantly, however, production losses were reduced dramatically, yielding a net increase in gross margin contribution that was five times the increase in maintenance costs in the first year. During the next four years, production losses were cut to 25% of their original level. Of course, as losses decreased and output increased, unit cost of production came down and customer deliveries improved,

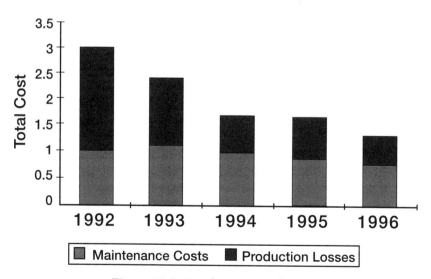

Figure 14-2. Total operational costs.

allowing for greater profits and return on net assets, as well and better market positioning. Ormandy[3] also reports that a pure cost-cutting strategy without changing basic practices also results in increased production losses. See Figure 14-3.

Kelley[4] reports results achieved by 500 companies that had implemented reliability and defect elimination programs as follows:

- Repair expenses increased by 30% during the first 12–18 months, then declined to 50–80% below original levels after 24–30 months.
- Machinery breakdowns declined by 50–60%.
- Machinery downtime declined by 60–80%.
- Spare parts inventory declined by 20–30%.
- Productivity increased by 20–30%.

Kelley also reports (verbally) that as these practices and results were being realized at his company, sales increased by 60%.

One final point on this, and that is that the typical "bow wave" may last one to two years before dropping below levels at the initiation of a reliability improvement effort. Several companies have worked with the shop floor to create "mini bow waves," that is, small efforts that provide a quick return, often within less than three months. The leaders of all organizations are encouraged to seek these small efforts, localized on the shop floor, such that the bow wave is a series of small ripples. Indeed, using *both* techniques is critical to maximize the prospective gain within a plant. Using both assures strategic management support, as well as shop floor support, shifting the culture of the company.

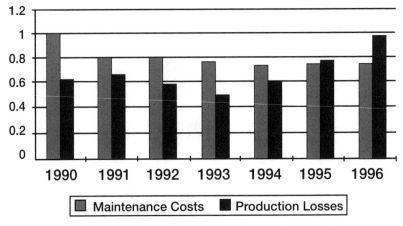

Figure 14-3. Effect of cost cutting on production losses.

The uptime optimization model described in Chapter 2, and demonstrated again in Chapters 10 and 12, provides a process for getting the implementation quickly started, and for beginning the development of your continuous improvement plan.

Implementation of these practices requires extraordinary leadership to enumerate a few basic principles and then encourage people to follow those principles to assure the company's success. Let's look at the details of Beta's Whamadyne plant and the process used to bring the plant to world-class performance.

Whamadyne's Journey to Manufacturing Excellence

Beta's Whamadyne plant, a continuous process operation, was essentially sold out, that is, it could sell all the product that it could make. It had relatively good operating performance at 86% uptime, and yet because demand was quite high, was having to work very hard to deliver on all customer orders in a timely manner. The failure of a bearing in one of its mixing reactors (and the loss of two days production valued at nearly $2M) lead to a reliability review of the entire plant's operation. As a result, an intensive reliability improvement process was established. This improvement process identified nearly $20M per year in improved gross margin contribution, most of which would convert into operating income. Minimal capital investment was required for assuring this improvement. Small increases were required in the operating and maintenance budgets (a small bow wave). After being presented with this opportunity, as well as a plan for its implementation, the president of the division said:

1. "Any questions?" (There were none)
2. "Is there any reason why we can't do this?" (None were offered)
3. "Let's get on with it."

And well we did. As the following indicates, the results were remarkable.

Whamadyne's Operational Characteristics

Whamadyne is a continuous process plant that manufactures a chemical for industrial use in other basic manufacturing requirements. It makes about 50 million pounds of product per year, generating some $322M per year in sales, and contributing a very healthy

$197M per year in gross margin to the company. Table 14-1 summarizes Whamadyne's sales, costs, and gross margin contribution.

Most of its manufacturing costs, about 55%, as shown in Table 14-2, are made up of raw materials. Other costs are typical of those expected in a manufacturing plant, include labor and fringes, overhead, energy, etc. It is interesting to note that when each cost category's labor is actually broken out, only 15–20% of Whamadyne's costs are directly associated with labor and fringes. This is highlighted because most managers seem to be highly focused on head count (reduction). Certainly, no one wants to employ more people than necessary, but a Pareto analysis of this data indicates a head count is not the place to begin. Rather, it may be more important to determine what is best for the business as a whole, or as illustrated in Chapter 1, to look at issues related to market share, uptime, return on net assets, and to put in place those practices and strategies that yield success. That done, head count will come down as a result, and not be a principle driver.

Whamadyne's maintenance operation is characteristic of what might be expected in most process manufacturing plants, with costs running at 10% of total manufacturing costs, a high level of reactive maintenance, and overtime (Table 14-3). Preventive and predictive maintenance are about average, and very little proactive effort is being exerted. Costs are split about evenly between labor/fringes and the sum of contractors and parts. Inventory turns on spare parts is 1. As shown in Table 2-1, this is pretty typical.

Whamadyne is currently operating at 86% uptime, and because it is sold out, there are no losses for lack of market demand (Table 14-4). Hence, its uptime is equal to its asset utilization rate, depicted in Figure 1-5. This uptime is actually better than the average value reported for most continuous manufacturing plants of about 80%. However, Whamadyne must achieve 92% to achieve its financial goals, and become the low-cost producer of its product, at least as low as is reasonably achievable. This 6% difference between actual and required represents 525 hours over a one-year period, or 3.3M pounds of product lost, which otherwise could have been sold at a profit.

Let's consider this 525 hours for a moment. That's a little less than 1½ hours per day over a year. It's also over three weeks during that same year. At Whamadyne, it had always been relatively easy to rationalize that it's no big deal to give up 20 minutes during one shift in delayed product changeover, or a half hour during another, or an hour for downtime because of a missing part, or a few percentage points lower than peak ideal rate, etc. These seemed to be daily occurrences. Being pretty good could be hindering Whamadyne from striving to be the best.

Table 14-1
Whamadyne Plant Business Profile

Throughput	50M lb/yr
Average price	$6.45/lb
Average cost of goods manufactured	$3.87/lb
Average gross margin	$2.58/lb
Annual sales	$322M/yr
Annual Gross Margin Contribution	$129M/yr

Table 14-2
Annual Manufacturing Costs

Description	Percent	Cost ($M)
Material	55%	$106.4
Equipment depreciation	7%	$ 13.5
Maintenance	10%	$ 19.4
Utilities	6%	$ 11.6
Direct labor	7%	$ 13.5
Environmental	5%	$ 9.7
Overhead	8%	$ 15.5
Other	2%	$ 3.9
Totals	100%	$193.5

Table 14-3
Maintenance Performance Profile

Budget:	$19.4M/yr
Consisting of $9.4M labor	
$5.0M parts	
$5.0M contractors	
Employees:	170
Work orders per week:	350
Maintenance practices:	
Reactive	45%
Preventive	35%
Predictive	15%
Proactive	5%
Overtime rate:	15%
Parts inventory turns ratio:	1.0

Few managers would "give up" 3 weeks of lost production. Then why are many plants so willing to give up this *three weeks per year a half hour at a time?* Let's not. Whamadyne isn't today.

The potential gain from best practices was estimated to be:

1. Increase in production from 86–92%, or 3.3M pounds additional throughput.
2. A reduction in overtime from 15% to 5%.
3. A dramatic reduction in rework losses from 0.5M pounds per year to 0.1M pounds.
4. A *minimum* reduction in maintenance costs of some $1.9M— prevent the maintenance from having to be done through reliability, don't just do preventive maintenance.

Rolling this information into a pro forma calculation results in the gains shown in Table 14-5. It illustrates that some costs are likely to remain constant, i.e., depreciation, environmental, overhead, and other. While environmental treatment costs may rise slightly, they were assumed as constant for this pro forma, likely offset by a slight reduction in "other" costs. However, if we achieve greater throughput, then unit costs will be reduced.

Material costs increase proportionally to increased production. Note that this does not consider other initiatives at Beta to work with suppliers to develop strategic alliances, and in helping them increase their plant reliability and performance, sharing in those gains. This initiative had only just begun when the reliability improvement effort began. Utility costs also rise proportionally with production, and this increase has not included any cost savings expected from a program to eliminate compressed air and nitrogen leaks, and steam leaks. Maintenance costs are expected to be reduced a *minimum* of 10%. As noted in Chapters 2 and 9, at some plants maintenance costs have been reduced by 30–50% and more with improved practices over a 3–5-year period. Whamadyne's improvement opportunities were expected to result in cost reductions of 10–20%, and possibly more, but credit was only taken for 10%. Finally direct labor costs were expected to be reduced by some 9% primarily through reduced overtime. No downsizing was anticipated as a result of this effort.

Finally, all the team members who participated in this effort concluded these gains were readily achievable, perhaps even conservative. However, as we all know, things happen, and the team wanted to present a plan in which it had high confidence.

Table 14-4
Production Performance Profile*

Planned production uptime:	92%
Actual production uptime:	86%
Lost production:	525 hr
Lost production:	3.26M lb/yr
Other production rework losses:	0.5M lb/yr

Since Whamadyne was sold out, uptime and asset utilization rate were synonymous.

Table 14-5
Pro Forma of Business Gains from Best Practice

	Percent	Before	After
Material	55%	$106.4	$113.4
Equipment depreciation	7%	$ 13.5	$ 13.5
Maintenance	10%	$ 19.4	$ 17.5
Utilities	6%	$ 11.6	$ 12.0
Direct Labor	7%	$ 13.5	$ 12.3
Environment	5%	$ 9.7	$ 9.7
Overhead	8%	$ 15.5	$ 15.5
Other	2%	$ 3.9	$ 3.9
	100%	$193.5	$197.8
Sales		$322.5	$346.4
Gross margin		$129.0	$148.6
Prospective Gain			$ 19.6M

Whamadyne's Reliability Improvement Plan

With this nearly $20M opportunity in hand, let's look at the improvement plan that Beta's staff developed and implemented for assuring these gains would be realized.

Background

A benchmarking exercise produced the following conclusions about Whamadyne:

1. The plant was in the middle to upper quartile in cost performance, plant availability, plant efficiency, and product quality— a pretty good operation, but not world-class.
2. Within the maintenance department, there was insufficient application of predictive, or condition-based, maintenance, reliability improvement teams, operator involvement in basic care and PM. Preventive maintenance, while on a sound foundation, needed considerable improvement. As noted, some 45% of maintenance was reactive.
3. The plant was running at 50% greater than nameplate capacity; achieved through a series of debottlenecking efforts, and further increases were underway.
4. The plant had a strong commitment to continuous improvement, good teamwork at the plant management team level, and had good leadership from the plant manager and his staff.

As noted previously, the plant was also sold out, and could sell everything it could make, when an unplanned downtime event (the bearing failure) lead to a reliability processes review. Perhaps as importantly, the company had a new CEO in Bob Neurath who was insistent on operational excellence to support new thrusts into marketing and R&D excellence. He had made it clear that "the company is competing in world markets where capacity almost always exceeds demand, necessitating that Beta be the low-cost producer of its products." Beyond operational excellence, Mr. Neurath also of course insisted that the company put together a good, sound corporate strategy, and, interestingly, he held a very strong view that once the strategy was established, "a bias for action would be far better than continued rumination about the strategy." His view was "let's get on with it"—marketing, R&D, and operational excellence, fully integrated. His expectations were quite high, and his staff rose to the occasion.

In Whamadyne's (and Beta's) view, operational excellence required that their plants be designed and operated using the reliability strategy depicted in Figure 1-4, the reliability process for manufacturing excellence, that is:

- Design equipment for reliability, uptime, and lowest life cycle costs (not installed cost).
- Buy equipment for reliability and uptime using good specs, histories, and alliances.
- Store equipment to retain its reliability, and operate stores like a store business.
- Install equipment reliably, with great care and precision and validating quality work.
- Operate the plant with great care and precision, using SPC, operator care, etc.
- Maintain the plant with great care and precision, integrating preventive, predictive, and proactive methods, with each other, as well as with design, procurement, and operating practices.

In particular, at existing operating plants Beta must use the knowledge base in operations and maintenance to continuously improve practices in each area.

Beta must also foster teamwork and communication; must assure training in the practices that will lead to operational excellence, and must regularly measure and display its performance against ideal standards. As one of its executives noted, "performance measures must also expose our weaknesses."

Improvement Opportunities

Notwithstanding its good performance, there were any number of opportunities, as the saying goes, otherwise disguised as problems, at Whamadyne, such as:

1. Performance measures focused on downgraded product vs. "lost" product. Whamadyne strongly subscribed to the product quality mantra, and had a heavy focus on downgraded product as a measure. However, this ignored other quality and reliability issues related to the total process and losses from ideal. The

value of product losses from ideal was 20:1 greater than down-graded product. Quality of processes, not just product, needed attention.

2. Condition monitoring, both of the process (precision process control) and of the equipment (predictive maintenance) was insufficient for world-class performance. Additional effort was needed in application of best practices, and associated training, staffing, and technology.

3. Critical equipment has been identified, but required detailed spares and histories at the component level to support Pareto and root cause analysis.

4. Improvement was needed in standards and procedures to improve reliability in:

   – New and rebuilt equipment
   – Equipment installation and commissioning
   – Balancing and alignment or rotating machinery
   – Root cause failure analysis (as a routine, not an exception)

5. Spare parts and capital spares inventory management needed a reliability-based focus. At the time there was a strong drive to make better use of working capital and to improve stock turns. This lead to predetermined parts reduction goals, which often ignored the plant requirements. Spares categorization and analysis (Chapter 6) led to a better strategy that supported reliability and capacity objectives.

6. While the plant was already operating at 50% greater than nameplate, even higher production rates were being planned to bring it to 100% greater than nameplate. There was concern that this would affect equipment reliability. Mitigating efforts included:

   – Reviewing the mechanical design in light of new operating conditions and loads.
   – Baselining equipment condition using predictive technology prior to the upgrade.
   – Recommissioning at the higher rates
   – Monitoring and trending, thereafter to verify adequacy of the upgrade

7. PM/overhaul practices were reasonably well planned, but needed documentation in an improved procedure, to include:

–PM/overhaul requirements driven more by equipment condition
–Before and after condition review
–Improved planning to minimize outage duration

8. Staffing levels and expertise were insufficient to support a world-class reliability program.

And, of course, capacity and reliability improvements were valued at: ~$20M per year.

Recommendations

The reliability improvement team put forth the following recommendations, which were subsequently approved and an action plan developed to include resources, responsibilities, and schedules:

• Performance measures

 – Expand performance measures to include asset utilization rate, and losses from ideal
 – Measure and display unit cost of production
 – Focus on minimizing the value of lost production (vs. just downgraded product)
 – Develop and display graphical trends of key monthly business performance measures

• Process monitoring and control

 – Develop and implement SPC methods
 – Explore, develop and implement advanced process control methods
 – Develop and implement greater operator basic care and PM
 – Integrate process and equipment condition monitoring for improved reliability

• Predictive measurements and techniques

 – Provide additional staffing for condition monitoring, including a reliability engineer
 – Improve predictive practices, training, instruments, software, and support
 – Improve communications; follow up on reliability activities

• Critical equipment prioritization

 – Continue to develop detailed listing of equipment to the component level; track machine failure histories, parts use, and lead times

- Proactive approach to minimize outage time

  – Develop and implement reliability-based procurement standards and specifications:
  – new and rebuilt equipment
  – bearing specs, gearbox specs
  – installation and commissioning
  – Develop methods for reducing duration of outages without affecting basic reliability, e.g. early insulation removal

- Spare parts/capital requirements

  – Complete categorization of MRO inventory
  – Develop strategy for MRO reduction in each area, factoring in:
  – equipment & parts use histories
  – reliability, capacity, & turns objectives
  – supplier alliances & reliability
  – Enhance procurement standards to include: physical data, PM intervals and basis, bearing data & B10 (L10) life, gear box service factor, vibration disks, lubricants needed, etc.

- Implement stores/motor shop supplier performance measures, including receipt inspection program; improve storage practices
- PM's (routine)

  – Review basis for PM's, revise; optimize PM's and align PM's to equipment condition.

- Higher rate effects on reliability/future requirements

  – Mitigate effects of higher rates through design review of equipment, and application of predictive and proactive tools, e.g., baseline, trend, recommission
  – Proactively use information to revise operation and/or design to mitigate effects

- Overhaul

  – Document overhaul planning and execution process into a formal procedure
  – Develop an improved machinery condition monitoring capability to establish details of overhaul work required, and success of overhauls/PM.

- Set up separate review team to develop CMMS action plan
- Manpower level and expertise

- Provide reliability engineer and technician resources
- Transfer non-reliability responsibilities out of reliability function, e.g., safety officer
- Provide intensive training in equipment reliability based principles/technologies:
  - predictive maintenance technologies
  - proactive methods

• Investment required—The incremental investment beyond existing capital and operating budgets was actually anticipated to be minimal, in light of the prospective gain. These included:

- Allocation of existing resources to develop standards and procedures, and lead the improvement effort
- Capital investment, instruments and software: $100K (capital)
- Operating budget for training, startup, etc.: $150K (startup)
- Reliability engineer and technician required: $150K per year

Amortizing the capital and start-up costs over a 5 year period given an estimated annual investment of: Annual investment ~$200K/year Further, the benefits of the improvement process were expected to accrue over 6–24 months.

Finally, perhaps the largest investment for Whamadyne was not in the budgets indicated, but rather in the allocation of existing resources to change the processes in place. This "intellectual and leadership capital" is perhaps the most expensive and difficult to come by. As Andrew Fraser opined, changing the habits of a lifetime is a very difficult process. Leadership at the plant in setting high expectations, and in creating superordinate goals will assure a common focus and facilitate changing these habits.

Unexpected Obstacle

An interesting issue developed shortly after the president of the division said "let's get on with it," and the management team proceeded accordingly. As indicated, the plan presented to the division president included hiring two additional staff, a reliability engineer, and a senior technician. Prior to the presentation, there was considerable concern that they were even being requested, because this same president had declared a freeze on new hiring. During the presentation, it was pointed out that there were no people within the plant who had the requisite skills to do the job of a reliability engineer; nor was there anyone adequately trained in vibration analysis. The training, was estimated to take one to two years to accomplish, substantially delaying the improvement process.

Unfortunately, however, the human resources department, as the saying goes, didn't get the word that the division president had said "let's get on with it." Resolution of this issue took several months and delayed the program implementation effort. In the interim the maintenance manager served as the reliability engineer, and contractors supported the vibration analysis effort.

Results—World-Class Performance

The results of the effort were remarkable:

1. Uptime improved to 93%.
2. Whamadyne became the low-cost producer (as low as reasonably achievable).
3. Production losses due to maintenance downtime were reduced to <1%.
4. Maintenance costs were reduced by over 20%.
5. Maintenance costs as % of plant replacement value were near world-class.

Constraints to the Improvement Process

In the Whamadyne example, much of the change and improvement was being driven from the top, making the change much easier. What happens when it's not being driven from the top, or even if it is, what if you don't agree with a particular change? What should you do? In *The Fifth Discipline* Senge[5] suggests that there are three basic constraints to organizational change:

1. Lacking the power to act.
2. Lacking the organizational support.
3. Lacking the deep personal commitment.

While there may be others, below are some thoughts on how to overcome these constraints in a manufacturing environment.

Lacking the power to act. If you feel that you lack the power to act, then go ask for it. A statement of the obvious. However, many are intimidated by doing the obvious things that may simply have not been done before. This action should consist of developing an improvement idea or plan, determining the benefit of the improvement, defining the key next steps which support achievement of the improvement, and estimating the investment required—people, money, time, etc. Take this to your boss, and/or go with your boss to your superiors and ask for the power to act on it.

Lacking the organizational support. Once you have approval, or even tentative agreement that your plan may be of value, seek the opinion and support of others. Modify your plan accordingly to suit their input. Getting some agreement on some issues is not likely to make the entire plan without merit. Don't let what you can't do be an excuse not to do what you can do. With that support, return to your boss or superiors and continue to take down the obstacles.

Lacking the deep commitment to the hard work necessary. This is perhaps the most difficult. Look in the mirror. Recognize there will be difficulties, especially if the plan is outside the norm. Keep your objective firm, even as you may be deterred in its achievement. Be a leader by the example you set every day.

Closing

Finally, which is as it should be, continuing improvements are in process at Beta's Whamadyne plant, that has created an environment that assured organizational success through:

1. Knowledge—of manufacturing best practices.
2. Training—in best practices to assure knowledge and understanding.
3. Teamwork—to assure communication and understanding.
4. Focus—on the right goals for business success.
5. Planning—to create a roadmap for knowing where you are and where you want to be.
6. Measurements—to provide feedback and control and most importantly . . .
7. **Leadership—to guide, direct, and sustain a continuous improvement environment.**

References

1. Wheatley, M. *Leadership and the New Science*, Berrett-Koehler, San Francisco, CA, 1992.

2. Thompson, R. et. al. "Taking the Forties Field to 2010," SPE International Offshore European Conference, Aberdeen Scotland, September, 1993.

3. Ormandy, D. "Achieving the Optimum Maintenance and Asset Strategy and Assuring They Are Aligned with Business Goals," IIR Conference, London, England, Sept., 1997.

4. Kelley, C. D. "Leadership for Change: Developing a Reliability Improvement Strategy," Society for Maintenance and Reliability Professionals Annual Conference, Chicago, IL, October, 1995.

5. Senge, P. *The Fifth Discipline*, Currency Doubleday, New York, NY, 1990.

Organizational Behavior and Structure

> Organizations . . . do best when they focus on direction and
> vision, letting transient forms emerge and disappear . . .
> information—freely generated and freely exchanged—is our only
> hope for organization.
>
> *Margaret J. Wheatley*

Experience has shown that almost any organizational structure within reason will work, if direction and expectations are clearly articulated by the leadership to create an environment for teamwork, common strategy, and common goals among all within the organization. Some of us recall reading about the Roman soldier who lamented about reorganizing the army every time they came into a serious problem to give the *illusion* of progress. In many companies that seems the case today. Reorganizing seems to be the thing to do, but often without adequate consideration for the results desired, or perhaps more importantly without having the patience to realize the results. This chapter reviews some experience and models used by Beta to assure good organizational behavior. Granted, there are times when organizational structure requires modification to more clearly define roles and responsibilities. But, most companies are in a reasonably good position to make those judgments, one hopes not just to give the illusion of progress. The way the boxes are arranged in an organization chart is far less important to an organization's success than is organizational behavior, which is driven by the leadership, who must develop and communicate a common strategy, create a common sense of purpose, and assure focus on common superordinate goals.

Leadership, Teams, and Teamwork

In the last several years and even decades, the autocratic, top down management style has given way to a more team-based approach for management. Most are probably thankful for this. We all have likely heard and used concepts such as self-directed work teams, empowerment, teamwork, high-performance work systems, etc. All these have the common attribute of teamwork, or working collectively toward a common goal. However, there have been several circumstances at Beta where the concept of teamwork has not been effective, and several where it has been. Let's look at their experience.

Empowerment appears to have come into popularity, and then waned, not because the concept isn't valid, but because it has been improperly applied. At one of Beta's small divisions the president routinely advised all the employees that they were closer to the problems than he or his management team, and as such they should solve them. This worked very well, save a notable exception. One of the employees felt that the health insurance policy for the company had several flaws. So he took it upon himself to rewrite the policy and distribute it to the entire company, without consulting the president, the human resources department, or anyone else, except perhaps his immediate associates. The employee was admonished, but not disciplined. Why not you may ask? The employee had taken the president literally and acted. Hence, he exposed a common problem with empowerment. As someone once remarked about empowerment, "The way we do empowerment, we get dumb decisions a lot faster." Some suggestions based on the Beta experience. To be effective, empowerment requires the following:

1. Relatively clear boundaries within which this power can be exercised.
2. Confirmation that those empowered have the skills to effectively exercise this power.
3. Performance measures in the context of the empowerment that measure its success.
4. A feedback loop to routinely review the successes, problems, changes needed.

5. Flexibility to allow the boundaries to grow and contract as necessary.
6. Leadership to assure clear direction for those empowered.

Leadership is a key component of empowerment, and here's one definition you may want to consider:

> Leadership is the art of getting ordinary people to consistently perform at an extraordinary level.

Leadership is about creating the environment wherein people are motivated to achieve very high goals and expectations. Management is about administering along the way. Both are necessary, and mutually supportive, but in the best organizations, leadership is superior for creating the environment in which success is a clear expectation. When asked, about 80% of a given company's employees will say they are above average in performance. This presents an extraordinary opportunity to motivate those employees to perform at that level.

Empowerment as a Disabler

Beta's Hueysville plant went through a team-building and de-layering exercise espoused by many. Unfortunately, this exercise did not have the effect desired. Uptime and unit costs did not improve, and a strong case could be made that it actually deteriorated. As a result of this de-layering and team-building exercise, one manager had 26 people reporting to him, another had over 30 reporting to him. After all, the logic said, self-directed work teams could figure out the problems and solve them, so there was no need for a lot of management structure. That would be true, except for some serious obstacles at Hueysville:

1. Work processes were not standardized in adequate detail to assure consistency of process among the staff.
2. Worker skills were at different levels, and as you might expect, understanding of work processes varied, resulting in different performance and outputs.
3. Many team leaders had little or no supervisory or leadership training or experience.
4. The plant management team changed completely about every 2–3 years, meaning that every 6 months, someone new (with new ideas and direction) would arrive.

5. A clear strategy and set of goals had not been communicated, other than something to the effect of "Do more better."

Until these issues could be addressed, supervisors were reinstated, a common strategy was created, clearer goals were established, and the corporation made the strategic decision to keep its manufacturing staff in their positions for longer periods to create more stability in the organization. Staying in a management position for too short a time can result in confusion about expectations and direction. Staying in a position too long can result in stagnation and a lack of new ideas. What's optimal? It depends. Generally, however, it is suggested that it's more than 2–3 years, but less than 8–10 years.

At Beta, it had long been held that they should hire the brightest minds from the best universities for their engineering and management ranks. Nothing is fundamentally wrong with this. Over time, Beta had also developed the practice of moving their bright new people into plant management positions fairly quickly. Many of these young managers viewed this 2–3 year stint in manufacturing management as part of a career path toward an executive position. Few expressed the desire to stay in manufacturing as a career. Many even expressed the opinion that if they stayed in a direct manufacturing position more than 4 years that their career was at a dead end. How can manufacturing excellence be established within a company where most of the best managers don't view manufacturing as a career, but rather as a stepping stone? Beta is working hard to change this practice, which has evolved over the years, including bringing the pay scale for manufacturing to a par with other career positions, and re-emphasizing the requirement for manufacturing excellence to assure business excellence. This institutionalized view, however, will take some time to change.

Teams

Most organizations believe in teams and recognize that teamwork and cooperation, with a focus on clear "super-ordinate" goals, or goals that transcend departmental goals, will more likely facilitate the organizations' success than will operating with a "silo" mentality. Information must be freely generated and freely exchanged if an organization is to prosper. One method for creating this free flow of information is creating a culture for teamwork. Below are several models for creating a culture of teamwork, based on an aggregate picture of

Beta International. Beta has yet to achieve the full sense of teamwork described here, but is working hard to do so.

Teams need common goals, strategies, rules, practices, and a leader or coach who can guide the team, foster a teamwork culture, and ultimately assure the team's success. The reliability process depicted graphically in Figure 1-4, and described in previous chapters, is fact-based, goal-oriented, and requires extensive cooperation between maintenance, engineering, production, purchasing, and human resources. It represents a strategy for creating teams and integrating the various functions into a comprehensive manufacturing process. As we've seen, the strategy itself consists of optimizing uptime and minimizing losses through the comprehensive integration of the processes in the way we *design, buy, store, install, operate,* and *maintain* our plants. Achieving excellence in this continuum requires that our staff work as a team, with the goal being to maximize production capacity and minimize production costs, allowing the company to be *the* low cost producer of its products.

An Analogy

Basketball is a team sport that makes a good analogy for developing a manufacturing team. If you don't like or understand basketball, feel free to pick your own sport and develop an analogy. At the broadest level, in basketball the primary **goal** is to score more points (**measures**) than the opposition in a given period of time. Of course, there are other *supporting* measures, such as percent shooting, rebounding, turnovers, etc. Achieving this goal requires an offensive and defensive **strategy,** such as a "run and gun" offense, a man-to-man defense, etc. The rules (**boundaries**) that provide a process for playing the game are generally well known, such as fouls, lane violations, 3-point lines, etc. The practices (**roles and responsibilities**) relate to execution of the strategy, such as high post, 3-2 offense, fast break, pick and roll, etc. But in the end the team must work effectively together to maximize the opportunity for success. Team members recognize that they must do both—execute their position well *and* support their team member's success through assists, rebounds, screens, guarding after a pick, etc. If each member doesn't play effectively at their position *and* as a part of a team, the team is not effective. For example, if each individual operates as if once the ball is passed, their responsibility is over; or as if the entire game rests on a single individual, then the team is more likely to be mediocre. Each team member recognizes a responsibility to emphasize their strengths, mitigate their teammate's weaknesses, and focus on the objective of winning. Finally, all teams have a coach or leader to whom they must report and be accountable, even those that are self-directed such as a basketball team. Likewise, in the best plants, the staff who make up self-directed work teams recognize the need for goals, measures, boundaries and rules, strategies, practices, and a reporting structure for accountability. And, even in the best companies, few argue with the coach, even when they are self-directed.

Current Teamwork Practices

Teams in a manufacturing environment should have much in common with basketball teams, but in most plants, the teamwork needs considerable improvement.

Let's take an extreme, although not uncommon example. The **goal** is to produce as much product as possible, at the lowest possible cost (**measures**). For that, production is the star—the principal burden of the company's success rests on production. The **strategy** is that each department has a specific function, and hand-offs occur between functions. Feedback and communication is frequently limited to crises. Production produces. Engineering engineers (generally in new capital projects). Purchasing purchases (getting orders placed, and parts and material delivered). Maintenance maintains (as quickly as possible to support production; some companies have even set up maintenance "swat" teams to quickly get equipment back on line). If everyone does their job right the first time, production could make all the product necessary. The **rules** are generally known, according to the culture of the organization, that is, certain things are done, others are not. The **processes and practices** tend to be historical and institutionalized—"that's the way we've always done it." The coach is the plant manager, who generally (and perhaps rightfully so) is closely aligned to the production manager, because his biggest interest is production and production costs, including maintenance.

This approach leaves several opportunities for improvement. Most people, most teams, are imperfect, and the problems associated with imperfection tend to be cumulative, having a compounding effect. Having very discrete definitions of job function, that do not include the interface and backup responsibilities can lead to unfulfilled expectations. Simply doing my job, or assuming that once I've completed my task and have passed the ball that I'm finished, ignores all the things that can happen in a complex environment. The best plants (1) follow up on the hand-off; (2) catch errors on the rebound; (3) signal a specific plan, etc.; and (4) constantly focus on working as a team to achieve the objective of winning.

When job descriptions are too definitive, however, it also creates a box mentality—"I can't stray very far from this box, or trouble can develop just the same as when job descriptions are too lax." Consider, for example, the maintenance box, whose job is to repair things; the purchasing box, whose job is to buy things; the engineering box, whose job is to engineer things. How often have we heard "if only maintenance would fix things right in the first place, we could make more product;" or "if production wouldn't run things into the ground, and would give us enough time to do the job right in the first place, we wouldn't have these problems;" or "if purchasing would just buy the parts we need, we wouldn't have these problems;" or "if engineering had included maintenance in the design, we wouldn't have these problems;" and so on. This box mentality can lead to poor teamwork, and mediocre performance.

The Reliability Process—A Better Way

The approach described would be better if defined in a slightly different, teaming-based relationship.

The **goal** is to be the low-cost producer for the company's products (the cost of quality is included in this concept). This might require an uptime level of 95%, and inventory turns on spare parts of greater than 2, with an OSHA recordable injury rate of less than 1. Alternatively, you may ask:

1. What unit cost of production do I need to achieve to assure superior performance?
2. What uptime will assure that? What are my losses from ideal uptime?
3. What other fixed and variable costs reductions are necessary to assure this?
4. Where are my next steps for eliminating the losses?
5. What is my personal responsibility for achieving this?
6. What do I need to provide to others, and from others, to assure meeting my responsibility?

Note that the last question is new and bridges the gap for assuring teamwork among individuals.

The **strategy** is to maximize equipment and process reliability, and therefore to maximize manufacturing capacity, and as a consequence to achieve minimum manufacturing cost. It is important to emphasize that when the primary focus is on maximizing equipment and process reliability, then minimizing costs will generally result as a consequence, especially when those expectations are created and supported.

The **rules** (boundaries and processes) are simple: focus on the goal of being the low-cost producer through maximum uptime, and do everything possible to work with the other team member to achieve that objective, even at times deferring to the greater good of the company what might otherwise be good for you or your department.

The **practices** (roles and responsibilities discussed in the following) involve doing those things that foster teamwork to achieve the objective of becoming the low-cost producer, and applying best practices so the goal of low-cost producer is achieved. Fundamental to this is that everyone is focused on this objective. Under the constraints of any given plant then:

1. Maintenance's job then becomes that of supplying maximum reliable production capacity. Repair becomes inculcated with reliability practices. With help from production, engineering, purchasing, and human resources, maintenance becomes focused on preventing maintenance, as opposed to preventive maintenance, putting reliability into the plant.

2. Purchasing's job becomes that of providing the most reliable, cost-effective equipment and supplies possible. Machine histories, for identifying suppliers with low reliability, are used as part of the purchasing process, and standards that include reliability requirements are defined. Low bid becomes secondary to value, as defined with the help of production, engineering, maintenance, and human resources.

3. Engineering's job becomes that of designing the most reliable (and maintainable) cost-effective system possible. Low cost becomes secondary to life cycle value, as defined with the help of production, purchasing, maintenance, and human resources.

4. Production facilitates the production process, with the plant manager coaching. Operators become involved in the reliability of their equipment through a sense of ownership (like owning a car and wanting it to run 300,000 miles), by doing simple rou-

tine maintenance, and by working with maintenance, engineering, and purchasing to get to the root cause of problems.

Production is still king, but everyone is an integral part of the king's team, and the king is fairly benevolent. Production no longer carries the entire burden of being "the star." Every member of the team supports the success of the organization and focuses on the objective—low-cost producer, which is achieved by high capacity, which is achieved by high reliability. Rather than having attitudes related to "if only *they* would just do their job," the team members are focused on supporting each other and providing constructive feedback for improvement. If *they* make an error, then *we* work with them to develop appropriate communications and solutions for these opportunities (often disguised as problems).

Reliability Improvement Teams

We've already seen reliability best practices and understand that the best plants have integrated the various functions and departments to achieve superior performance. Let's review the details of these reliability improvement teams and practices that lead to this. Note that not all Beta's plants had all the practices, so the discussion below is a composite—"the best of the best."

First, we might view the concept of teamwork and organizational structure as the three circles in Figure 15-1. The organization depicted has three functions (it could have more)—maintenance, production, and engineering. Each function has a zone in which it operates autonomously without help from others. Each function also has zones wherein there are overlapping responsibilities and communication necessary—the teamwork zone. Finally, there is a common goal for all the functions, one that must be met by all the functions—making money is the goal—even if an individual function has to defer for the greater good of the organizational goal of making money. Further, there are times when the production function plays a stronger role or has stronger influence, as in Figure 15-1b. It still needs support and communication from engineering and maintenance. There are also times when maintenance may play a larger role, as in a shutdown or turnaround, and there are times when engineering may play a larger role, as in a major plant expansion or other capital project. The size of the circles and the overlap between circles will pulsate between two different sizes and amount of overlap depending on the circum-

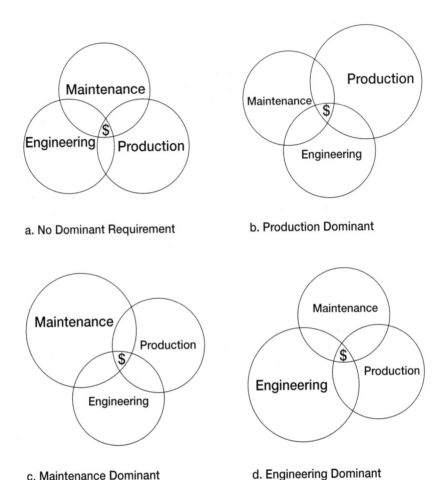

a. No Dominant Requirement

b. Production Dominant

c. Maintenance Dominant

d. Engineering Dominant

Figure 15-1. Organization models.

stances. The organization is dynamic, but is always focused on the goal of making the most money over the long term.

Let's consider several different team behavior models with this strategic team model in mind.

The Maintenance Team

In the best plants the maintenance team was reliability focused. In some rare instances, the maintenance department was called the reliability department, or the maintenance and reliability department, to emphasize the need for reliability. In general the department was organized into four functions, a maintenance planning function, a predictive/proactive function, a stores/spares function, and a skilled trades function. The functions varied from plant to plant, that is, in some plants they may have been, de facto, split into teams to focus on the reliability of a given line or area, but not always. Most of all, the maintenance team worked closely with production to maximize capacity, not simply run machines until a failure required emergency turnaround. And, they worked with engineering and purchasing to maximize future opportunity for improved reliability.

In this teamwork environment, while the organization chart still had fairly definitive boundaries, the lines of responsibility became more like overlapping bands of responsibility, and distinctions became "fuzzy." For example, operators (in production) became responsible for significant routine PM's and assumed a sense of ownership for their equipment, but called in the predictive maintenance team or the design engineering team to help with routine monitoring and diagnostics—the maintenance team in this circumstance might be the operators and predictive technicians. They made decisions about what equipment needed what work, and estimated when. In turn, they worked with the maintenance and production planning to schedule and plan the effort. They worked with the stores staff to make sure the parts were available, which were often kitted and delivered to the job location. Once repaired, they then used condition monitoring of the process and of the equipment to verify proper installation and operation. If a problem was recurring, they asked engineering to review the design and operation to develop a long-term solution. If training was key to improved reliability and productivity, they worked with human resources to develop a training program. They worked as a team focused on maximum plant reliability, each function supporting the other to achieve this objective.

The Maintenance Planning Team

Typically, the maintenance planning team uses a computerized maintenance management system, CMMS, to perform the maintenance planning function. However, in the best organizations, the CMMS is not simply a maintenance work order and scheduling function. It goes well beyond this typical approach, and includes the routine review of machinery histories and repair costs to identify those machines or areas which cause most of the loss of capacity or increased costs. It facilitates Pareto analysis (e.g., the so-called 80/20 rule for finding 80% of the problems (opportunities) caused by 20%

of the equipment). It assures maintenance planning, not just scheduling, by helping to identify and order the right parts, assure that staff and support resources are available, assure that the steps for the job and procedures are in place and understood, assure that appropriate drawings are available, etc. And most importantly, it works with the other team members to assure optimal allocation of resources and the plant's success. A job description for a maintenance planner is provided in Reference 2, and a good behavioral model for a maintenance planner is provided in Reference 3.

The Reliability Engineering Team

The predictive and proactive technologies were typically organized into a single function for reliability engineering, and typically included vibration, oil, infrared, motor current, ultrasonic, and other technologies. This group had the responsibility for knowing machinery condition, and using that knowledge to work with maintenance planning to plan maintenance based on condition, not interval, and to support maximum production capacity. Further, they used this knowledge to be proactive, to seek the root cause of problems, to diagnose problem machinery, and to support commissioning of equipment at start-up to verify proper repair. They supported training of crafts in techniques such as precision alignment and balancing. Finally, they worked directly with engineering and purchasing to support the procurement process such that reliable equipment was purchased—specifications for balance and alignment, L10 life for bearings, gear box service factor, cross-phase impedance imbalance for motors, jacking bolts, machinery configuration drawings, lubrications requirements, etc. This group was also responsible for writing procedures that assured that maintenance and repair work was performed consistent with good reliability practices. *Note:* it has been found that when these technologies are spread across the company in different departments, they are not as effective, losing the synergism the technologies bring when focused in a single department that must assure equipment condition knowledge and reliability. And most importantly, it works with the other team members to assure the plant's success.

The Stores Team

Sometimes a single person in a small plant, the stores team was responsible for assuring that stores provides the spare parts and tools for maintaining the equipment. Stores in the best plants was run like a store—clean, well stocked (not excessive), reliable. Imagine going into a department store that was dirty, had few of the parts you needed and what they had was in the wrong place, and on inquiring about ordering your needs, you found a long delay before receipt. Would this meet your needs? Would you go back? The store manager in a modern plant must view his/her function much like a store manager anywhere—clean, efficient, everything in its place, and just the right amount of stock to satisfy their customers and manage their cash flow. Moreover, they must do simple things that help assure equipment reliability, e.g., like storing bearings on isolation pads to minimize deterioration from ambient vibration, rotating shafts periodically to preclude shaft sag and bearing deterioration, not picking up equipment by the shaft, keeping spare motors and pumps covered, verifying that critical spares are in fact correct, etc.—basic care, like we would exercise with our automobiles. Granted the competition doesn't exist within a plant to drive conformity, but the attitude must be the same. And most importantly, the focus of the stores team is the overall success of the plant.

The Skilled Trades Team

In the best plants the skilled trades consider themselves true craftsmen, a part of a team that assures high reliability in the equipment to which they have been assigned. Very often they are assigned to an area or a given set of equipment. If something fails unexpectedly, they take a personal role in understanding the problem and being proactive about taking corrective action to assure reliability. They constantly seek skill improvement through training and experience. They take great pride in their work, but not so much that a team member can't suggest an area for improvement.

The Production Team

Members of the production team understand what the peak demonstrated production rate is for a given process, its losses from ideal, and what is at the root cause of each. When a piece of equipment fails, the production supervisor and/or operator works with the skilled trades to explain the failure, diagnose the problem, and facilitate learning so that it doesn't happen again.

In many of Beta's plants, particularly the batch and discrete plants, there were far too many times when the operator would call in a work order and then leave for a break while the equipment was being repaired. The operator only provided minimal input to the work order—"equipment broken." Most of us as operators of our cars would not treat them this way, that is, drop it off at the garage, and say fix it, leaving a blank check to be filled in later. We'd explain what happened, ask questions, and generally participate in the process. At Beta's better plants the operator stayed with the equipment to explain the problem, to work with the mechanic, technician, etc., to clean, calibrate, tighten, etc. while the repair was being made, and then helped bring the equipment back of line during start-up, in effect commissioning the quality of the work.

At Beta's better plants, operators also were very diligent about using SPC methods and trend charts, about understanding how to properly start up and shut down pumps, about valve operation, about the process itself, and the "recipes" for production. If they didn't, they felt free to call maintenance, design engineering, or process engineering to better understand the process and equipment, and to assure process and equipment reliability. Their shift handover procedure was excellent, and there was minimal competition between shifts. Rather they focused on how best to assure the company did well.

Production planning worked closely with maintenance planning, and with sales, to balance the need for delivery of product to the customer in a timely manner against the need to assure key maintenance requirements were met. Production planning and sales had learned the hard way that one of the easiest ways *not* to meet customer expectations was to ignore good reliability practices, and let the plant deteriorate to where very few customers were happy, with price or delivery.

The Capital Project Engineering and Design Teams

These teams focused on how to assure minimum life-cycle costs, working with the production and maintenance staff to understand where losses from ideal production were occurring and how to better design and install the equipment so that the losses didn't occur in new capital projects for the existing plant, or for new production lines and plants. To illustrate the point of how far many have come, at one of Beta's batch plants a project engineer was attending a reliability improvement workshop with a focus on design and project practices. This engineer, on being prompted with a question, replied "You mean you want me to go into the plant to check out my design?" Incredulous at the reply, the instructor made this a memorable moment for the engineer. After the initial embarrassment, he thanked the instructor for helping him to understand the need for communication and teamwork with production and engineering.

In particular project engineers are now more attuned to requirements for contractors during and at completion of a major project, especially since many capital projects are done with contractors. These include the issues covered in Chapter 12, and in particular assuring that contractors work closely with the production and maintenance function to commission the process and equipment, and to make sure that all housekeeping is done at completion. At one of Beta's sites, the contractor's 5% final payment is contingent on the project engineer signing off on contractor housekeeping.

Good enough rarely is, and when teamwork is an integral part of the plant culture, and reliability is the focus, then processes are readily established that assure:

1. Engineering designs for reliability and maintainability. The engineering team works to make sure that equipment is designed and specified for minimal life-cycle costs, not just for process inputs and outputs, but also for maintainability and reliability.
2. Purchasing buys reliable equipment. The purchasing team works with production and maintenance to develop specifications for reliability, and vendors that supply reliable equipment.
3. Equipment is stored to maintain reliability. The stores team works to make sure that stores supports reliability, using those methods mentioned.
4. Maintenance and contractors install and maintain equipment to assure reliability. The maintenance team works to make sure that equipment is installed properly, developing standards and procedures for equipment reliability—bearing handling and installation, grouting, shimming, alignment, hookups, etc.; and for checkout and acceptance testing by using standards and procedures for vibration, infrared, oil, motor current, and ultrasonic analysis to assure equipment is operating in a like-new condition (based on condition, not just looks). In particular the proactive and predictive technologies and methodologies help assure the maintenance team maximizes equipment reliability and capacity.
5. Production operates reliable equipment reliably. The production team works with all the other teams to maximize output at a

minimum cost—the low-cost producer, facilitated through a spirit of teamwork, communication, and continuous improvement.

6. Human resources trains for reliability. The human resources team works with all the teams to develop programs to assure proper training, both in regulatory driven matters, and in skill development.

And, the leadership of the organization makes sure that the organization operates as a team to achieve common goals.

Some Rules

It is important in any team-based environment that the team members assigned to a given task understand the following:

1. Their individual and team roles and responsibilities.
2. Who the team leader is to facilitate the focus and effort.
3. The time table for their efforts.
4. The reporting mechanism for their progress.
5. The measures for determining their success (more on this in the next chapter).
6. Their common goals and common rewards.

These "rules" will help create a teamwork culture for assuring world-class performance.

It is emphasized that teams facilitate teamwork, but teamwork is more important than teams per se. We could go into substantial detail for particular kinds of teams—rapid response teams, repair teams, area teams, the teams previously described, etc. Most organizational structures will work, and most teams will work, so long as teamwork permeates the mentality of the organization, so long as adequate, fact-based information is available to make informed decisions, and so long as clear goals are understood throughout the organization. The coach(es) as leaders must assure that this culture is established, set those goals, develop a team spirit, and foster teamwork throughout.

Organizational Structure

As we said, organizational behavior and culture are generally more important than organizational structure. Before the purists debate the issue, however, there are certainly times when structure matters, some of which follow.

Centralized Manufacturing Support Specialists

At the corporate level, Beta has been served well by a group of manufacturing specialists that provide support in the key manufacturing methods, e.g., statistical process control, advanced process control, all the predictive and proactive maintenance methods, TPM, RCM, and RCFA methods, as well perhaps softer issues such as training methodologies, team building, project management, concurrent design, benchmarking, etc. For example, this department of specialists has one or more experts in each of the methods or technologies, who are recognized as leaders in their specialty, and facilitate the implementation of the technologies throughout Beta. Their specific functions would include, for example surveying a given plant to assure that the technology applies, assessing the prospective benefit, working with the plant to set up a program—equipment, database, commissioning, trending, integration with other technologies and with process monitoring, continuing quality control and upgrade, problem solving and diagnostics, and last, but not least, training in the technology to assure excellence in its use.

Further, they would also seek and demonstrate new or improved technologies, identify common problems and opportunities, communicate successes and improved methods, facilitate the virtual centers of excellence discussed in the following section, and overall work as a facilitator for improved communication and implementation of a common strategy. These individuals would not necessarily *do* the technology, except perhaps in a start-up mode, but rather would facilitate getting it done, and may from time to time identify and use contractors for certain support functions. In other words, these specialists would facilitate the review and implementation of appropriate methods and technologies that are considered to provide benefit to a given manufacturing plant.

Finally, this corporate level function also conducts routine assessments of plants against a best-practice standard. The plant manager and his staff are also participants in the assessment process and commit to an improvement plan after each assessment. Reports and improvement plans go to the vice-president of manufacturing, signed off by the plant manager, both of whom follow up to assure implementation of the improvements.

Virtual Centers of Excellence

At one of Beta's divisions so-called virtual centers of excellence have been created to facilitate process improvement. This method involves defining four or five key areas that must be addressed corporate-wide for that division to achieve manufacturing excellence. Note that this process can also be used for marketing and sales, or other functional requirements. In manufacturing, these might be process control, capital projects, maintenance practices and stores practices. One representative from each plant is selected to serve on the center of excellence for that issue. Meetings are conducted on a periodic as-needed basis to define what the major issues are, what best practices are, what technologies will help assure best practice, what the obstacles are, etc. Each individual is expected to contribute to helping answer these questions and formulating best practices, and at their plant, for assuring that best practice is implemented. Best practice and a summary of the division's position relative to best practice is provided back to the plant manager and the vice-president of manufacturing. The plant manager has the responsibility to follow up on the implementation of best practice through the designated representative and working with his staff, and to integrate these issues with those from the periodic assessment and improvement plan for his/her plant. The vice-president oversees the entire improvement process.

Reliability Managers/Engineers

At one of its divisions Beta is currently training a minimum of one reliability engineer for each of its plants to meet the job description summarized here and detailed in Appendix A. This individual is being trained in manufacturing reliability best practice to include use of uptime/OEE measurement and loss accounting, RCFA, RCM, and TPM methods, maintenance planning and scheduling, predictive technologies, stores management, proactive methods (described in Chapter 9), and operational best practice. This individual's job is not necessarily to do the effort identified, but rather to understand best-practice applications and act as a facilitator and communicator for their implementation at the plant level, and in particular between production, design, and maintenance for eliminating the losses that result from poor practices. As time passes, it is expected that this position may become unnecessary, or certainly will change in form, as best practices become inculcated in the organization.

Predictive Maintenance

Finally, at Beta's best plants, all the predictive maintenance technologies were under the leadership of one manager, often the reliability engineer. In large plants this was typically a department of some 5–6 people, typically 2–3 vibration analysts, a tribologist (lube specialist), thermographer, and an ultrasonics specialist. In some cases one individual had multiple skills, e.g., thermographer/ultrasonics. In smaller plants this might be one individual who managed contractors. Their job was to assure that the appropriate technologies were being applied to know equipment condition and to use that knowledge to assure maximum reliability. Specific tasks included equipment commissioning, routine monitoring and trending, prevention of catastrophic failures, and diagnostics for root cause failure analysis. This information would be routinely shared with the maintenance planning and scheduling function for better planning. Further, they would routinely review equipment histories and work with the maintenance planner to better allocate resources for improved reliability and higher uptime. In plants that had the technologies scattered throughout the plant, that is, the vibration analyst in mechanical, the thermographer in electrical, the oil analysis in the laboratory, etc., the data that resulted were not used nearly as effectively as when they were in one group, whose job it was to know equipment condition and to use that knowledge to improve plant reliability.

Centralized vs. Decentralized Organizations

Focused factory concepts, as well as agile manufacturing and its typically attendant decentralization, have recently demonstrated their value in manufacturing organizations, including Beta's batch and discrete manufacturing plants, and particularly when the marketing and product mix have been well integrated with the focused factory, and when maintenance has been developed as a hybrid with some functions centralized and some decentralized (see Chapters 3 and 9). However, the concepts do not appear to be as effective at their large, continuous process plants. For example, it's difficult to have focused factories at a process chemical plant, a refinery, an electric power plant, a paper plant, etc. What you can have at these type facilities is teamwork, as previously described. Taking a given task or activity to the lowest competent level in the organization, the level at which the task is performed, is generally a good idea. Whether to centralize or decentralize depends on the circumstances, the competency at which decentralization is desired, and a host of issues.

Centralizing the manufacturing support specialist's function at Beta is generally a good idea. Centralizing the virtual centers of excellence is generally a good idea. Decentralizing, and aligning along business product lines and markets is generally a good idea and provides better focus. And so on. "It depends" on your objectives, business and personnel competency, business processes, etc. What Beta has found, in general, is that some hybrid form, which fluctuates with time and circumstances, appears to work best.

Key, however, in any organization is the leadership's ability to create a common sense of purpose and goals, and contrary to some harsher philosophies today, to "pet" employees a bit, that is expect and instill *pride* and craftsmanship, to encourage people to *enjoy* their work, and to develop a sense of *trust* between management and the shop floor that everyone has the same goal—to prosper over the long term—at the personal level, at the functional level, at the plant level, and at the corporate level. If any one level fails, the risk that they all fail is greater.

Mission Statements

Properly done, mission and vision statements create a common sense of purpose and a common set of values within an organization. They also force senior management to articulate its "vision" of the company in 5–10 years. However, the reality may be more akin to the Dilbert cartoon character's concept of a mission statement—management obfuscation that demonstrates its inability to think clearly. While it's not that bad, and it is important to articulate company goals and issues, roughly 1% of Beta employees in each of its divisions know its mission statement. When asked if they have a mission statement, most all reply yes. When asked what it is, about 99% cannot state it. They know it's on the wall, or they know it has something to do with . . . (fill in the blank), but they're just not sure what it is. How do we create a common sense of purpose in an organization where only 1% of the people know what it is?

The mission of the United States Army Infantry is "To close with and destroy the enemy." There's nothing ambiguous in this statement. The sense of purpose is understood. Notice that it doesn't talk about weapons, tactics, strategy, teamwork, etc., because that's covered elsewhere; or as businesses might, it doesn't mention the environment, shareholders, safety, profits, quality, community, etc. Of course you want to make money. Of course you want to be a good corporate citizen. Of course you want to do any number of things associated with running a world-class business. Articulate those important issues, and state them elsewhere, perhaps in your vision statement. Those may also change from year to year, in spite of your best vision. The mission should not. Certainly it shouldn't change very often (as measured in decades or generations). It should also be short, to the point, and create that sense of purpose. Everyone in the organization should know the mission statement.

At one of Beta's smaller divisions, the new president had written the division's new mission statement. Each new president apparently has to make his/her mark. He was quite proud of it. It had all the right words, and had been compared to several other mission statements, and was, at least in his view, better than all the rest. Good stuff!

This president (a people person) was walking through the manufacturing area and stopped to talk with one of the shop floor employees about a new process and its product. The process was working well, lower costs and higher quality were being met, etc. Toward the end of the discussion, which of course was very pleasing, the president asked the employee what they thought of the new mission statement. The employee replied that it was good, with surprised enthusiasm. Next, the president asked pointedly "What is it?" To which the employee replied that it was "Uh, to uh, make the uh, best, uh, product, uh..."

It was clear that the employee, a long standing, loyal, highly competent individual didn't know. Rather than embarrass the employee further, the president brushed it aside and said "Don't worry about it, it's not that important. Keep up the good work here." Walking away, the president reflected that the mission statement wasn't important, at least not to some of the best employees in the company. After some thought, he concluded that the mission statement had to be changed to a short concise statement that captured the essence of the company's mission. After much discussion with the board, many of whom liked the existing statement, it was finally resolved that the mission would be "To be the preferred supplier." After that, most all people in the company knew it, because it was easy to remember, and knew how they could help assure achieving it by what they did in their daily jobs. They lived the company's mission statement every day.

Finally, it also seems that this same president's father was a lifelong member of the International Brotherhood of Electrical Workers, and that his mother was a clerical worker all her life. His philosophy in management was to treat everyone, especially those on the shop floor, with the same respect, care, and dignity that he would treat his mom and dad. That said, however, he also expected them to work as hard as his mom and dad did all their lives for the success of the company. It seems to have made a good philosophy for motivating and instilling that sense of pride, enjoyment, and trust throughout the organization.

Implementing Reliability and Manufacturing Excellence in a Union or Non-Union Plant

Beta has a slightly higher proportion of union plants than non-union, but all things considered, there does not appear to be a substantial difference between the two in getting best practices in place. More crucial is the leadership and expectation for best practices focus than whether a plant is one or the other. The history and culture of the plant is also important. There are both union and non-union plants that have a long standing history and culture for "that's the way it's always been" and a reluctance to change. That said, however, the improvement process may require slightly more effort in a union environment, primarily because existing work rules and contract issues must be addressed. In this light it is critical that the union leadership be brought in at the beginning of the improvement process. The business issues and objectives must be explained, and their advice and counsel must be sought. You won't agree on everything, but you will earn their respect in the process. The more common objectives can be articulated, the more likely the buy-in from the union.

It is also important, if possible, that you pledge to the union that the improvement process will not be an exercise in head-count reduction. It should be made clear, however, that you expect to need fewer people per unit of production as a result of the process, and that you will manage that need through natural attrition, reductions in contractors, re-allocation of resources to a modified plant functionality, improved business position with more volume, etc. Take the high road and work with the unions to assure their security through business success.

Finally, additional works on organizational behavior and team building may be of benefit. Senge[4] takes a systems approach to organizational behavior. Frangos[5] goes through a team-building exercise and case history at a business unit of a Fortune 500 company. Galbaraith and Lawler[6] review anticipated changes in concepts related to learning organizations, value adding efforts, and team building. Donnithorne[7] stresses character, honor, teamwork, and commitment to group and institutional goals. All provide good food for thought in developing leadership and teamwork within any organization.

Summary

As Margaret Wheatley has so eloquently stated

"Organizations . . . do best when they focus on direction and vision, letting transient forms emerge and disappear . . . organizational change, even in large systems, can be created by a small group of committed individuals or champions . . . information—freely generated and freely exchanged—is our only hope for organization."

The flexibility to operate as a team and to be somewhat transient as the need dictates will serve Beta well. Beta must create a few simple goals that are readily understood by all, and then allow the organization to form around those goals through a team-based environment, led from the top.

Small teams and local leaders working to create a reliability-based culture and having a common sense of purpose for manufacturing excellence have yielded extraordinary gains for Beta.

Beta must forever more foster open lines of communication and teamwork to truly benefit from free information exchange and achieve manufacturing excellence.

References

1. Wheatley, M. *Leadership and the New Science,* Berrett-Koehler, San Francisco, CA, 1992.

2. *Reliability,* directory issue, Knoxville, TN, 1996.

3. "A Day in the Life of a Maintenance Planner," *Maintenance Technology,* Barrington, IL, April, 1995.

4. Senge, P. *The Fifth Discipline,* Currency Doubleday, New York, NY, 1990.

5. Frangos, S. and Bennett, S. *Team Zebra,* Oliver Wight Publishing, Essex Junction, VT, 1993.

6. Galbraith, J. and Lawler III, E. *Organizing for the Future,* Jossey-Bass, San Francisco, CA, 1993.

7. Donnithorne, L. *The West Point Way of Leadership,* Doubleday & Company, New York, NY, 1993.

16

Training

. . . and the absolutely decisive "factor of production" is now
neither capital nor land nor labor. It is knowledge.

Peter Drucker

At Beta International, far more often than not, when the subject of
training is brought up, a wave of cynicism sweeps the audience. The
vast majority do not feel that their training is adequate, either in
quantity, or in quality, or both. Some point out that "when push
comes to shove" in the budgeting process, training is often one of the
first things to be cut. Others point to the boring or misguided nature
of the training they receive. Only a few have admitted that they don't
personally put a lot of effort into the training process, expecting to be
"spoon fed." Learning from training, as we all know, requires hard
work from both the student and the instructor.

Such cynicism and pessimism may in fact be well founded. According to a survey published in 1994 by the National Center for Manufacturing Science,[1] training does not appear to be a very high priority,
at least for US companies. In this survey only some 10–20% of the
employees of US companies were reported to routinely receive formal
training. This stood in sharp contrast to Japanese companies where

60–90% of employees of Japanese companies routinely received formal training. The quantity of training varied with company size, with the larger companies providing more training. Of those employees of US companies that did receive training, the types of people receiving training were characterized as follows:

Personnel	Percent Receiving Training
Managers/Supervisors	64–74%
Customer Service	52%
Sales People	41%
Production Workers	37%

These are remarkable statistics in two ways. One is that they demonstrate a huge lack of perceived, or perhaps actual, value for training within this group of US companies. The other is that they demonstrate a lack of perceived value in the need to train production workers more fully. Note that 64–74% of the managers and supervisors received formal training, while only 37% of the production workers received formal training, or training for managers was about twice that for production workers. The question to be posed with this data is who needs training most? After all, if production workers don't perform well because management hasn't provided adequate training, how can we possibly hope to succeed in our efforts to become world-class companies and assure our business success. Nothing is wrong with having highly skilled managers and supervisors. In fact, as we'll see below, one company insists that its managers be the principal trainers. However, this needs to be formalized in practice to be effective. This lack of perceived value in training and learning brings to mind an old cliché—"If you think education is expensive, try ignorance." One hopes that much of this lack of appreciation for training and learning has changed in recent years with the advent of several books about learning.[2,3]

One model to follow in any situation when trying to improve a given process, in this case training, is to return to first principles. We've returned to first principles many times in this book, and focusing on getting the basics right is almost always the first order of business. Let's use that approach in this instance for training. What is training? learning? educating? According to Webster, the following definitions apply:

- Educate—to provide schooling; to train or instruct; to develop mentally and morally.
- Train—to teach so as to be qualified or proficient; to make prepared for a test of skill; to undergo instruction, discipline, or drill.
- Learn—to gain knowledge, or understanding of, or skill in by study, instruction, or experience. (In Chinese, to learn means to study and practice constantly.[2] This constancy of purpose about learning and improving would serve most of us well.)

For our purpose, we'll narrow this a little further. Educating is more broadly cast as mental and moral development. Training is targeted at developing a specific proficiency or qualification. Learning is gaining a specific skill or proficiency by study, instruction, or experience.

At Beta, there are several things that could be improved in their training processes, much the same with the US education system today. Perhaps the first is to create clear expectations in the trainers and in the students. For example, it should be stated that "I expect that when you leave here at the end of this training week, you will be able to (fill in the skill). There will be a test at the end of the week of your proficiency to determine if this learning has occurred." This does two things: (1) it sets the expectation, and (2) it makes sure that the students understand that there will be a test of having met the expectation. If students want to be deemed proficient, they must pay attention, participate, and study. If trainers want to continue as instructors, they must provide the proper input to the students to assure proficiency in those who are willing to work. Granted, there are always criticisms of the trainer, the students, the time, etc. This is just more opportunity for improvement. Beta's experience has been that when expectations are clearly expressed, they are more often met. Let's consider some strategic and tactical approaches used by Beta for improving the training process.

The Strategic Training Plan

At Beta's Langley plant, a large discrete parts manufacturer, they established a strategic training plan directed at meeting their corporate objectives. The process proceeded as follows:

1. Establish corporate objectives, e.g., RoNA of 20%, average plant uptime of 85%, unit cost of production, etc.

2. Analyze the skills required to achieve these objectives, given your current position compared to benchmarks, and in particular relative to your current losses from ideal.
3. Identify your current skills—types and quantities.
4. Review anticipated attrition, work-force demographics, and its effects.
5. Review planned changes to processes and equipment and training needs thereto.
6. Review "soft" skill needs—supervisory, team building, communication, conflict resolution.
7. Review regulatory and legal training requirements.
8. Perform a gap analysis of the shortfall between skills/quantities, as well as specific regulatory type requirements, and define training needs to minimize losses from ideal.
9. Develop a strategic training plan, including budgets, timing, numbers, processes, priorities, etc.
10. Establish clear expectations and outcomes from the training effort.
11. Repeat steps 1–10 annually.

This process is providing a framework for establishing strategic training goals and for assuring training which supports manufacturing excellence. Beta is currently applying this process, and is satisfied with the improved skill level of its employees.

Boss as Trainer

As a practical matter, Andrew Grove[4] makes a very strong case for the boss as trainer, as opposed to hiring training specialists. His case is also strongly supported by Intel's success, where 2–4% of every employee's time is spent in training every year, and where training is required to "maintain a reliable and consistent presence," and not be something for solving immediate problems. As a result, training is viewed as a process, not an event. In his view, a manager's success, as measured by output, is the output of the organization they manage. Thus, a manager's productivity depends upon increasing the output of the team under his/her direction. The two ways in which to accomplish this are (1) increase the motivation of the team, and (2) increase the capability of the team. He makes the case that a manager's job has always been to assure strong motivation of the team, so training should be no different, especially in light of the leverage of training. The example he provides to illustrate this leverage of using the boss as trainer is quite telling:

> "Say that you have ten students in your class. Next year they will work a total of about twenty thousand hours for your organization. If your training efforts result in a 1% improvement in your subordinates' performance, your company will gain the equivalent of two hundred hours of work as the result of the expenditure of your twelve hours."

The other, unspoken point in this example is that when training is provided, expectations should be articulated about the consequences of the training on improved productivity, output, etc. Training for its own sake, while philosophically satisfying, may not be in the best interest of the business. An example of this is discussed in the following.

Grove goes on to distinguish the difference in training required for new employees and veteran employees, offering the example of a department having a 10% turnover rate, and a 10% growth rate. This necessitates training 20% of the department in the specific skills needed to for their jobs. On the other hand, training everyone in the department in a new methodology or skill, requires training 100% of the entire department. When the two are combined, the task becomes even more daunting. But, remember the leverage in training. His suggestions for developing the training requirements include defining what the training needs are, assessing the capability to provide the training, and in identifying and filling the gaps, both in training required and in instruction available.

Training Versus Learning

Roger Schank[3] makes the point that:

> "The way managers attempt to help their people acquire knowledge and skills has absolutely nothing to do with the way people actually learn. Trainers rely on lectures and tests, memorization and manuals. They train people just like schools teach students: Both rely on 'telling,' and no one remembers much that's taught . . . we learn by doing, failing, and practicing."

His view appears to be fairly cynical about most educating and training done today, in that it does not foster learning. While this has considerable validity, a strong case could be made that studying and memorizing even the most mundane facts in itself develops learning skills and good habits, such as discipline and hard work, which are useful in themselves. Studying and listening to instruction, properly done, also provides a framework from which to practice and gain the experience we need to develop a given skill. The Japanese have demonstrated that discipline and hard work needed for the rote style of learning that is part of their culture can lead to a very successful economy.[5]

The very definition of learning, whether you adopt the 'Webster' version of study, instruction, and experience, or the 'Chinese' version of study and practice, both require study, presumably under some instruction, and both require practice and experience. Given this, it is recommended that training be accomplished in the context of mutually supportive methods:

- First, classroom instruction should have a specific objective in mind and should assure that those objectives are met through some sort of validation process, e.g., a test. This will encourage study, paying attention, good instruction, etc., and will create the framework for learning.
- Second, workshops or hands-on sessions should accompany most training wherein the instruction or principles are actually practiced in a forum that is not threatening. Practicing in this type environment should at least begin the skill development.
- Third, recognize that the skill is not fully developed until it has been practiced in an operating environment for a period of time. Allowing for this transient time and for complete learning and proficiency to develop is essential.
- Finally, expectations should be clearly stated when training is provided, both for a given course of instruction, and for the training program as a whole. To understand these expectations, try answering the questions: "What business benefit will result if we do this training? What are we going to get in return? What do I expect my people to be able to do as a result?"

Training for Pay

Beta's Bosco and Maytown plants at one time adopted a policy of paying for skill development. While paying for skills is generally a part of any market-driven economy, in this particular circumstance, it did not lead to the anticipated result. At these plants, it became standard practice that for every skill demonstrated that was generally consistent with their job, an increase in pay was awarded. However, as with many things, the policy became abused in that at times the sole purpose of some employees was to demonstrate the skill, and receive the pay increase, without applying the skill to their jobs. Several employees were receiving pay for skills that were so old, and out of practice, that the skill had become a skill on paper only, all the while costing the company additional money.

In this case, this not only created additional costs, without additional benefit, but could also create a safety risk. This could be particularly true if a person was perceived to be qualified for a job, but had not performed the job in an extended period, and then was called upon to do the job. The increased safety risk results because of skills assumed to be present but are not. Pay for skill should have a business purpose in mind, and a process for verifying the need for the skill, and that the skill itself has been acquired.

Training in Appropriate Methodologies

If you are seeking to be a world-class company, many of the technologies and methods described in this book will be necessary. However, a key reason these technologies fail to provide the expected benefit is the failure to recognize the need for extensive training and start-up effort for their implementation. As a rule of thumb, you can expect to spend an additional 2–5 times the initial cost of the instrumentation and software for the start-up and training effort needed to fully implement these technologies. Plan on it and you'll be happy with the result. If you don't plan on it, then don't waste your money.

Finally, all training programs must recognize the need for what might be termed "soft" skills—teamwork, communication, conflict resolution, supervisory methods, leadership, regulatory and legal issues, etc. Make sure these are incorporated into your training program. However, as one Beta division found, these soft skills aren't very productive in and of themselves, and must be combined with determining the "things you're going to do" to improve performance, and how that performance will be measured.

How Much Training Is Enough?

As we all know, training and learning is a continuing effort. You're never done, whether you're advancing existing skills, or training on new technology or equipment, or refreshing existing skills that have become rusty, or training for a new role or position, etc. However, how much training is enough is very problematic.

If you're currently well below world-class performance, or even below average, it's likely that you're going to require much more training per year than those who are above average or world class. As an engineer might say, you're likely "behind the power curve" and require an extraordinary amount of training to get over the skills requirement "hump." At one Beta plant, the maintenance manager trained everyone in maintenance basics first, and then in best practices for an average of 160 hours per year for two years to "catch up" in their skill level. Over the following 2–3 years, it is expected that this will decline to 40–80 hours per year. Below are some guidelines for deciding how much training is enough. Train sufficiently to:

1. Eliminate or minimize the gaps in the losses from ideal.
2. To ensure that processes are in statistical control;[6] this is especially true of operators.
3. To inculcate best practices.
4. To eliminate worst practices.
5. Or train about 40–80 hours per year[4]—but only after you're at a high level of performance.

Multi-skilling and Cross-functional Training

Much has been said about multi-skilling and cross-functional training. Some of Beta's plants have reported very good results with this concept. Others have reported less than satisfactory results. Some even sneer when either word is mentioned.

Based on anecdotal evidence, the plants that have had the greatest success appear to be those that did not try to take multi-skilling too far. That is, they didn't expect a senior mechanic to become a journeyman electrician, or vice versa. Rather, for example, they expected the mechanic to be able to lock out and tag out a motor, disconnect it, replace the bearings, check the stator and rotor for any indication of problems, etc., and put the motor back on line in 90% of the cases without having to call in an electrician. Likewise, they expected the electrician to be able to change bearings, too, normally a mechanic's job. Multi-skilling had to do with making sure all the skilled trades could perform basic tasks of the other trades, and yet retain the craftsmanship needed in their trade to assure that precision and craftsmanship in the work being done. These basic skills also varied from site to site, depending on any number of factors. They also worked *with* the unions to make sure that common objectives for productivity improvements were established, that safety considerations were observed, and that all were appreciative of the success of the business.

Closing

If you're an average manufacturing plant, or even above average, putting together a training plan that supports your strategic objectives, that puts in place the proper resources and time for your employees to learn, and that assures minimizing the gaps from ideal performance will serve you well. Your training must "maintain a reliable and consistent presence," not just be done as a reaction to a problem. As Senge so aptly put it, "Generative learning cannot be sustained in an organization where event thinking predominates." Your managers must view themselves as trainers, leveraging their skills across their organization. Clear expectations must be established for the training to be done, and "craftsmanship" must become a part of the culture of the organization. Learning must become a part of the continuous improvement process at your organization, providing your employees with both the direction, and simultaneously the freedom, to learn.

References

1. *National Center for Manufacturing Science,* newsletter, Ann Arbor, MI, July, 1994.

2. Senge, P. *The Fifth Discipline,* Currency Doubleday, New York, NY, 1990.

3. Schank, R. *Virtual Learning,* McGraw-Hill, New York, NY, 1997.

4. Grove, A. *High Output Management,* Vintage Books, 1983.

5. Reid, T. "The Japanese Character," *SKY* Magazine, Atlanta, GA, November, 1997.

6. Walton, M. *The Deming Management Method,* Dodd, Meade and Company, New York, NY, 1986.

Performance Measurement

"If you don't measure it, you don't manage it."

Joseph Juran

If you do measure it, you will manage it, and it will improve. With this in mind, it is critical that the measures selected be the correct ones, and that they be effectively communicated. Thus far we've covered the basics of practices for assuring manufacturing excellence. This done, however, we must make sure we measure those things that are supportive of our corporate objectives, including those measurements that establish our objectives. The following is a case history of one of Beta's divisions that achieved exceptional results by implementing a process for measuring and continuously improving their manufacturing methods. It provides guidance for an active, participative management style for most organizations in assuring continuous improvement.

The new vice-president of manufacturing for Beta's small start-up instrumentation division questioned the plant manager about the quality of the plant's new products. The plant manager assured the vice-president that quality was good, even very good. When asked for the measures of quality, however, the plant manager admitted that their focus was on finished product quality. Because there was a strong commitment to customer satisfaction, and new products tended to get "buried" in the total statistics, the more mature products usually represented the greatest volume. Soon thereafter measurements were intensified on all products, and the vice-president focused on two key measures: (1) for internal purposes—first-pass yield; and (2) for external purposes—DOA's, or equipment that was "dead on arrival" or failed to meet any critical function within the first 30 days of shipment. Supporting measures were also implemented, but these two were considered key measures of success.

After collecting the information for several months, it turned out that quality was not good in either of the key measures for new product success. DOA's were >3%, or 3 of 100 customers could not fully use the product because of defects that rendered a key function useless. This was particularly painful, because it was their belief that dissatisfied customers will tell 10–20 people of their bad experience, and therefore the potential existed for some 30–60% of potential customers not to view the company favorably. It also turned out that first-pass yield was only about 66%, meaning that effective costs for manufacturing were 50% (1.0/0.66) above ideal.

The good news was that critical data were now being measured and could be managed toward improvement. Clearly the next step was to examine the causes for DOA's and low first-pass yields. Upon investigation, causes were determined to be mechanical failures, component failures, assembly failures, software failures, etc. A Pareto analysis was performed, which identified the principal causes of the failures, and provided a basis for establishing priorities for solving them.

A team was formed to evaluate, on a prioritized basis, the cause of the failures, and then to quickly implement change for eliminating failures, all failures. For example:

1. Each instrument was fully powered for a period of time sufficient to minimize start-up and early life failures, and a series of tests were developed and documented in a procedure (check-off) to assure mechanical and electrical performance. Non-conformance judgments were placed in the hands of each technician who had the authority to reject any equipment under test. Technicians were also encouraged to work directly with manufacturing and engineering personnel to improve processes to eliminate failures.

2. Review of the Pareto analysis and a root-cause failure analysis indicated vendor quality problems were at the source of many problems. Components incurring a higher rate of failure were

reviewed directly with the vendor to develop corrective action. A receipt inspection program was also implemented to assure quality products were received.

3. Mechanical defects were particularly troublesome. In reviewing the data, specific patterns emerged as to failure modes. Design modifications were implemented. Procedures were rewritten (engineering and manufacturing) to eliminate failures. Each instrument was put through a mechanical shake test to simulate several severe cycles, validating the mechanical reliability of the equipment.

4. Software was rewritten and test procedures were made more stringent to assure system functionality.

5. A customer service line was established to provide details of failures, failure modes and effects, and these were entered into a data base for use in future designs and design modifications.

The measurement and analysis process continued forward (continuous improvement). Over the course of 2 years, first-pass yield increased to over 85% (a 21% cost reduction), and the DOA rate dropped to 0.15%, a twenty-fold improvement. While neither of these was considered world-class, the trend was clearly in the right direction, and the division expected that in time, world-class performance could be achieved.

When new products were introduced, these measures would sometimes show a deterioration in performance, but the impact was immediately recognized, analyzed, and corrective action taken to improve the quality of the product and the processes. Customers received higher quality products; and first-pass yield increased (costs were reduced).

Using this success as a model, performance measures were implemented throughout the plant with comparable results. For example, in customer support, measures of customer satisfaction were implemented and routinely surveyed. Customer support staff were strongly encouraged to use their own judgment and take the steps they deemed necessary to satisfy customer needs. Likewise they were strongly encouraged to seek help from and give input to engineering, manufacturing, and sales departments. If in their judgment, they felt the problem needed senior management attention, they were encouraged to immediately contact the president or other officer of the company to seek immediate resolution. This was rarely necessary, but demonstrated corporate commitment to customer satisfaction. Over time, the staff became outstanding and handled essentially all situations to the customer's satisfaction, achieving a 93% overall approval rating.

Other departments, likewise, showed substantial improvement in their performance—accounting improved cash flow from 53 days aged receivables to 45 days aged receivables, cut billing errors in half, provided month-end reports within five days of the end of the month, etc.; engineering had fewer design defects, improved design cycles, etc. Some additional lessons learned include the following:

• Simply measuring data is not sufficient to assure success. Performance measures must be mutually supportive at every level within the company and across company departmental lines. Measures that encourage an attitude of "I win if I do this" only alienate other departments and individuals. Measures that focus on the customer winning, and therefore the company winning will assure a greater degree of success. They must not, as the management-by-objectives (MBO) strategy tended to do in the '70s, create narrowly focused interests and the loss of teamwork. The least desirable measure is one that results in a reduction or loss of teamwork. As such, measurements must be integrated into a hierarchy supportive of overall corporate objectives, and does not conflict with other departmental measures. Measurements must be mutually supportive between departments.

• Measures must be displayed clearly, openly, and unambiguously. This provides an emphasis of the importance to the company, to the customer, and therefore to the individual. It also gives employees feedback on individual, department, and company performance and allows employees to adjust their activities to improve their performance according to the measures. Processes and methods can then be revised to assure continuing improvement.

At Beta's Watergap plant, key performance measures related to output, quality, and unit cost were boldly and clearly displayed for all to see. However, on closer review, the data were nearly three months old. When questioned about this, the production manager replied, "We'd had a couple of bad months and we didn't want to concern people." The philosophy should be that when you have bad news, get it out right away. If you don't, the rumor mill will capture it anyway, and amplify it. More importantly, the employees could take the view that management doesn't trust the people well enough to be honest with them. Of course, we all want to hear good news, but the real test of a company is often how it manages bad news, and particularly the plan of action to assure employees that the problems will be resolved.

• For a given functional unit, limit the number of measures displayed to five. More than this gets very cluttered and confuses any message of importance trying to be conveyed. People can only respond to a few measurements effectively. Any particular manager may want to track other measures that support the key three to five, but displaying them will likely detract from the goal of using measurements to reinforce or modify behavior.

At Beta's principal divisions, the following were chosen as key measures, which cascade from corporate to plant level:

• Corporate Strategic: Earnings per share/growth
                         Return on net assets
                         Safety (injury rate)
• Plant Operations: Asset utilization rate
                         Return on net assets
                         Unit cost of product
                         On time-in full rate
                         Inventory turns on product and stores
                         Safety (injury rate)
                         Percent operations downtime
                         Operations cost as a percent of
                           production costs
•Plant Maintenance: Maintenance cost as percent of asset
                           replacement value
                         Maintenance cost as percent of
                           production costs
                         Maintenance downtime production losses
                         Percent reactive work
                         Overtime rate
                         Safety (injury rate)
                         Average equipment life

The following are additional possible measurements for establishing key performance indicators (also see Reference 1). Again, select the three to five that are most important to the functional group and display those.

Sample Production Measures

- Total production throughput (pounds, units, $, etc., total and by product line)
- Asset utilization (% of theoretical capacity)
- Overall equipment effectiveness (Availability × Efficiency × Quality)
- Conformance to plan (%)
- Total costs ($)
- Cost per unit of product ($/unit)
- Maintenance cost per unit of product ($/unit)
- Equipment availability by line/unit/component (%)
- MTBF of production equipment (days)
- Scrap rate ($ or units)
- Rework rate ($, units, number)
- Quality rate ($ or units)
- Finished goods inventory turns
- Inventory "backlog" (weeks of inventory available)
- Work in process (non-finished goods inventory, $ or units)
- Overtime rate (% of $ or hours)
- Personnel attrition rate (staff turnover in %/yr)
- Product mix ratios (x% of product lines make up y% of sales)
- Energy consumed ($ or units, e.g., kwh, Btu, etc.)
- Utilities consumed (e.g., water, wastewater, nitrogen gas, distilled water, etc.)
- On-time deliveries (%)
- Returns ($, units)
- Set-up times (by product line)
- Cycle times (plant, machine, product)
- First-pass yield (product, plant)
- Process efficiency(s)
- OSHA injury rates (recordables, lost time per 200K hours)
- Process capability (to hold specification, quality)
- Training (time, certifications, etc.)
- Productivity ($ per person, $ per asset, etc.)
- Scheduled production and/or downtime
- PM work by operators (%)

Sample Maintenance Measures

- Equipment availability (% of time)
- Overall equipment effectiveness (Availability × Efficiency × Quality)
- Equipment reliability (MTBF, life, etc.)

- Planned downtime (%, days)
- Unplanned downtime (%, days)
- Reactive work order rate—emergency, run-to-fail, breakdown, etc. (%, %hrs, %$)
- Product quality (esp. in equipment reliability areas—rolling mills, machine tool, etc.)
- Maintenance cost (total and $ per unit of product)
- Overtime rate (% of $ or hours)
- Personnel attrition rate (staff turnover in %/yr)
- Rework rate ($, units, number)
- Spare parts/MRO inventory turns
- Overtime rate (% of $ or hours)
- Personnel attrition rate (staff turnover in %/yr)
- OSHA injury rates (recordables, lost time per 200K hours)
- Process capability (to hold specification, quality)
- Training (time, certifications, etc.)
- Productivity ($ per person, $ per asset, etc.)
- Scheduled production and/or downtime
- Bearing life—actual vs. L10 life
- Mean time between failure, average life
- Mean time to repair, including commissioning
- Planned and scheduled work/total work (%)
- PM/work order schedule compliance (% on schedule)
- Hrs covered by work orders (%)
- PM work by operators (%)
- PM's per month
- Cost of PM's per month
- "Wrench" time (%)
- Average vibration levels (overall, balance, align, etc.)
- Average lube contamination levels
- Schedule compliance for condition monitoring
- PDM effectiveness (accuracy of predictive maintenance by technology)
- Mechanics, electricians, etc. per
  support person
  first line supervisor
  planner
  maintenance engineer
  total site staff
- Total number of crafts
- Training hours per craft

- Maintenance cost/plant replacement value
- Plant replacement value $ per mechanic
- Stores $/plant replacement value $
- Stores service level—stock out %
  critical spares
  normal spares
  Contractor $/total maintenance $
  Maintenance $/total sales $
  Maintenance $/value added $ (excludes raw material costs)

Other Corporate Measures

- Return on assets
- Return on equity
- Return on invested capital
- P:E ratio
- Percent profit

Industry Specific Measures

- Refining—dollars per equivalent distillate capacity
- Automotive—hours per automobile
- Electric Power—equivalent forced or unplanned outage rate

Return on Net Assets or Return on Replacement Value

Many corporations use return on net assets (RoNA), or some comparable measure as part of determining operational and financial performance. While this is an excellent measure, it may be more appropriate to measure specific plants on the basis of return on replacement value. In those cases where a plant has been depreciated to where it has a low book value, return on net assets may not truly reflect the plant's performance, as compared to a new plant. It is probably more appropriate to put all plants on a normalized basis and truly judge the plant's operational performance.

Plant Age and Reliability

For those who think allowances should be made for older, less reliable plants, data from continuous process plants indicate that older plants are no less reliable than newer plants.[2] Ricketts found no correlation between plant reliability and plant age, location, capacity, or process complexity. Beta's experience has been that there is some reduced reliability, as measured by uptime, during the first two years or so of a new plant operation, and there is some reduced reliability after about thirty years into operation, if the plant has not maintained its infrastructure, e.g., its piping bridges, tanks, roofs, etc. If it has, then there is nor correlation between age and plant reliability.

Measure for Weaknesses

One of Beta's divisions also subscribed to the philosophy that measurements should also expose their weaknesses, not just their strengths. There is a natural tendency in almost everyone to want to look good. Hence, if measurements are made, we want to score high, looking good. However, this tendency can at times lead to a false sense of security. For example, at one Beta plant, the plant manager reported an uptime of 98%. However, on closer review, this was being measured against an old production rate that was established before a debottlenecking effort. After considering this, and factoring in all the other issues, the plant was more like 70% and indicating a 30% opportunity versus a 2% opportunity.

Benchmarking against the best companies will help minimize the tendency to use measures that assure looking good. Making sure that you're setting very high standards for your measurements will also help in this. As stated, measurements should expose your weaknesses, not just your strengths. Only then can these weaknesses be mitigated, or converted into strengths.

If you measure it, you will manage it, and it will improve.

References

1. Haskell, B. *Performance Measurement for World-Class Manufacturing,* Productivity Press, 1991.
2. Ricketts, R. "Organizational Strategies for Managing Reliability," National Petroleum Refiners Association, Washington, DC, Annual Conference, New Orleans, LA, May, 1994.

18

Epilogue

There is a tide in the affairs of men which, taken at the flood, leads on to fortune.

Mark Anthony from
Shakespeare's Julius Caesar

Beta International is at a major juncture in its corporate history. It can, through the proper leadership and direction, re-establish itself as a world class performer. For those who achieve superior performance, global competition whets the appetite, pumps the adrenaline, and spurs them to new levels of performance. For those who do not rise to the occasion, this ever intensifying competition represents a threat from which to retreat. Bob Neurath is convinced that the globalization of economic forces is an opportunity waiting for the best companies. He is also determined that Beta will rise to this challenge by creating clear expectations for excellence in all business activities.

Thus far, several divisions are in fact rising to this challenge and meeting these expectations. Manufacturing performance has improved substantially—at one division uptime is up 15%, unit costs are down 26%; at another division, OEE is up 35%, unit costs are down 27%; at another division, maintenance costs have been reduced by over $40M. At these particular divisions, this has all been done without any downsizing. When combined with other improvements related to restructuring its market focus and new product development, stock price has risen substantially, more than doubling for one division.

Prior to Mr. Neurath's arrival, Beta International had suffered from overconfidence and a lack of investment, focusing too much on making the short term look good. This approach had not served Beta well, ultimately resulting in a downturn in corporate performance, and creating a sense of retreat in the organization. Reestablishing a well founded sense of confidence, pride, and trust in senior management's leadership has been a daunting task. With these successes in hand, Beta's plan for this follows the processes outlined in this book, but also includes continued improvements in marketing and advances in research and development. Some markets or market segments have been abandoned, either in the form of sell-offs of businesses or by discontinuing certain products. This has been done where there was a lack of confidence in Beta's technology, performance, or leadership to achieve excellence in those markets. Other changes are also likely. Beta will also be looking for businesses in which to invest, particularly in those markets where it feels strong. Research and development will be enhanced and tied more closely to those markets that represent Beta's strengths. Manufacturing excellence is now a requirement, not an option, and the marketing and manufacturing strategies will continue to become much more closely aligned and mutually supportive.

Beta's 10-Point Plan

Beta has had success in several of its divisions. However, these individual success stories must be transformed into the corporation's overall behavior. Bob Neurath's expectations, like many corporate leaders today, is that Beta should be first or second in all its markets, or have a clear, measurable path for achieving that position. And, trying to be all things in all markets only dilutes management focus, leading to mediocrity. The plan for accomplishing this is clearly described in the following section and begins with reviewing all of Beta's markets and current market position, world-wide. Strengths and weaknesses will be reassessed in those markets, and a plan for achieving market leadership will be put forth, including the integration of R&D requirements, as well as manufacturing performance and strategy. Beta's *10-point plan* for manufacturing excellence is:

1. Integrate the marketing and manufacturing strategies, establishing the manufacturing performance necessary for market leadership—unit cost, quality, uptime, on-time deliveries, etc.
2. Establish performance benchmarks as the *beginning* of the process for achieving and sustaining manufacturing excellence in all markets. Compare all manufacturing plants to this standard of excellence.
3. Measure uptime/OEE and losses from ideal performance. Establish the root cause of these losses from ideal. Use these losses as the basis for establishing improvement priorities.
4. Develop a plan of action for minimizing these losses from ideal; and assuring that best practices are being applied to that end. The culture of Beta must be changed from one of having to justify applying best practice to one of having to justify *not* doing best practice. Best practice and manufacturing excellence are requirements, not options. Getting the basics right, all the time, is fundamental to making best practice an inherent behavior.
5. Establish and apply best practices, using the models developed at successful plants, for the way Beta designs, buys, stores, installs, operates, and maintains its plants, i.e.:

   a. Capital projects must be designed with lowest life-cycle cost in mind, not lowest installed cost, incorporating the knowledge base from operations and maintenance to minimize costs through better up-front design.
   b. Buying decisions must incorporate life-cycle cost considerations. Design, operations, and maintenance must use their knowledge base to provide better specifications and feedback. Supplier strategic alliances must be developed that focus on operational and business success, not just low price.
   c. Stores must be run like a store—clean, efficient, low stockouts *and* minimal stock, high turns, low overhead, accurate cycle counts, and driven to support manufacturing excellence.
   d. Installation must be done with great care and precision, and to an exacting set of standards. Commissioning to validate the quality of the installation must likewise be done to an exacting set of standards, both for the process and for the equipment. These exacting standards apply to both skilled trades and contractors.
   e. The plants must be operated with great care and precision. SPC principles must be applied by operators who are trained

in best practices related to process and operational requirements. Good shift handover practices, operator basic care and PM, common set points, ownership, and teamwork become standard.

f. Maintenance must become a reliability function, not a repair function. Working with design and operations to minimize equipment failures is a requirement. Balancing preventive, predictive, and proactive maintenance methods to assure maximum equipment life and minimum reactive maintenance is also a requirement. TPM, RCM, PM Optimization, RCFA and CMMS models, as well as other tools, will be used to facilitate the effort.

6. Contractors will be held to the same high standards as the balance of the organization, and a policy will be established for the use of contractors. In particular, safety performance expectations will be strengthened, as well as commissioning and housekeeping standards.

7. Each division, and each plant within each division, will be expected to put forth its current performance relative to these benchmarks and best practices, and its plan for improvement, along with the anticipated value of these improvements and the investment required to achieve them.

8. Organizational behavior and structure will be modified to facilitate teamwork for applying manufacturing excellence principles. The clear goal of the teams is to assure manufacturing excellence. These efforts will be facilitated by small structural changes to the organization that will include a corporate manufacturing support function for benchmarking and best practices in operations/maintenance; virtual centers of excellence; and reliability engineers at each plant. Beta's mission statement will be reviewed, and made clear and easily remembered, creating a common sense of purpose.

9. A corporate strategic training plan will be established in cooperation with the divisions and plants, which supports continuous learning and manufacturing excellence. Skill requirements will be established in each of the major elements for manufacturing excellence.

10. Performance measurements that assure manufacturing and business excellence will be reviewed, and modified as necessary, to assure that Beta measures, manages, and improves every step

of the way. These measures must cascade from the executive office to the shop floor in a mutually supportive manner.

Bob Neurath is determined to assert his leadership and make Beta International a premier company world-wide. He understands that manufacturing excellence is a necessity for Beta's success, and that there is no "magic bullet." Costs must come down, not so much as a consequence of cost cutting, but rather as a consequence of best practice that includes clear expectations about cost reductions. This view has only been reinforced by an analysis of Beta's plants, described in Appendix A, which demonstrates how management support and plant culture, organization and teamwork, as well as applying best practice day to day, in operations, maintenance, training, performance measures, etc. have a positive influence on performance, but none dominated. Conversely, not doing best practice had a negative impact. Business success requires a solid strategy that integrates marketing, manufacturing, and R&D, and assures excellence in each. Beta International is well on its way to superior business performance.

Manufacturing excellence is about doing all the basics right, all the time. Business excellence requires this, but it also requires excellence in marketing, sales, customer support, and distribution systems, as well as research and development, and a host of things. If marketing and sales is the beacon of light for your products, then manufacturing is the cornerstone of the lighthouse, and R&D is the power supply. And generating the capital required to put all those systems in place demands adequate gross margins from your manufacturing systems. I know of no single plant that is doing all the basics right, all the time, though there may be some. Always there is room for improvement, with Utopia being only a concept not a reality. So, please don't be discouraged about not doing everything perfectly.

As McCarthy said in *Blood Meridian,* "No man can put all the world in a book." Likewise, all the issues related to manufacturing excellence cannot be captured in this book; and clearly there are many, many additional models and issues related to manufacturing; to marketing; to research and development; to corporate training; to safety performance, etc., which are necessary for business excellence. I hope this has helped get you started in improving your manufacturing performance, giving you a map for doing the basics well, so that you "will not lose your way." Manufacturing excellence, indeed excellence in any area requires leadership to create the environment for excellence, a good strategy, a good plan, and good execution. All are necessary; none are sufficient; and leadership, the art of getting ordinary people to consistently perform at an extraordinary level, is the most important.

I have a concern relative to leadership as it is practiced in most organizations. With all the downsizing and threat of downsizing, albeit some of it necessary, it's not likely that people will consistently perform, even at an ordinary level, when threatened with their jobs, cost cutting, down-sizing, etc., nor are they likely to be very loyal. Extraordinary performance requires that people be instilled with a greater sense of purpose, or as David Burns has said, "superordinate goals" that transcend the day to day grind most of us endure. People also need to believe that their employer has their best interest at heart and be treated with dignity. At the same time employers must insist on high standards and set high expectations. If this happens, it is more likely they will rise to the occasion and achieve excellence. Saving money is good, but it's just not likely that you can save your way to prosperity. Prosperity over the long term takes a long-term vision, regular positive reinforcement, doing value adding activities, assuring growth, etc.

This vision and sense of purpose is captured in the story of three men working in a rock quarry. The first was asked what he was doing, to which he replied "I'm just breaking up rocks. That's what they pay me to do." The second on being asked, replied "I'm making a living for my family, and I hope some day they'll have a better living." The third replied "I'm helping build a temple for the glory of God." Notwithstanding any religious inclinations you may or may not have, who has the greater sense of purpose? Who is more motivated? Who, according to Maslow, is 'self-actualized'? Clearly, those leaders who create in their employees a sense of purpose in their daily lives, and help them to feel that they are contributing to the success of the organization, are more likely to be successful. Some executives don't have enough understanding of this—they are managers, not leaders, and what people need in most organizations is leadership. I encourage you to work harder at being a leader, creating the environment for success, giving people a sense of purpose, and something to be proud of.

Yet, we still have to live with the short term. I often do small workshops for shop-floor people. One of the questions I almost always ask—Do you have a retirement plan, like a 401K, or some other plan? Most all do. What's in your plan's portfolio? Most have a large chunk of mutual funds of publicly traded stock. What do you expect of your mutual fund? Marked growth in value at a rate substantially higher than inflation. So, when you open your quarterly statement, you expect it to be up, and if it's not, you start fretting, right? Yes. What happens if your company is not one of those companies considered worthy of your fund manager investing your money? Its stock price goes down. Then what happens? The company starts cutting costs. Who's creating this expectation of ever increasing performance? As one man said, "You mean we're doing it to ourselves?" You tell me. Capitalism is a harsh task master. We have to succeed in the short term, while planning for success in the long term, so that we can all meet our own demanding expectations.

When you begin your improvement effort, as with most systems, things are likely to get worse before they get better, and all new systems have a lag time before the effects are realized. Putting new systems in place just seems to be that way. With this in mind, patience may need to be exercised as new processes are put in place; this is difficult for most executives. Oh, and please go easy on using the phrase "world-class." It becomes so common as to be trivialized and meaningless in many companies, particularly on the shop floor. If you do use the phrase, mean it, and give it specific meaning—for example 50% market share; 87% uptime; $2.00 per pound; 1.5% of plant replacement value, etc. might be best in class benchmarks, or *real* world-class goals.

Change is a difficult thing to manage for most organizations. Having little or no change is not healthy. Alternatively, too much change is not healthy. As humans we like stability, and we like change. Too much of either, and we become bored, or stressed out, neither of which is effective. So it is with organizations. Try to use the principles in this book to promote change, but at a rate and under circumstances in which people feel in reasonable control, and which provides a sense of self satisfaction. After good practice in one area becomes habit, then it's time to add something new, and to continue to learn and improve.

As noted earlier in this book, physics teaches that for every action there is an equal and opposite reaction. Seemingly for every business strategy, there is probably an equal and opposite strategy—economies of scale for mass production vs. cell, flexible, and agile manufacturing for mass "customization"; out-sourcing vs. loyal employees for improved productivity; niche markets vs. all markets and customers; centralized vs. decentralized management, and so on. These strategies are often contradictory and add credibility to what someone once said—"There are no solutions, only consequences." I trust this book will help you select those models, practices, and systems that optimize consequences in light of your objectives.

Thank you for considering my suggestions. I wish you every success.

Appendix

World-Class Manufacturing—A Review of Several Key Success Factors*

There are no magic bullets.

R. Moore

Introduction

What are the critical success factors for operating a world-class manufacturing organization? How much influence does each factor have? What should be done "first"? How are these factors related? And so on. The following analysis below confirms what we've known intuitively for some time. That is, if you put in place the right leadership, the right practices, and the right performance measurements, superior performance will be achieved. It also demonstrates there is no "magic bullet" for superior performance. All the factors had some influence, and many factors were interrelated. While it's almost impossible to review all the factors for success, the following characterizes the relative influence of several key success factors for manufacturing excellence.

*The author is grateful to Mike Taylor and Chris Crocker of Imperial Chemical Industries for their support in the above analysis.

For several years now, data have been collected regarding critical success factors as they relate to reliability practices and manufacturing excellence. These factors are defined in the following section.

Definitions of Key Success Factors

• Uptime. Critical to manufacturing excellence, uptime is the focal point of the following factors. Compared to a theoretical maximum annual production rate, at what rate are you operating? For purposes of this discussion, uptime has been defined in this manner. However, some companies refer to this as utilization rate. It is understood that uptime typically excludes the effects of market demand. For example, if your utilization rate as a percent of theoretical maximum were 80%, of which 10% was due to lack of market demand, then uptime in some companies would be adjusted to 90%. As noted, the choice has been made here to define uptime more stringently as a percent of maximum theoretical utilization rate.

Leadership and Managment Practices

• Management Support and Plant Culture—Measures how much plant personnel believe that management has created a reliability-driven, proactive culture in the plant, and the degree to which management is perceived to be supportive of good operating and maintenance practices.
• Organization and Communication—Measures how much plant personnel believe that a sense of teamwork, common purpose, and good communication has been created within the plant.
• Performance—Measures how much plant personnel believe that key reliability and manufacturing excellence measures are routinely collected and displayed, and used to influence improved performance.
• Training—Measures how much plant personnel believe that the plant has developed a strategic training plan that supports business objectives, and is implementing the plan in a comprehensive manner to assure skills for good operating and maintenance practices.

Operating and Maintenance Practices

• Operational Practices—Measures how much plant personnel believe that the plant is operated with a high degree of consistency, and applies good process control methods, e.g., common set points, SPC, control charts, good pump and valve operation, etc.

- Reactive Maintenance—Measures how much your organization's maintenance is reactive, i.e., what percentage of your maintenance effort is reactive, e.g., run-to-failure, breakdown, emergency work orders, etc.?
- Preventive Maintenance—Measures how much plant personnel believe that preventive maintenance (interval-based) practices are being implemented, e.g., use of a maintenance management system (typically computerized), routine inspections and minor PM, comprehensive equipment histories, comprehensive basis for major maintenance activities, etc.
- Predictive Maintenance—Measures how much plant personnel believe that condition-monitoring practices are routinely being employed to avoid catastrophic failures, optimize planned maintenance, commission the quality of newly installed equipment, etc.
- Proactive Maintenance—Measures how much plant personnel believe that the maintenance organization works diligently to eliminate the root cause of equipment failures through improved design, operating, and maintenance practices.
- Stores Practices—Measures how much plant personnel believe that stores is well managed, i.e., it is run like a store—clean, efficient, few stock outs (but not too much stock), good inventory turns, etc.
- Overhaul Practices—Measures how much plant personnel believe that overhauls, shutdowns, turnarounds, etc. are well performed, e.g., advance planning, teamwork, condition monitoring to verify the need for maintenance, commissioning afterward to verify the quality of the work, etc.

It should also be noted that the workshops tended to consist mainly of maintenance staff, which could bias the data in some instances.

Summary data reported in each factor are provided in Tables A-1 and A-2, and graphically in Figure A-1. The data were collected from a survey of attendees of reliability-based manufacturing workshops in which the attendees were asked to assess their uptime (or more accurately, plant utilization rate), and to judge, on a scale from "0 to N," the quality of their leadership and management practices, as well as their operating and maintenance practices. The study comprises data from nearly 300 plants. These practices were then analyzed as to their potential influence.

Table A-1
Summary of Reliability-based Manufacturing Seminar Scores

Measurement	Average Score of Continuous Plants	Average Score of Batch/Discrete Plants	Typical Score of World-Class Plants[1]
Management support and plant culture	57%	51%	80%+
Organization and Communication	59%	50%	80%+
Performance	60%	44%	80%+
Training	50%	48%	
Operations practices	57%	50%	80%+
Reactive maintenance	46%	53%	10%[2]
Preventive maintenance	57%	47%	80%+
Predictive maintenance	54%	27%	80%+
Proactive maintenance	50%	31%	80%+
Stores practices	47%	36%	80%+
Overhaul practices	68%	50%	80%+

Notes:
[1] *These scores are typical of plants with superior levels of performance, typically reporting 80–85%+ OEE for batch plants, and 90–95%+ uptime for continuous plants. In fact, the best plants typically reported scores in the upper quartile in essentially all categories. The fact that a given individual or group reports a high score in any of these area does not necessarily mean the plant is world-class.*
[2] *Generally, the lower the score in reactive maintenance the better the plant is operated. The best plants operate at 10% or less reactive maintenance.*

General Findings

Perhaps the most striking thing about Table A-1, and its graphical depiction in Figure A-1, is the marked differences in scores between continuous manufacturers and batch/discrete manufacturers. These scores are not limited to management practices, but are apparent throughout the entire spectrum of management, maintenance, and operating practices, and are in some cases quite substantial. This is more than just the nature of the manufacturing process; it represents

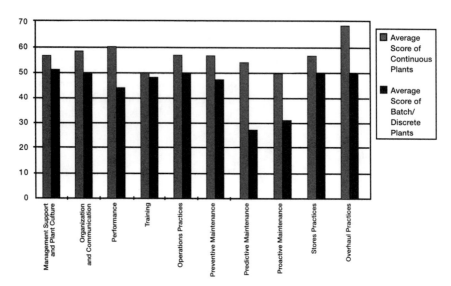

Figure A-1. *Comparison of operational practices—batch and continuous plants.*

a fundamental cultural difference between the two types of manufacturers. For example, continuous manufacturers understand fully that if the plant is down, production losses and their attendant costs are huge, and they appear to work harder to put practices in place to avoid those losses, much more so than do batch manufacturers. Whereas, batch manufacturers tend to believe that if a batch or line is disrupted, they can always "make it up." It should also be emphasized that time lost is time lost *forever*. You don't ever really make it up, and inefficiencies in manufacturing show up as additional costs, or poor delivery performance, or waste, or increases in work in process and finished goods, etc. which in the long run are intolerable.

Additional analysis using principal components analysis (not detailed here) reinforces the belief that practices between the two types of plants are fundamentally different. The data strongly indicate they operate in two different, almost exclusive, domains of performance and behavior. Further, this difference also exhibits itself in other ways. These practices need not be fundamentally different. However, they are, and the consequence is that batch and discreet manufacturers typically have much farther to go in establishing world-class performance in the categories shown than do continuous manufacturers.

As shown in Table A-2, it was also found that a typical continuous manufacturer, e.g., paper, chemicals, refining, etc., would report uptimes averaging 80%, while the best (highest) would report uptimes in the range of 95%+. A typical batch or discrete manufacturer, e.g., automotive, food, etc., had an average uptime of 60%, whereas the best would report 85%+. It was also found that generally the manufacturers with the highest uptimes would also report the lowest levels of reactive maintenance, e.g., 10%, while the typical continuous manufacturer averaged 46% reactive maintenance, and the typical batch or discrete manufacturer averaged 53%.

Table A-2.
Uptime for Typical and Best Manufacturing Plants

Type of Manufacturing Plant	Uptime	Reactive Maintenance
1. Typical continuous process manufacturer	80%	46%
2. Best continuous manufacturers	95%+	10%
3. Typical batch or discrete manufacturer	60%	53%
4. Best batch or discrete manufacturers	85%+	10%

It was also found that for the group of plants studied, *for every 10% increase in reactive maintenance reported, a 2-3% reduction in uptime rate could be expected—the higher the reactive maintenance, the lower the uptime.* While there was considerable scatter in the data, this scatter was often explained by the fact that in many cases the data itself may have lacked precision; that installed spares helped to mitigate downtime, though installed spares were sometimes unreliable themselves; that many plants were reported to be very good (fast) at doing reactive maintenance; cyclical demand also increased the data scatter in some plants. However, for most plants, two factors added even further significance: (1) the impact of reactive maintenance on lost uptime was often worth millions of dollars in lost income, not to mention out-of-pocket losses, or the need for increased capital (to add equipment for making up production losses); (2) reactive maintenance was reported to typically cost as much as two times or more than planned maintenance. An additional consideration, which is perhaps as important but more difficult to measure, is the defocusing effect that reactive maintenance has on management, taking away from strategic management, and forcing far too much time spent on "fire-fighting."

For the plants studied, *uptime was positively correlated to all leadership/management practices, and to all operating/maintenance practices, except one—reactive maintenance.* That is to say, all factors, with the exception of reactive maintenance, provided a positive influence on uptime—*the higher the score in good practices, the higher the uptime.*

Further, all those same factors were negatively correlated with reactive maintenance. That is to say, *when reactive maintenance levels were high, all leadership and management practices, as well as all operating and maintenance practices were poorer.*

Finally, all factors except reactive maintenance were positively correlated with each other, that is, they influenced each other in a positive way in daily activities. Indeed management and operating practices were significantly more positively correlated to each other than they were to uptime, indicating the increasingly positive influence these factors have on one another to create a positive culture within a given organization. See Figures A-2 through A-7 for details.

As shown in Figure A-2, uptime was positively correlated to all the factors under consideration, except reactive maintenance of course, and were typically in the range of 0.3–0.4, with no factor being particularly statistically dominant, suggesting the need to do many things well at once. It also begs the question of whether management being supportive of good maintenance and operating practice creates a cul-

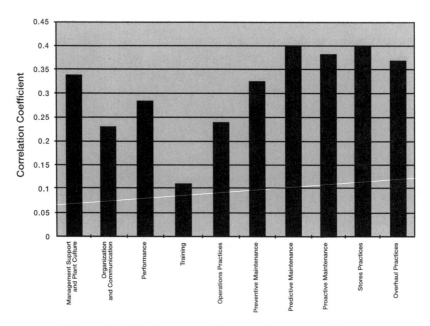

Figure A-2. Uptime—correlation to key success factors.

ture where it is more successful, or whether operating and maintenance practices alone are sufficient. In my experience, plants with high
uptime always have strong management support for good practice, in
both operations and maintenance. The reverse is not always true, that
is, plants that have reasonably good (though not the best) maintenance

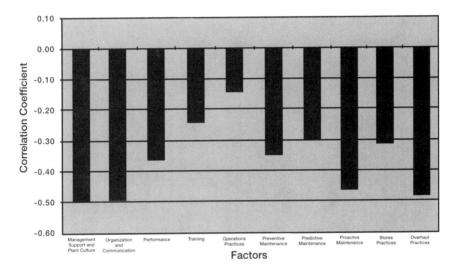

Figure A-3. Reactive maintenance—correlation to key success factors.

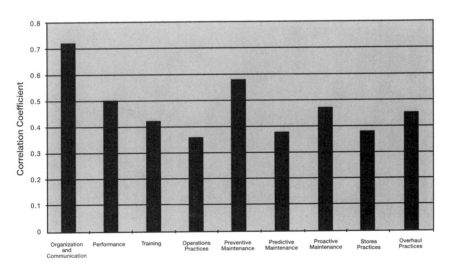

*Figure A-4. Management support and plant culture—correlation to key
success factors.*

practices, will not necessarily have high levels of management support, or good uptime. In these cases, the people at the lower levels of the organization have worked hard to put in place some good practices without benefit of strong support of senior management, and have achieved some improvement. Unfortunately, they are generally limited to a level of performance that is less than world-class.

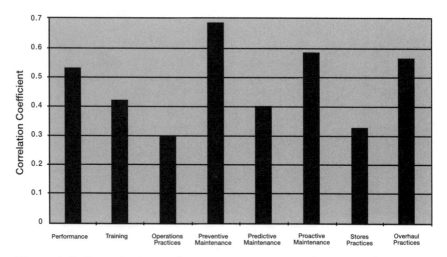

Figure A-5. Organization and communication—correlation to other success factors.

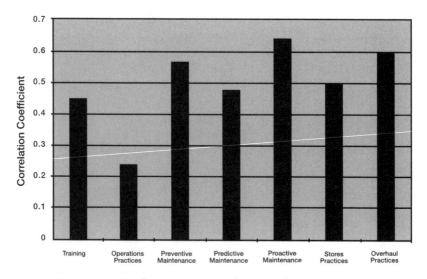

Figure A-6. Performance—correlation to key success factors.

Apparently numerous factors affect uptime and help lower operating costs. None alone appears sufficient. All appear necessary in some degree. What can be said with high confidence is that the best plants create an organizational culture in which the leadership of the organization is highly supportive of best practices, both from a managerial perspective of promoting teamwork, performance measurement, training, craftsmanship, etc.; and from an operating perspective of fostering best operating and maintenance practices.

Further, the "less than best" plants appear to focus more on arbitrary cost cutting, e.g., head count reduction, budget cuts, etc., without understanding fully and changing the basic processes that lead to "less than best" performance. In these plants arbitrary cost cutting is believed to be likely to have a positive effect on manufacturing performance. However, this perception is not necessarily supported by the data presented in Chapter 1, which concluded that a cost-cutting strategy is not a high probability approach for long-term success.

The best plants focus on putting in place best practices, empowering their people in such practices, resulting in unnecessary costs not being incurred, and costs coming down as a consequence of good

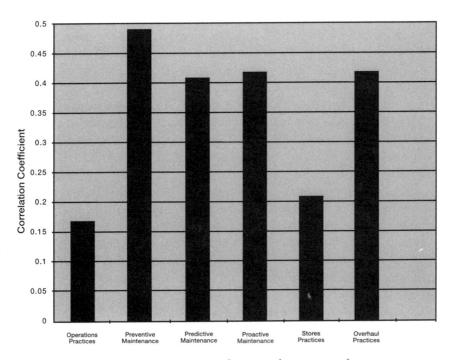

Figure A-7. Training—correlation to key success factors.

practice. This is also considered to be much more readily sustainable over the long term.

It must be emphasized that these data represent typical data and ranges, and should not necessarily be considered conclusive about any particular business. For example, a best-practices paper plant manufacturing coated paper might have an uptime of 87%, and be considered world-class, even though it is not at a 90–95% rate. This can be because of any number of factors, including the nature of the process, the product mix and number of products being made, management policy regarding finished goods stock, on-time/in full, etc. These other business factors must also be considered in determining what uptime is optimal for a given manufacturing plant. Likewise, the same could be said for all other types of plants.

Summary

These data lend strong support to what we've known intuitively for some time—put in place the right leadership, the right practices, the right performance measurements, create an environment for teamwork and a common sense of purpose about strategy and performance, and superior performance will be achieved.

Not all factors that could influence world-class performance were reviewed. For example, marketing and/or research and development that lead to superior products and market demand, or ease of manufacture, were not considered in this study. Nor were operational issues such as the level and application of redundant equipment and in-line spares, nor just-in-time policies, nor on-time delivery policies, nor specific design policies, etc. These and other factors will clearly affect uptime and other operating and maintenance practices, and ultimately plant performance. However, the factors that were analyzed do indicate that a major portion of the variability can be accounted for in the parameters measured, and providing compelling reasons to assure that these practices are in place.

Finally, this effort is on-going and continuously being improved. It is anticipated that this additional analysis and information will be available at a later time. In the interim, it is hoped that these results will be beneficial to you and your organization.

Reliability Manager/Engineer Job Description

Insanity is doing the same old things in the same old way and expecting different results.

Rita Mae Brown

The following is offered as a model job description for a reliability manager, engineer, or specialist who facilitates the change process. Many of Beta's plants are implementing this position, or a variant thereto, to assure focus and facilitation of the reliability improvement process for manufacturing excellence. While likely useful, it is not essential that the individual be an engineer, but it is strongly recommended that they have 10+ years experience in an operating plant, have a strong work ethic, and be capable of being both team leader and team member. It is likely that the individual will not be able to initially do everything identified below, and that the role will evolve as the improvement process takes effect. Ultimately, the role may not even be necessary, if and when, the practices become second nature and habit. In any event, this individual might be expected to be performing the following kinds of tasks:

Loss Accounting. One of the fundamental roles of a good reliability engineer is to focus on uptime/output losses and the causes of those losses via Pareto analysis. This does not mean that they would necessarily create the data base for identifying the losses, but rather would use existing data bases to the extent possible for the analysis. For example, a review of a given plant might indicate that most of the unplanned losses are a result of stationary equipment; the second biggest loss may be related to instrumentation; the third due to rotating machinery, etc. A good reliability engineer would focus on those losses on a priority basis, do root-cause failure analysis, develop a plan for eliminating those losses, assure the plan's approval, and then facilitate its implementation. In doing this, he or she would work with the production, engineering, and maintenance departments to assure buy-in, proper analysis, support teams, etc. for the planning and implementation process. Some issues may not be in their control. For exmaple, the need for a full-time shutdown manager to reduce losses related to extended shutdowns (e.g., issues related to organization, management, long-range markets, etc.) would generally be passed up to managment for resolution.

Root-Cause Failure Analysis (RCFA). Once losses have been catgorized and a tentative understanding developed, the reliability engineer would begin to perform, and/or facilitate, root-cause failure analysis and prospective solutions for major opportunities for improvement. Note that root-cause failure analysis is a way of thinking, not something that requires the individual to have all the answers or be an expert in everything. Some of these RCFA issues may be equipment specific, e.g., redesign of a pump, while others may be more programmatic, e.g., the need for a procedure for precision alignment. The reliability engineer would be responsible for analyzing losses, and then putting forth a solution based on root-cause analysis.

Managing the Results of Condition Monitoring Functions. In some of the best companies around, the so-called predictive maintenance technologies (condition monitoring) have all been organized under the direction of a single department manager. That is not to say that the individual or his staff actually collects all the data or has all the technology. In some cases, they may contract the analysis to external or internal suppliers, and in some cases all the data collection may be done by contractors. Rather, it is to say that they are responsible for the quality of the data provided by the suppliers, for the integration of the data, and more importantly for the decision-making process that results from the data. Generally, they would be responsible for assuring that the following types of technologies are applied and used in an integrated way to improved reliability:

• Vibration
• Oil
• Infrared
• Ultrasonic (Thickness, Leak Detection)
• Motor Current
• Corrosion Detection
• Other NDT Methods

Overhaul/Shutdown Support. Further, they would work to correlate process data (working with process and production people) with condition monitoring technology to "know equipment condition," and to use that knowledge to help:

• Plan overhauls and shutdowns—do what is necesary, but only what is necessary; link equipment condition and maintenance requirements to stores, tools, resources, etc., in cooperation with maintenance planning.
• Commission equipment after shutdown—in cooperation with production for commissioning of the process, but also of the equipment quality, using applicable technologies, e.g., vibration, motor current, oil, etc., and specific standards for acceptance.

Proactive Support. Finally, and perhaps related to the above efforts, the reliability manager would also provide proactive support in the following areas:

• Work with the design staff to eliminate root cause of failures through better designs.
• Work with purchasing to improve specifications for reliability improvement, and to improve the quality and reliability of suppliers' scope of supply.
• Work with maintenance to assure precision practices in installation efforts—precision installation of rotating machinery, and in particular alignment and balancing; precision installation of piping, of infrastructure; precision handling and installation of electrical equipment; precision calibrations; precision power for instruments and equipment, etc.

- Work with stores to assure precision and quality storage practices for retaining equipment reliability, e.g., proper humidity, temperature and electrostatic discharge control for key, applicable components; proper storage of equipment to preclude corrosion; turning of shafts on motors periodically; proper bearing and critical equipment storage and handling.
- Finally, but perhaps most importantly, work with operations to identify losses related to lack of process consistency, e.g., poor process chemistry control; poor process parameter control (temperature, pressure, flow, etc.); poor control of transition modes for both process chemistry and physical parameters; poor valve and pump operational practices; and the application of basic care by operators to the production equipment.

Facilitator/Communicator. Perhaps the most important role of the reliability engineer/manager is to facilitate communication between production, design, and maintenance related for eliminating the losses which result from poor practices. Often these practices are not attributable to a single person or department, but somehow are "shared" among two or more groups. The role of the reliability engineer is to facilitate communication and common solutions, without seeking to "find fault" anywhere. Their goal is to help create common "superordinate" goals related to uptime, reliability improvement, without seeking to blame anyone for the current losses.

It is understood that the reliability engineer can't do all these things at once, and that's why the loss accounting is so important for providing a sense of priority and purpose for the limited time and resources available.

Index